IMAGES
of America

FROM AVALON TO EDEN

A POSTCARD TOUR OF ROCKINGHAM COUNTY

IMAGES
of America

FROM AVALON TO EDEN

A POSTCARD TOUR OF ROCKINGHAM COUNTY

Piper Aheron

ARCADIA
PUBLISHING

ISBN 978-0-7385-6883-6

Published by Arcadia Publishing
Charleston, South Carolina

Printed in the United States of America

For all general information contact Arcadia Publishing at:
Telephone 843-853-2070
Fax 843-853-0044
E-mail sales@arcadiapublishing.com
For customer service and orders:
Toll-Free 1-888-313-2665

Visit us on the Internet at www.arcadiapublishing.com

This book is dedicated to Richard Lee Aheron.

Contents

ACKNOWLEDGMENTS

Although it is impossible to tell the entire story of Rockingham County in this book, I am grateful to those who so kindly shared with me their time, their photographs, their homes, and their memories. Without their support and generosity, this book could not have been completed.

My most heartfelt thanks goes to Jerri B. Griffin, the president of the Rockingham County Historical Society. Jerri spent tireless evenings and afternoons with me, sorting and identifying and explaining the history of western Rockingham County. She drove me to Avalon, a place I would have never found on my own. Her perspective added depth and dignity to this work, and when I was overwhelmed, Jerri's genuine vision—to educate the children and grandchildren about the history of Rockingham County—was a great source of inspiration.

Likewise, I wish to thank Mary Cheek, a precious, beautiful woman. Her husband Lavender, a Sunday school teacher to my husband in his youth, died after a long-term illness before we completed this project. With difficulty and grace, Mary recounted the history of Leaksville in Lav's absence. Her love is strong, her memories are dear, and her guidance sweet. Zelma Joyce Scott, the city historian of Stoneville, is a woman of uncommon vitality. Zelma also spent hours with me patiently sharing the facts and history pertinent to Stoneville's development. Harold Francis of Francis Photography Studios and Jeff Bullins of Mayodan answered my questions and reproduced vital photographic material that could not be found elsewhere. Jimmy Waynick of Reidsville and Roscoe Hankins of Eden were also patient and supportive of this project. Their good humor and stories made my days bright after puzzling in the dark over newspaper clippings and archival reports. Special thanks are extended to writers Lindley Butler, Majorie Walker, Peggy Osborne, Ola Mae Foushee, Vera Dillion, Ruth McCollum, and Jean Harrington for their published materials on the history of Rockingham County. Also, I would like to thank the staff of the Eden Library, *The Eden News, The Reidsville Review, The Madison Messenger,* and the Rockingham County Community College Library and Archives were most helpful.

I would also like to give many thanks to Jo Ann Peters for travel arrangements; George Aheron and Lisa Shaffer Wylie for lodging arrangements; Tidge Aheron, Bertha Vestal Aheron (Nanny), Iris Aheron Earps, and William Aheron for their support and verification of facts; Ann McCollum Aheron for her input and support; Lou Ann Aheron for her photographic contributions; and Lou Ann Cooper, Kenneth C. Newell, James C. Stewart, and C. D. "Pete" Peters for their understanding and clarification of structural/architectural terms. Also, I would like to extend my special thanks to Catherine Joseph and Aerial Photo Services, Charlotte, NC, for their generous contributions.

Lastly, I deeply appreciate the patience and work of Sarah Maineri and the entire staff at Arcadia Publishing. I also extend a heartfelt thanks to the ever-encouraging Frye Gaillard, a unique historian and writer with a deep, spiritual conviction and unwavering commitment to make this world a better place.

INTRODUCTION

The history of Rockingham County, North Carolina, is inseparable from the history of its streams and the textile communities which gradually formed around them. From the mighty Mayo, the location of the ill-fated mill fortress of Avalon in the early 1900s, to the birth of sweet Eden along the calm Smith River in the late 1960s, the residents of Rockingham County entered the twentieth century with an economy fueled by water and by the sweat of the people—men, women, and children dedicated to working hand-in-hand in the Southern spirit of cooperation for the betterment of their neighborhoods and towns.

These small, friendly communities were originally seated on the river basins surrounding the hills and mountains that were drained by the northward flowing Dan River and its tributaries, the Smith, the Mayo, and their many creeks. Although it is not known who first settled the area, the Sauras Indians (sometimes called Saras) were contacted by the Spanish under DeSoto in the 1540s. Between 1728 and 1733, William Byrd II, a Virginia planter and author, chronicled a survey commission's journey that established the North Carolina-Virginia boundary. Byrd, in an effort to promote the area he eventually would purchase, described the previously unexplored Dan River Valley as the "Land of Eden." He purchased 20,000 acres and soon after, European settlers came to the region. The first farmers in Rockingham County were immigrants from Pennsylvania, New Jersey, Maryland, and Virginia. They traveled down the Shenandoah Valley into the Carolina Piedmont. These newcomers—English, Germans, Scots, and Irish—spread and their population quadrupled in the next two decades.

By the early nineteenth century, gristmills that ground flour and cornmeal were established on the Mayo and the Smith Rivers. Attorneys, accountants, and doctors were also coming to the area to set up practices. In 1813 the textile industry of Rockingham County was founded at the junction of the Dan and Smith Rivers in present-day Eden. John M. Morehead built the first cotton mill. This mill was one of the earliest in the state of North Carolina. By 1818, Leaksville (now Eden) was permanently graphed on cartographers' maps. At the same time, the railroad interests were drafting expansion plans into the South. After the Civil War, Francis H. Fries directed the completion of the Roanoke and Southern Railroad, which is now a part of the Norfolk and Western rail system. The son of a textile manufacturer, Fries noted the fine mill sites along the Mayo River. With the backing of W.C. Ruffin, Fries began Mayo Mills (also known as Washington Mills). The village that benefitted from this development is now known as Mayodan. By 1904, Fries, a visionary, built Avalon, but his dreams of prosperity for the region nearly perished in a ball of fire. Fortunately for Fries, Avalon was fully insured. Its principals literally and physically relocated Avalon employees to Mayodan, where Washington Mills continues its productivity under the name of Tultex.

Commercial photography was beginning to enjoy success as a legitimate profession during this period in Rockingham County. A man could make a living with a camera instead of working in the mills. Rockingham County had several commercial photographers. They included men like Mr. Wannamaker, Mr. Gilley, Mr. Jackson, Mr. Adams, and Mr. Francis. Mr. Francis has a few of the glass plates today, but most have not survived the times. Supplies were limited in the early 1900s and photographers like Mr. Wannamaker, for example, would take a photo, print a few copies, then wipe the emulsion from the glass negative, and begin again. Other photographers' plates survived them, "Picture" Price's work among them; he is best known for photographing eastern Rockingham County. Allen Benton was the local master of western Rockingham County. He frequently photographed businesses and their patrons in Madison and Mayodan. Jesse G. Seay of Leaksville (now Eden) was also a great cameraman. Seay's notoriety befell him after he visited Avalon to drum up business. He did not have much success on that hot day in 1911. He was walking the railroad tracks to Mayodan when Avalon Mills ignited. Seay, running northward down the tracks, stopped, set up his box, snapped the flash, then ran closer to the burning mill. That day he created one of the more fascinating postcard series of the early 1900s, a series that documents a tragedy with a great, happy ending.

Among the pros, of course, were the laymen, gentlemen employed by the cotton mills. They also took pictures for postcards, unknowingly documenting the optimism and the hardships, the architecture and the landscape of village life in Avalon, Stoneville, Mayodan, Madison, Reidsville, Eden, and Wentworth. These mill men were C.B. Daniels, J.M. Suttenfield, and Dan Aheron, just to name a few. This is a sampling of their work as much as it is an incomplete history. It is a pictorial designed to provide the reader with a sense of evolution in Rockingham County as seen by these photographers. It is primarily comprised of postcards, a direct-mail device now used almost exclusively in promoting tourism and industry. In the past, however, postcards were a popular method of fast and easy communications. Whenever possible, after verification by two or more sources, the photographers are identified with their work. It is my hope that after the reader enjoys these pictures, this brief trip down memory lane, he or she will be prompted to investigate Rockingham County and actually visit the sites illustrated and preserved by local historical societies. History is not merely a chronology of events. Our past is always viewed amidst the realities of the present. Through history we make a connection with the dreams and schemes of real men and real women who have gone before us. Their success is our reward. Their failures are our opportunities, and by sharing their history, we entice our children and grandchildren to reach for a better future, to explore their visions and create a better world both abroad and at home in Rockingham County.

Piper Aheron
June 1997

One

Avalon

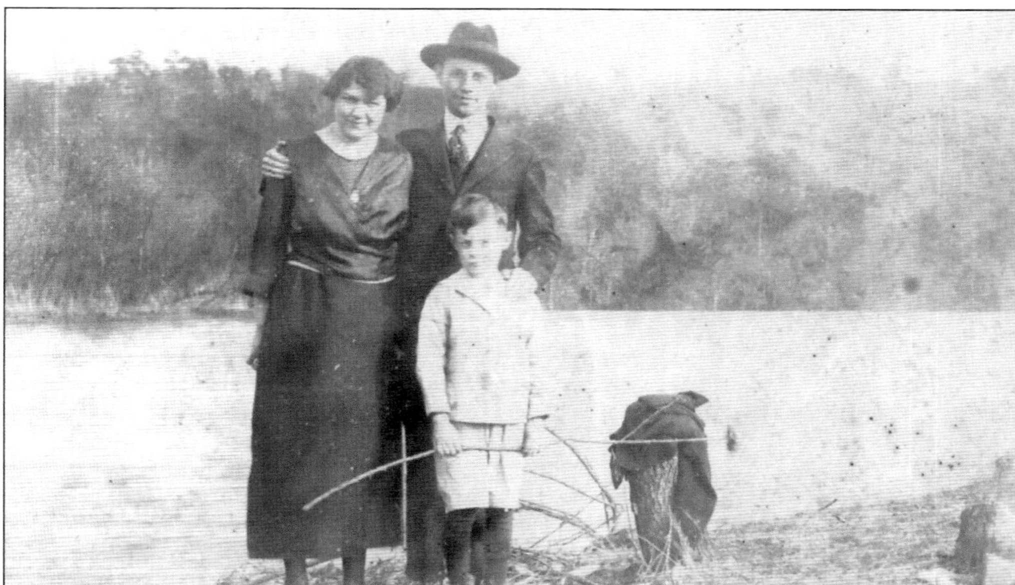

This early 1900s postcard depicts a family outing along the Mayo River two miles south of Avalon, a village that existed on the cartographer's map for approximately ten years. One dismal day in 1911 everything changed, and all that remained in Avalon was the river itself. (Courtesy of the Jeff Bullins Collection, Mayodan, NC.)

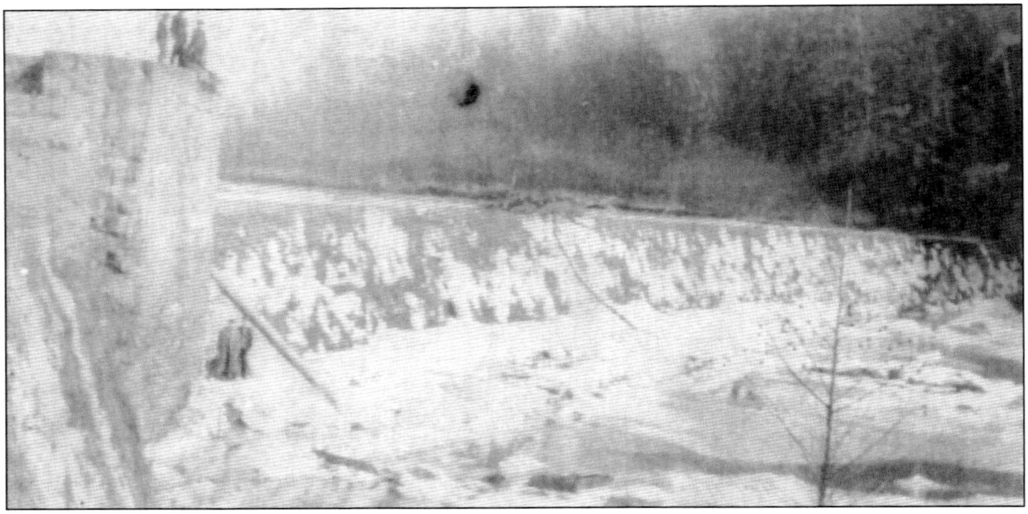

The village of Avalon was developed after Avalon Mills in 1900. Pictured above are the dam and canal near completion (1899). Note the two men inspecting the foundation at the lower left of the image. Three gentlemen are also perched at the top of the lock. This black-and-white postcard offers no clues as to the men's identity, but the formality of the professional frame suggests it was commissioned by Francis Henry Fries (pictured below), the man responsible for building Avalon. (Top postcard courtesy of the Jerri B. Griffin Collection, Madison, NC. Portrait of F.H. Fries courtesy of the Jeff Bullins Collection, Mayodan, NC.)

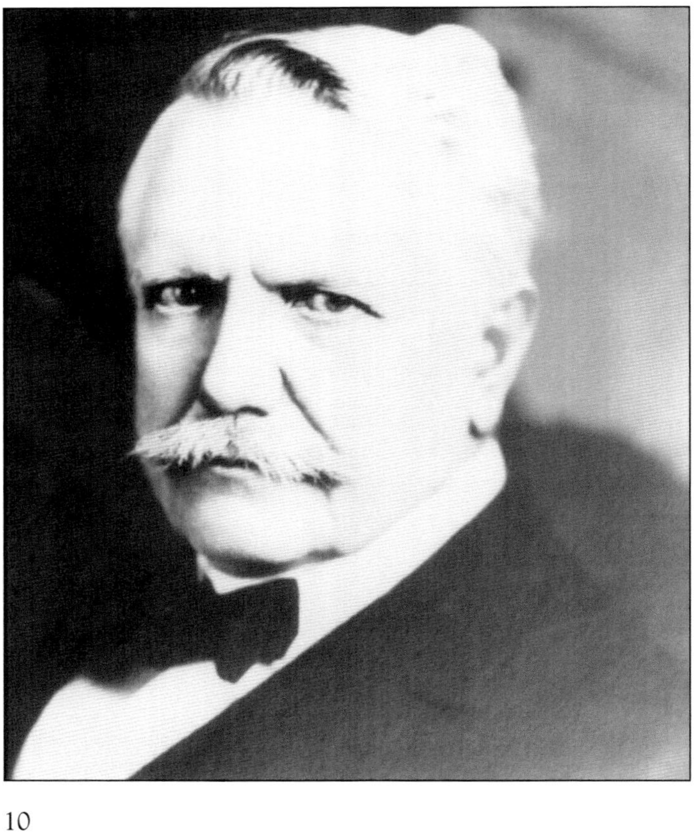

Avalon was a multifaceted project documented by postcard photographers. The Avalon Mill Dam, constructed on the Mayo River, was the first phase of the project. The black-and-white postcard below reveals the beautiful man-made falls that inspired William Cain Ruffin (pictured on the right) of Mayodan to name the place Avalon. (Postcard below courtesy of the Zelma Joyce Scott Collection, Stoneville, NC. Portrait of W.C. Ruffin courtesy of the Jeff Bullins Collection, Mayodan, NC.)

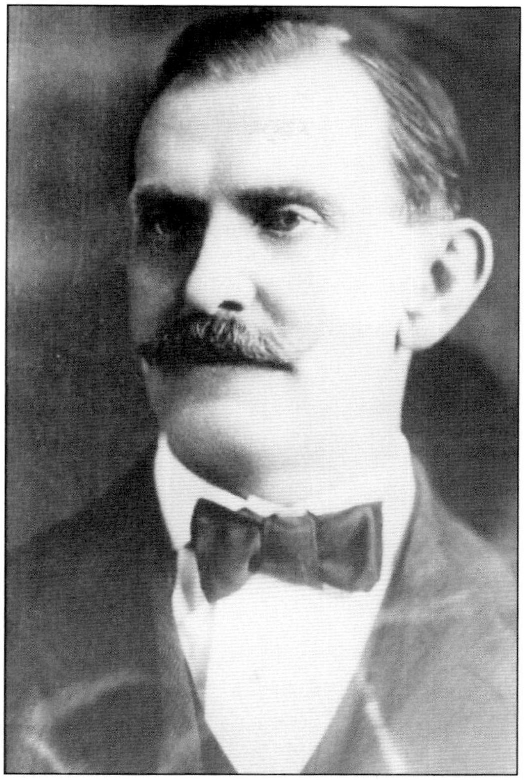

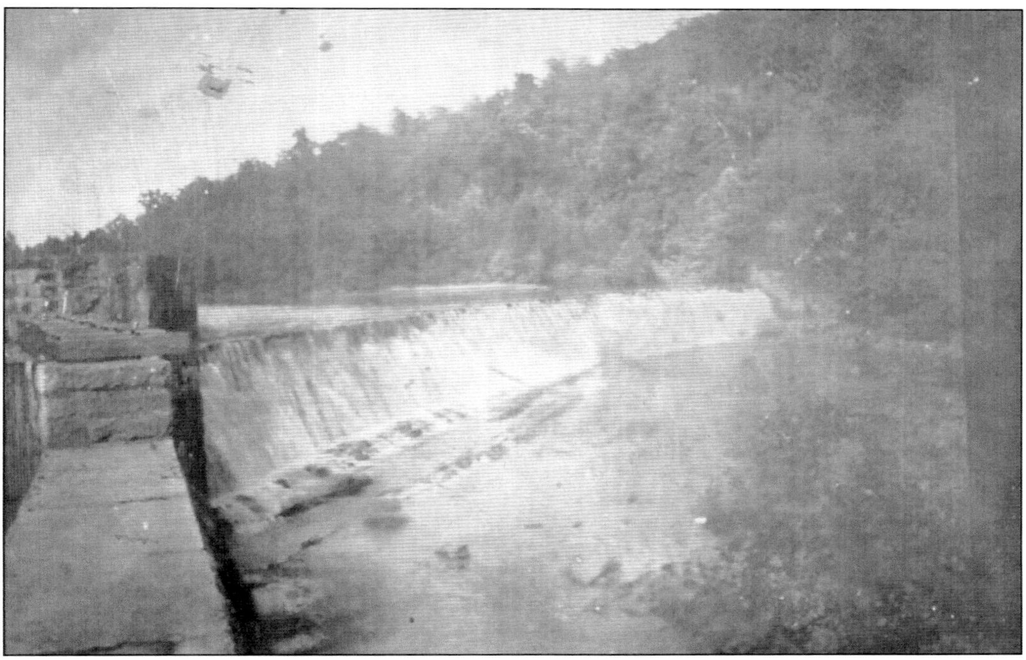

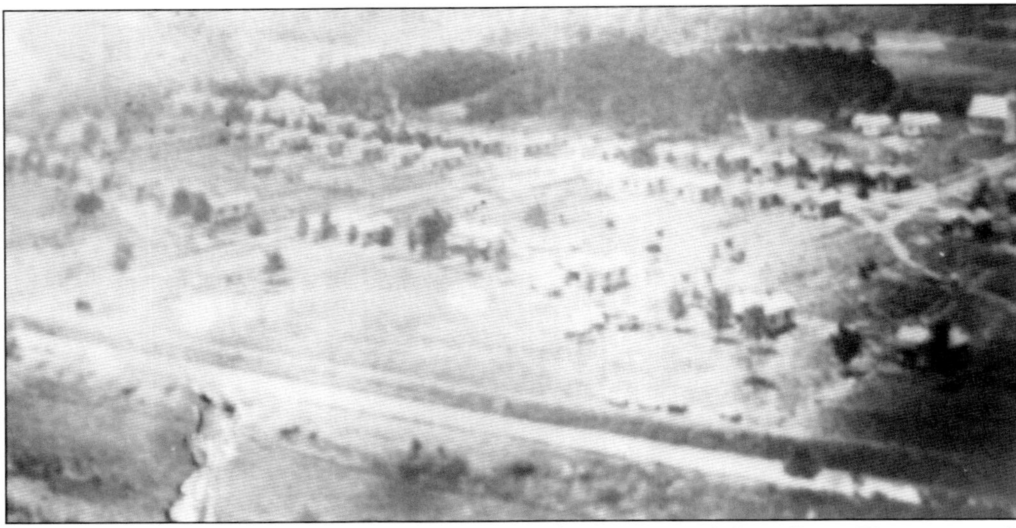

This black-and-white postcard features a rare, bird's-eye view of the village. The man-made canal is in the foreground. The Moravian Church is to the far right of the image. Photographers were lifted by balloons in the 1900s in order to take aerial shots. Some would hike to nearby Mayo Mountain or Cedar Point Mountain to get the breathtaking landscapes. (Courtesy of the Jeff Bullins Collection, Mayodan, NC.)

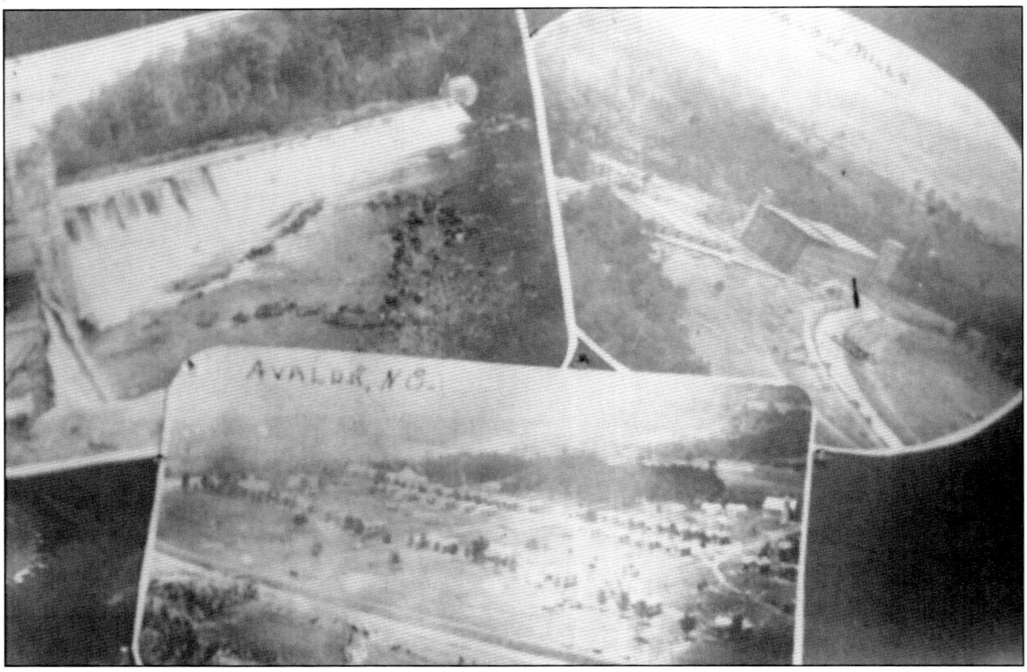

This singular black-and-white postcard was created by combining three cards into one, an unusual photo technique in 1910. Note that the right image is the northern elevation or the back of Avalon Mills. One can see the cotton warehouses with the winding canal meeting the mill at the centerpoint of the image. At the bottom is the aerial view of the village. The ruins of Avalon are about a mile off Highway 220 on private property. (Courtesy of the Jeff Bullins Collection, Mayodan, NC.)

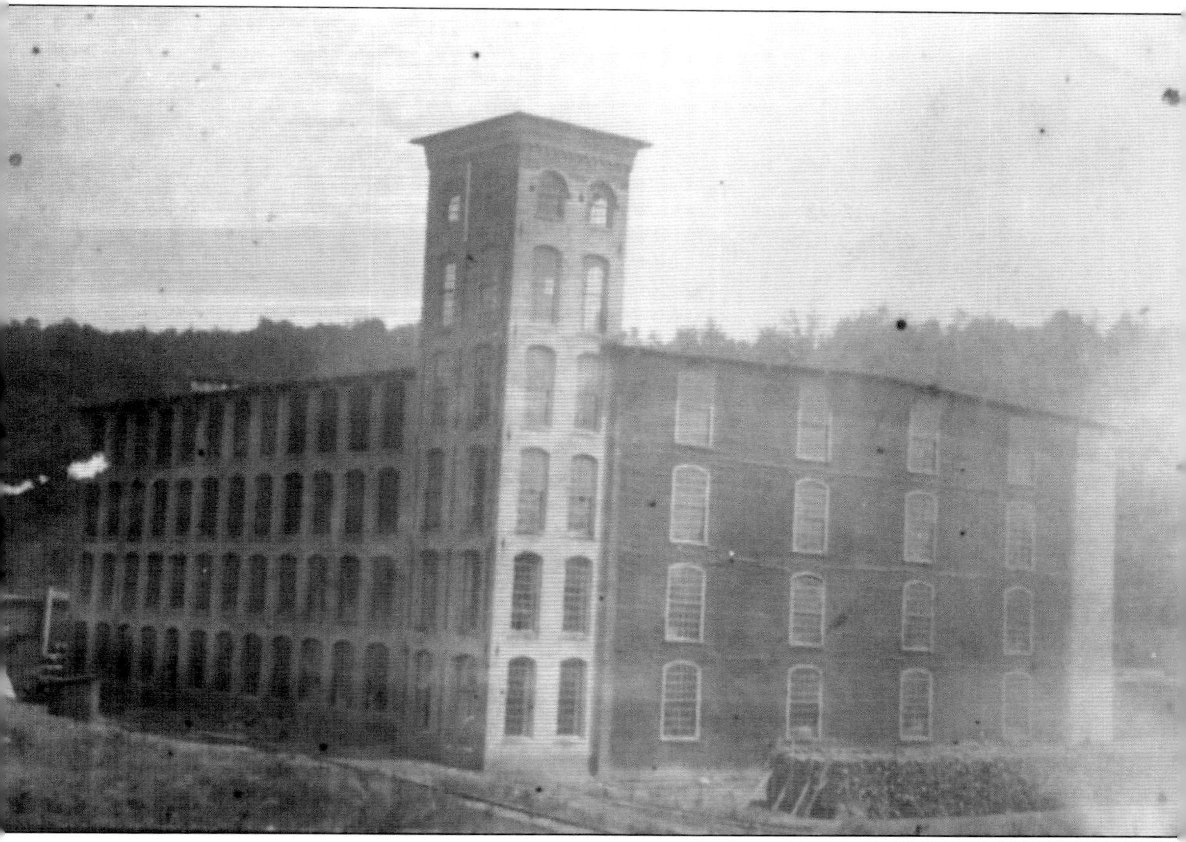

This postcard depicts Avalon Mills, the Mayo Mills' great expansion project . Note that the south walls were wood planks easily removed for renovations and additions. Avalon Mills was four stories, and at the time (1910) was the largest textile mill in North Carolina. (Courtesy of the Jeff Bullins Collection, Mayodan, NC.)

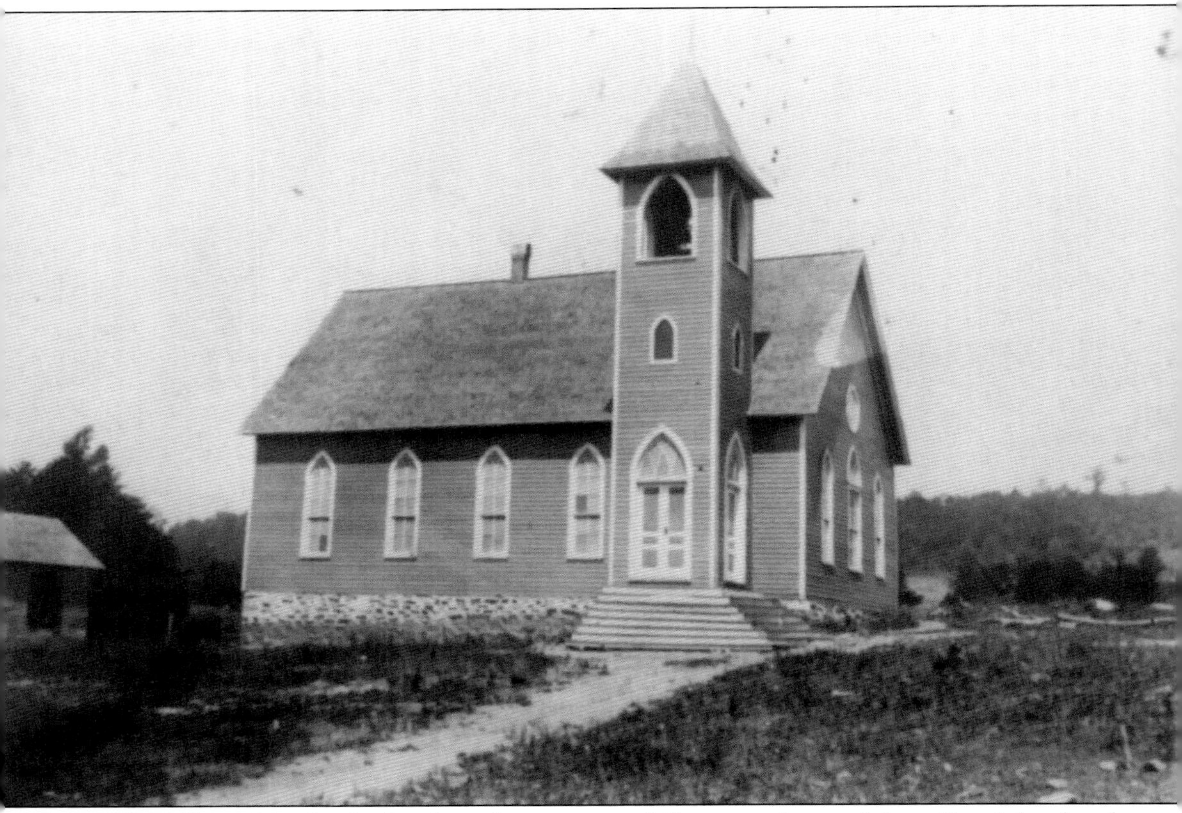

The village of Avalon had no formal government. Life centered around the mill and the church. The photo above shows the Moravian Church (1910). It was a handsome structure on a solid rock foundation. It was situated just off Main Street. After the fire, the sanctuary was torn down and its lumber recycled into various structures in the town of Mayodan. (Courtesy of the Jeff Bullins Collection, Mayodan, NC.)

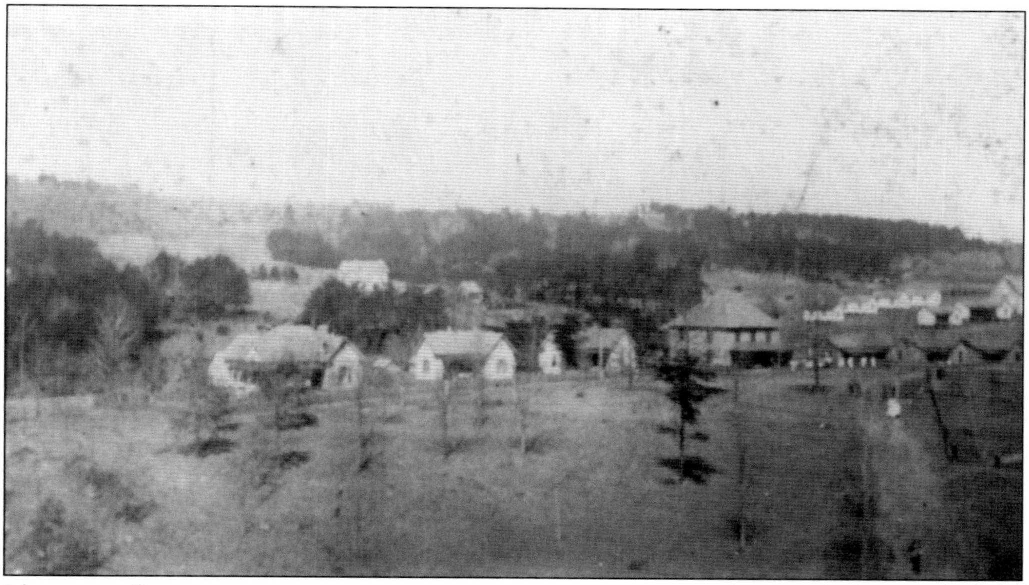

This is a village scene photographed from the mill's tower. From left to right are the Hedge House, the Suttenfield House, the Bailey House, and the two-story Avalon Hotel. They were the most prominent structures in a town largely ignored by professional postcard photographers. This picture and the preceding one may have been taken by E. Suttenfield, an employee of the mill. The houses pictured and the Avalon Hotel were relocated to Mayodan after June 1911. (Courtesy of the Jeff Bullins Collection, Mayodan, NC.)

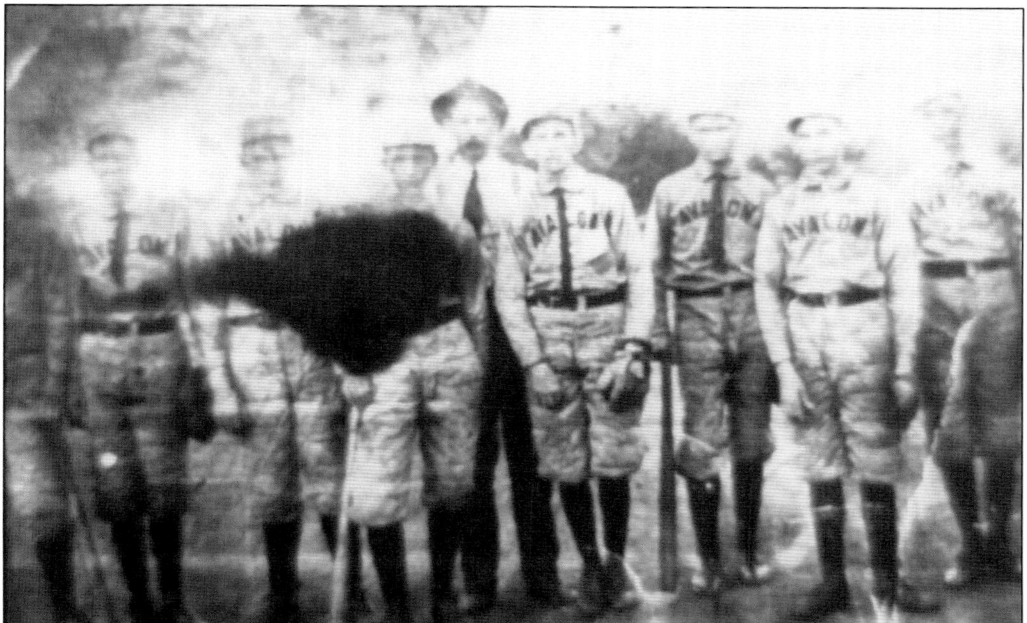

The Avalon baseball team included Hunt Smith, John McGee, Sherman Reynolds, Charlie Griffin, Troy Shropshire, and others now unidentifiable. (Courtesy of the Jeff Bullins Collection, Mayodan, NC.)

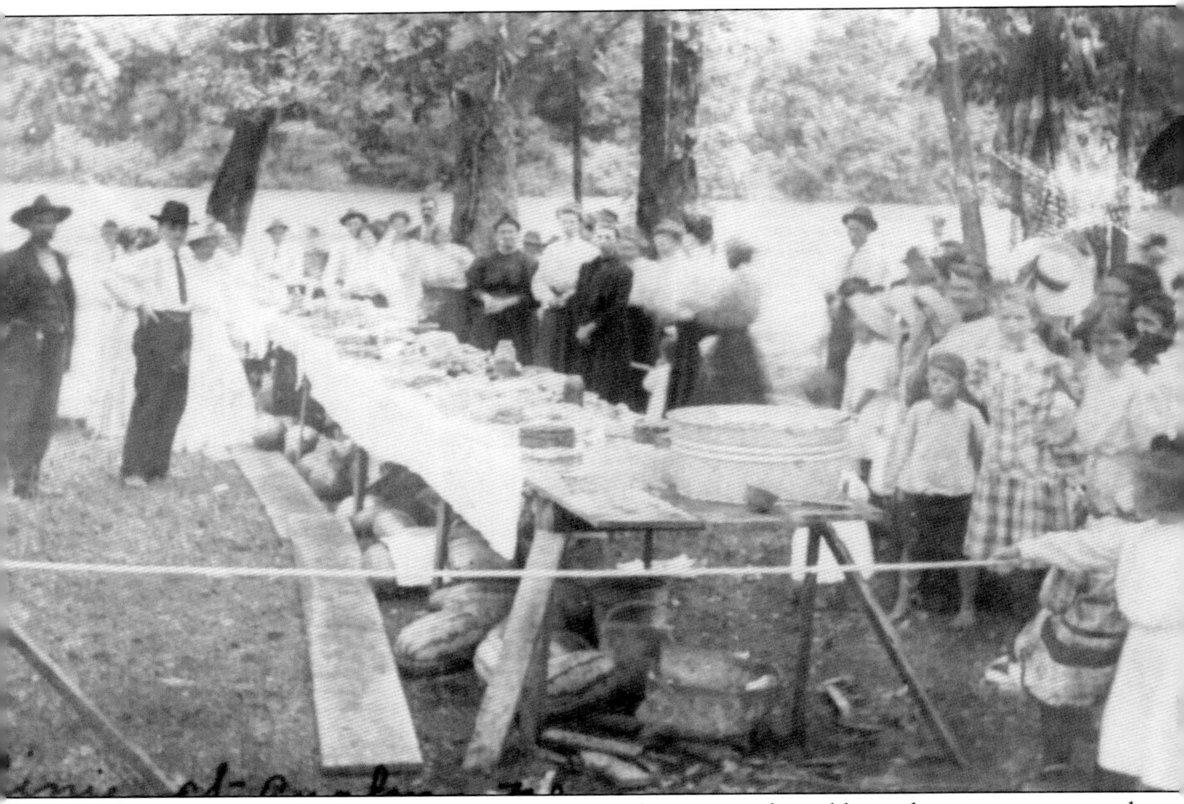

Reportedly, the Avalon picnic area was only used one time after tables and swings were erected along the banks of the lazy Mayo River. When the mill burned, the town was literally and physically moved to Mayodan. This area was abandoned. (Photo courtesy of the Jeff Bullins Collection, Mayodan, NC.)

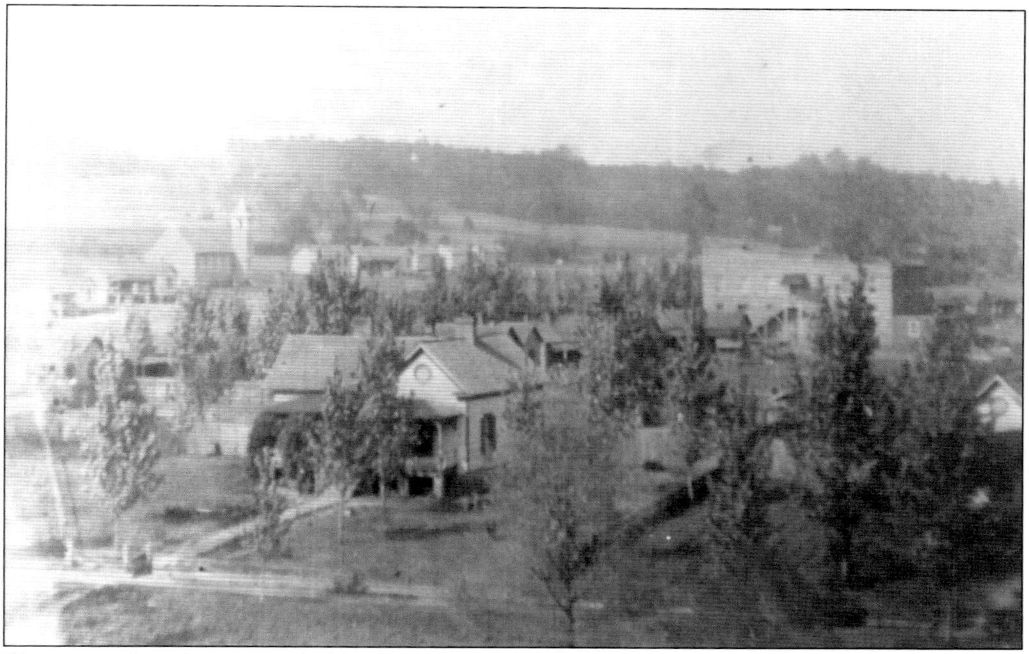

This view of Avalon was probably photographed from the tower. It is thought that some informal photographs of the town were the product of C.B. Daniel. Daniel, an overseer at the mill, enjoyed part-time photography and also documented the fire that destroyed the mill. (Photo courtesy of the Jeff Bullins Collection, Mayodan, NC.)

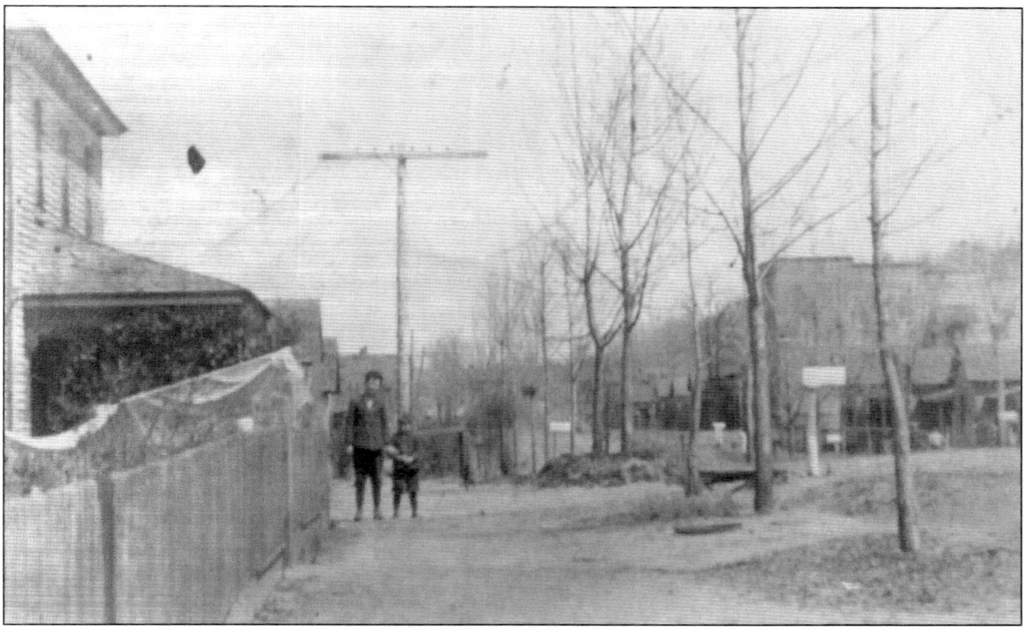

Main Street in Avalon was dominated by the Avalon Hotel (on the left, in the foreground) and the two-story Mill Store (on the right, in the background). The hotel was operated by Belle Carter. This picture featuring Charlie Smith (left) and Claude Bailey(?) was snapped in 1911. (Courtesy of the Jeff Bullins Collection, Mayodan, NC.)

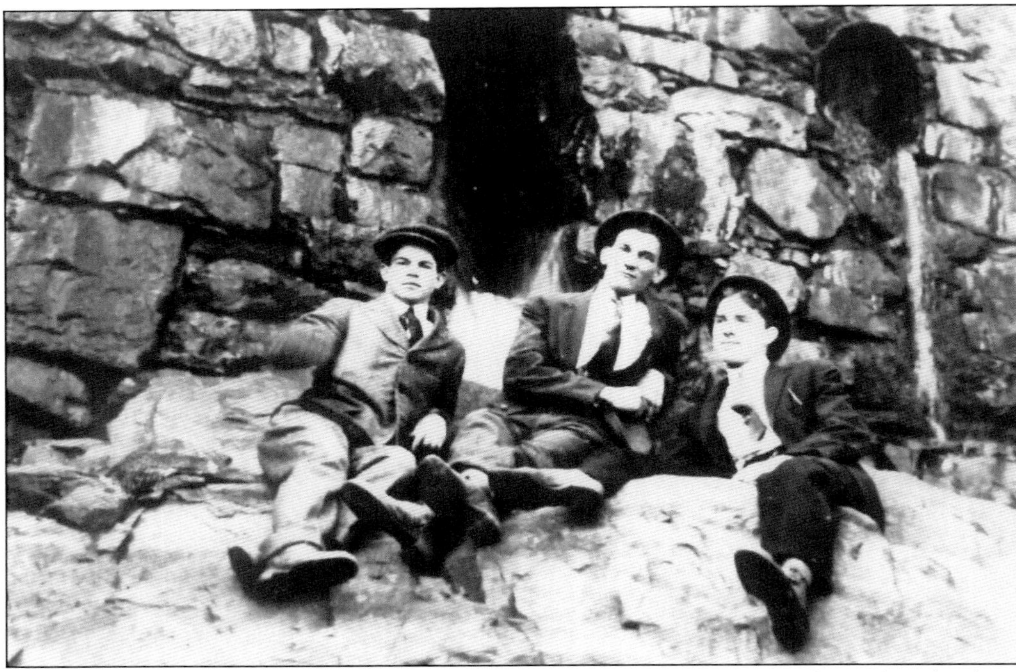

One of the outstanding architectural features of Avalon's water system is the rockwork—huge boulders probably from the NC Granite Corporation in Mount Airy. Above is an image of Booner Meyers (the gentleman in the middle) with friends at the base of the bulkhead where small waterfalls would flow. It was an area popular with courting couples and teenagers. (Courtesy of the Jeff Bullins Collection, Mayodan, NC.)

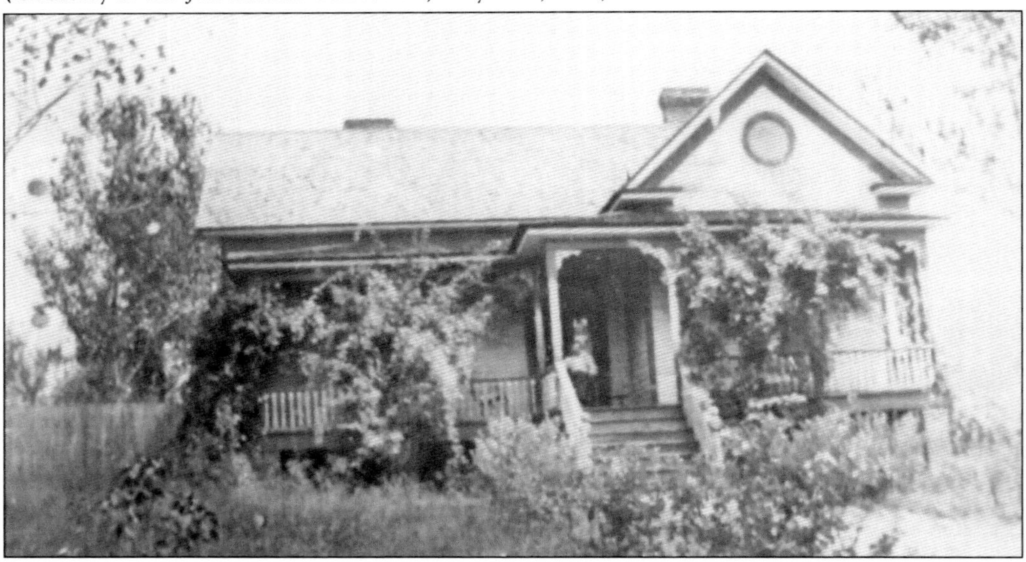

The Robert C. Smith House and the J.M. Suttenfield House (not pictured) literally faced Avalon Mills. They were located upon a hill, which made them a good spot for a photographer to shoot a series of pictures about the disastrous fire. Jesse G. Seay, a professional photographer from Leaksville (now Eden) is accredited with many scenes that comprise the postcard series. (Courtesy of the Jeff Bullins Collection, Mayodan, NC.)

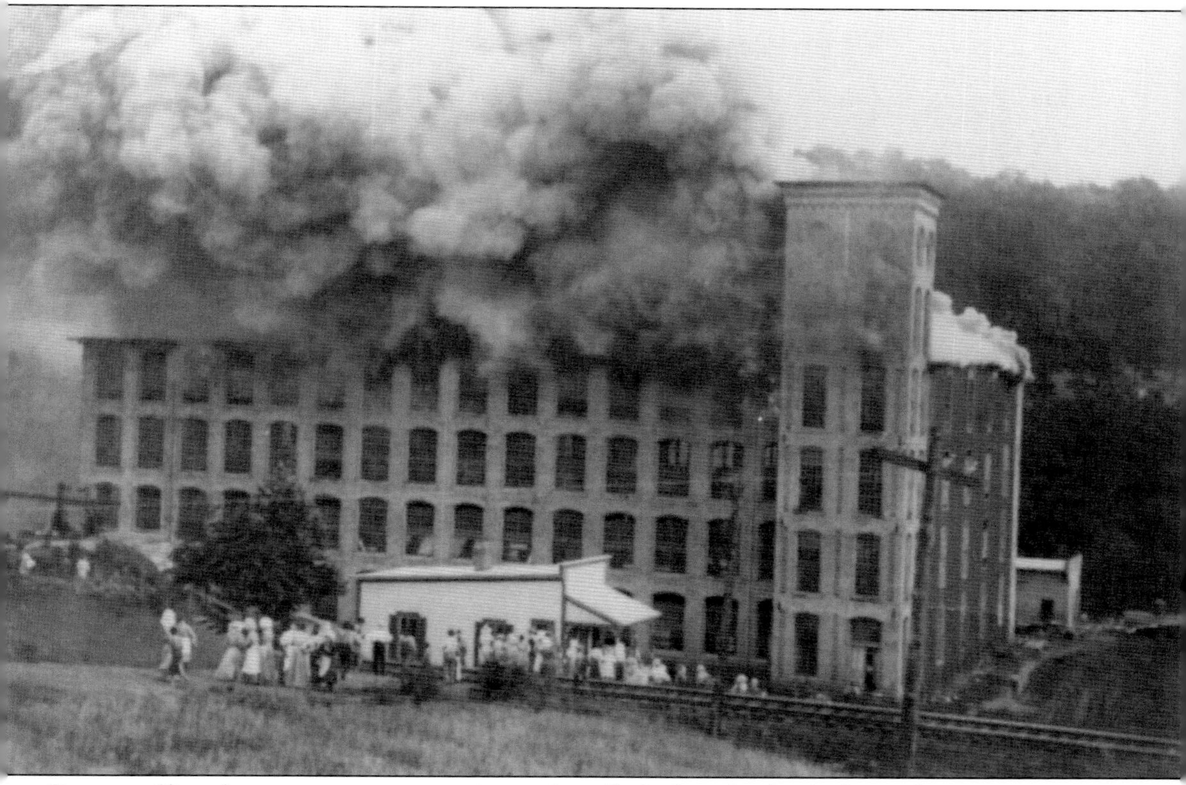

Because of lint, fire was not uncommon in textile mills. In fact, Avalon had a modern automatic sprinkler system throughout the factory. When its water pumps failed due to lack of proper maintenance, a summer breeze fanned a fire from the sparks of hot equipment and the flaming cotton lint spawned an uncontrollable blaze. The black-and-white postcard above depicts the fire on the floor where it originated—the fourth. The fire started at quitting time on June 15, 1911. (Courtesy of the Jeff Bullins Collection, Mayodan, NC.)

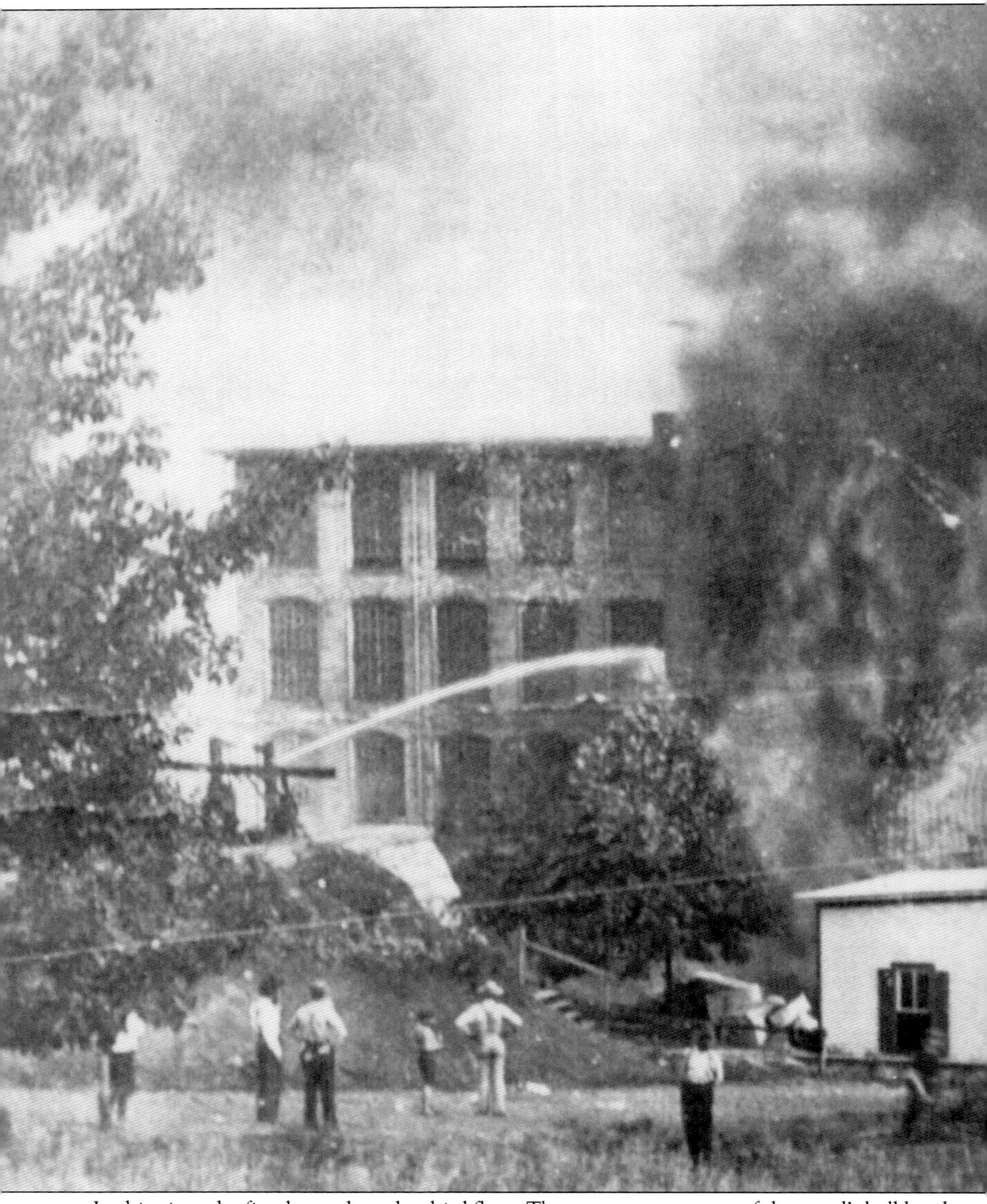

In this view, the fire descends to the third floor. The water spout on top of the canal's bulkhead was aimed at the factory once it became clear the interior sprinklers had not activated. In the foreground is the white mill office. At the far right in the background is the powerhouse (non-

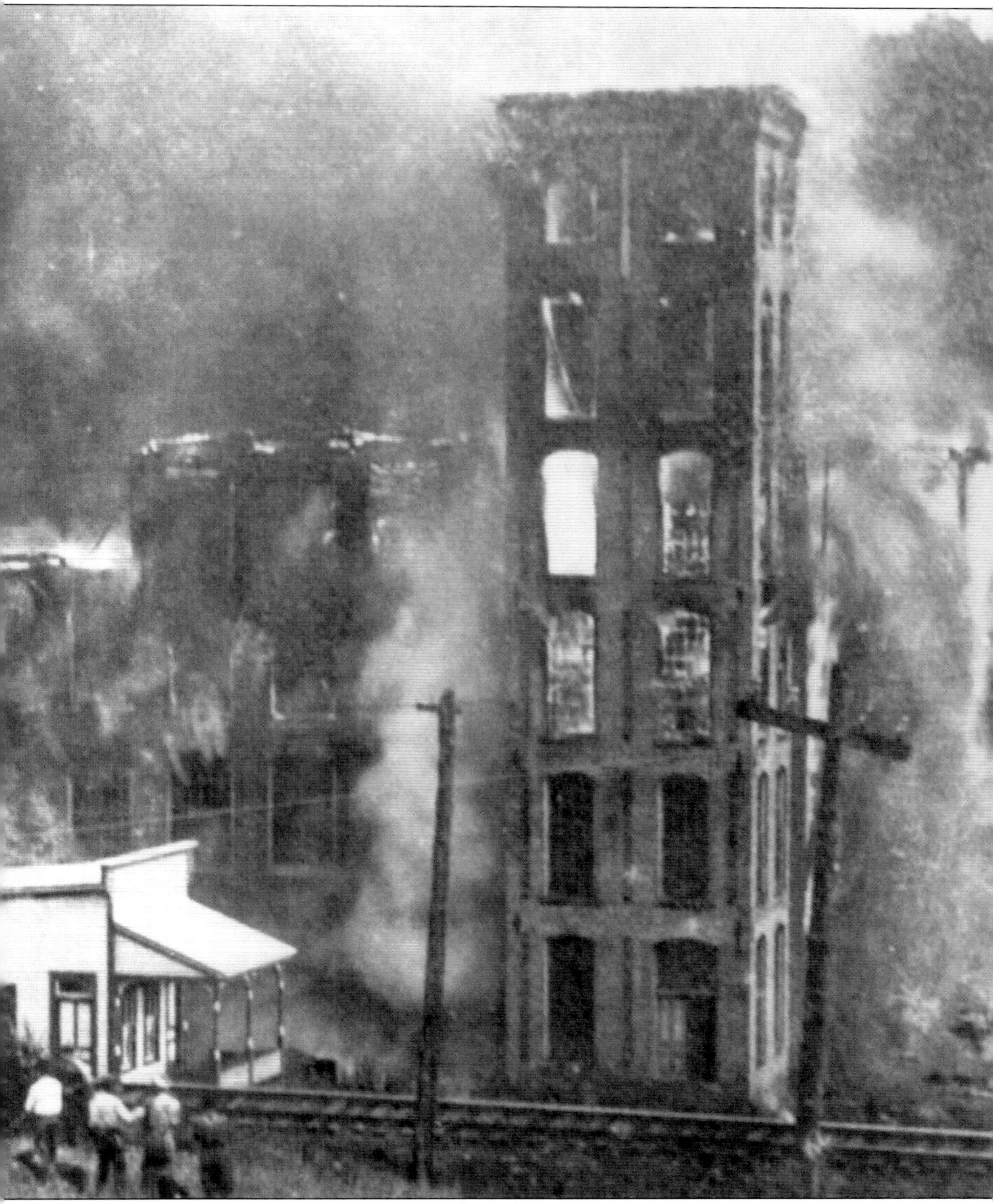

electrical); it survived the fire, as did the bulkhead. The ruins are now on private property. (Courtesy of the Jeff Bullins Collection, Mayodan, NC.)

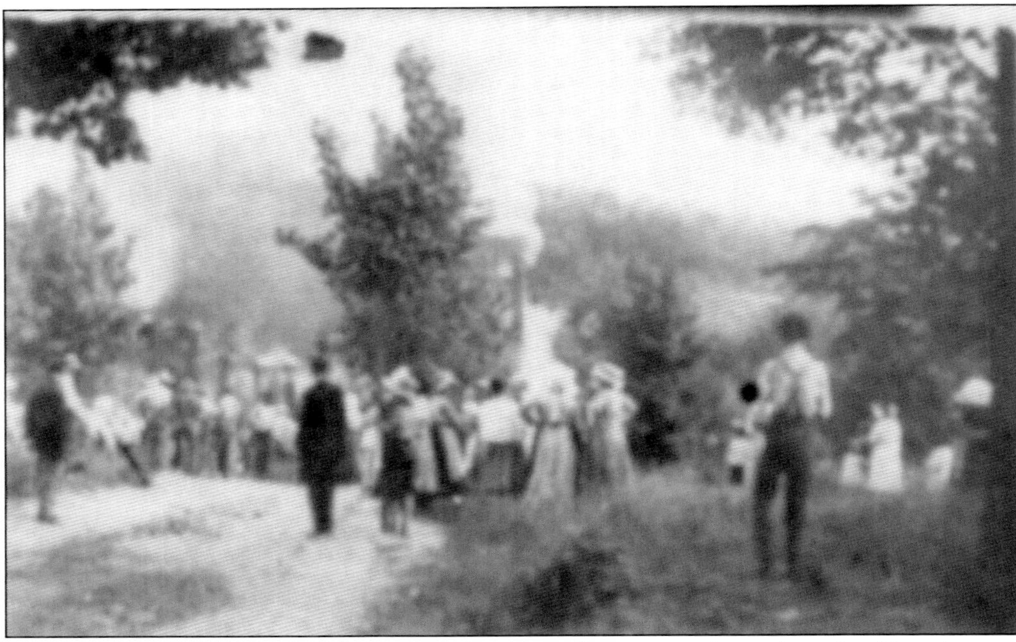

This black-and-white postcard portrays Avalon villagers watching their livelihood go up in smoke. The man in the black suit (center, left) is the chauffeur that drove Washington Mill's superintendents to the site once the telephone call came that all was lost. (Courtesy of the Jeff Bullins Collection, Mayodan, NC.)

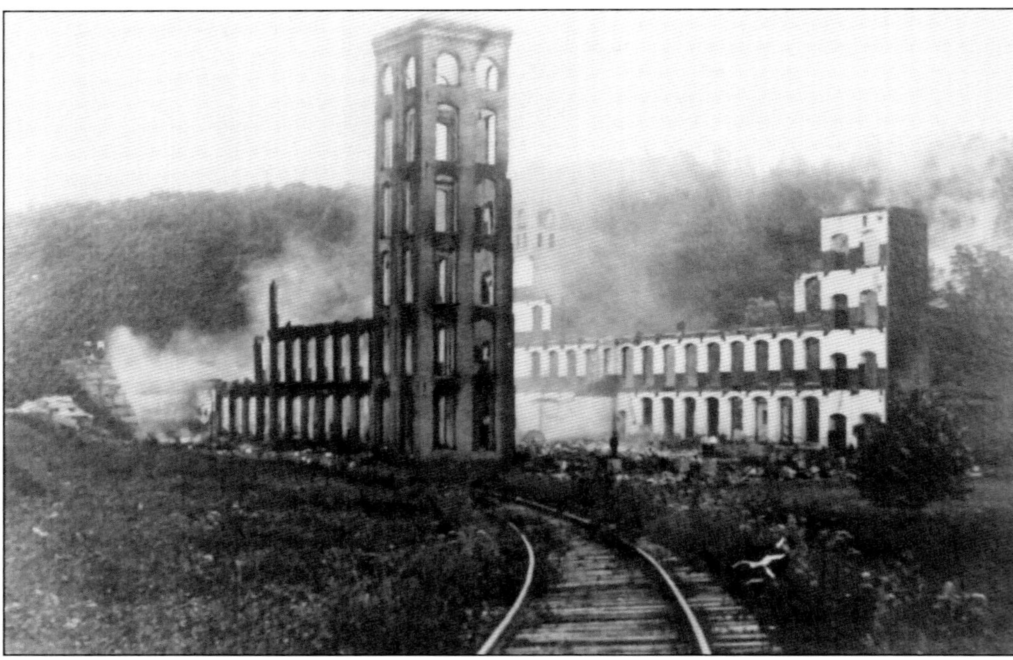

As bad as the fire appeared, few to no injuries occurred. Most employees had gone home for the day. This black-and-white postcard depicts the south elevation. (Courtesy of the Jeff Bullins Collection, Mayodan, NC.)

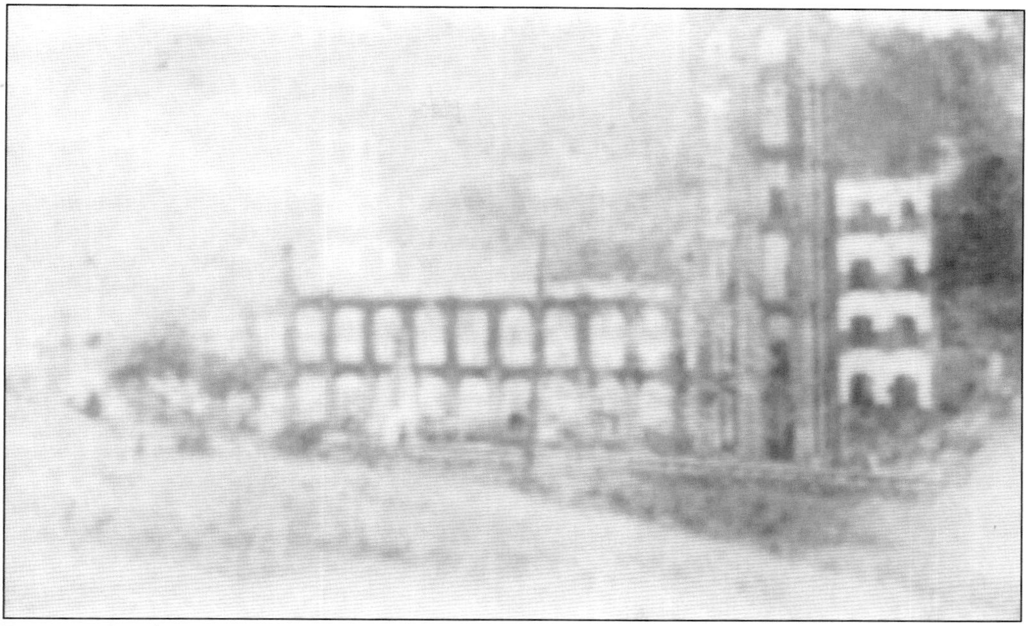

Fortunately, the structure was totally covered by insurance. This postcard shows the west elevation, the area where the Norfolk and Western Railroad tracks laid. (Courtesy of the Jeff Bullins Collection, Mayodan, NC.)

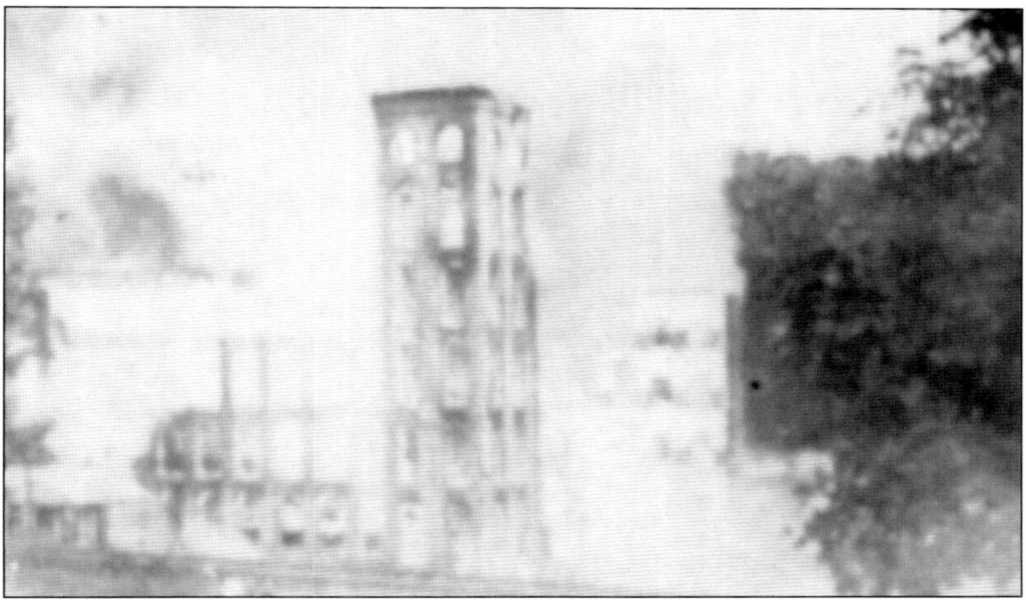

This postcard shows the mill office (far left) in front of the tower that was on the southwest corner of the facility. Amazingly, the planked office withstood the heat, protecting valuable records that were eventually destroyed in Mayodan at Washington Mills in the late 1950s. (Courtesy of the Jeff Bullins Collection, Mayodan, NC.)

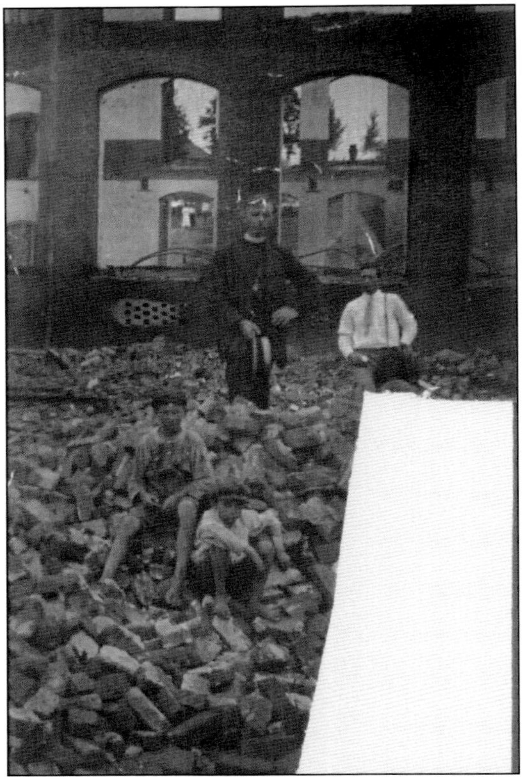

Perhaps this black-and-white postcard is one of the rarest in the Avalon Mills series. It depicts the east elevation, the side of the mill closest to the Mayo River and the area least damaged by the fire. The town can be seen through the windows and the doffers. The children who worked in the mill pose among the brick rubble in the shadow of a preacher man. One of the boys has been removed from the image. None of the persons have been identified despite the owner's efforts. (Courtesy of the Jeff Bullins Collection, Mayodan, NC.)

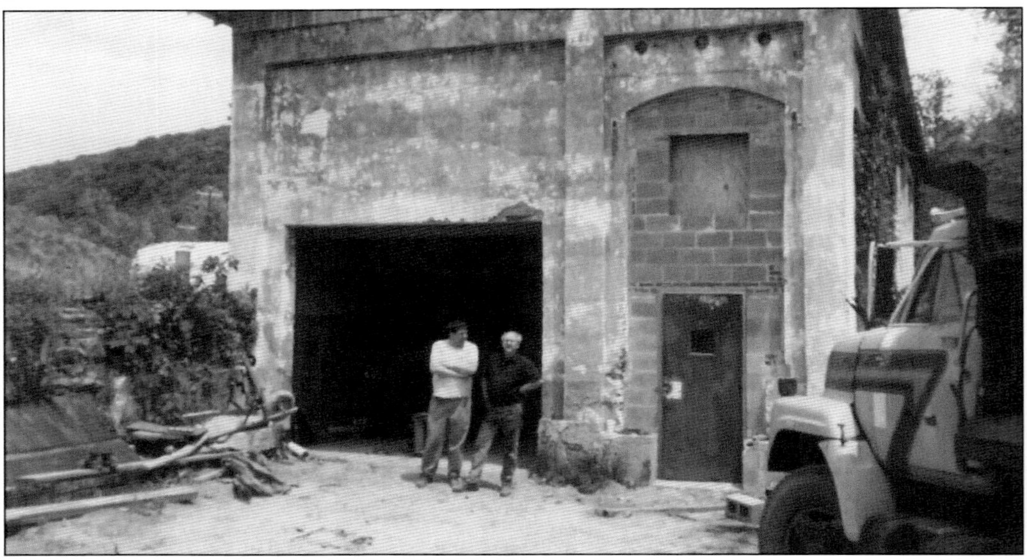

This photograph shows the powerhouse that survived the fire. It is located on the east elevation. Ironically, this structure housed the defunct pumps of the sprinkler system that could have saved Avalon. Today, this block building next to the Mayo River contains a turbine that generates electricity into the Duke Energy network. At the far left of the image, beneath honeysuckle vines, lies the brick and concrete foundation that was the southeast corner of Avalon Mills. (Photograph by Piper Aheron, Belmont, NC.)

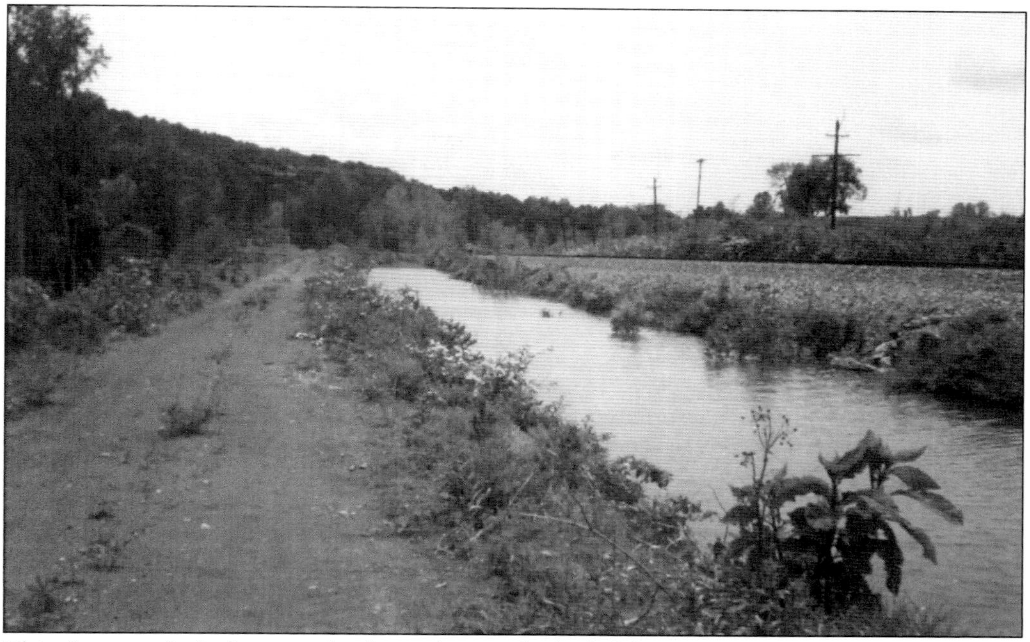

This photograph, looking south, shows the canal which followed the tracks utilized by Norfolk and Western Railroads after their completion in 1892. The tracks are still used today. Avalon Mills was located at the junction where the road bed, canal, and tracks seemingly meet in the background. On the right, across the tracks, is the hillside where the village was located. (Photograph by Piper Aheron, Belmont, NC.)

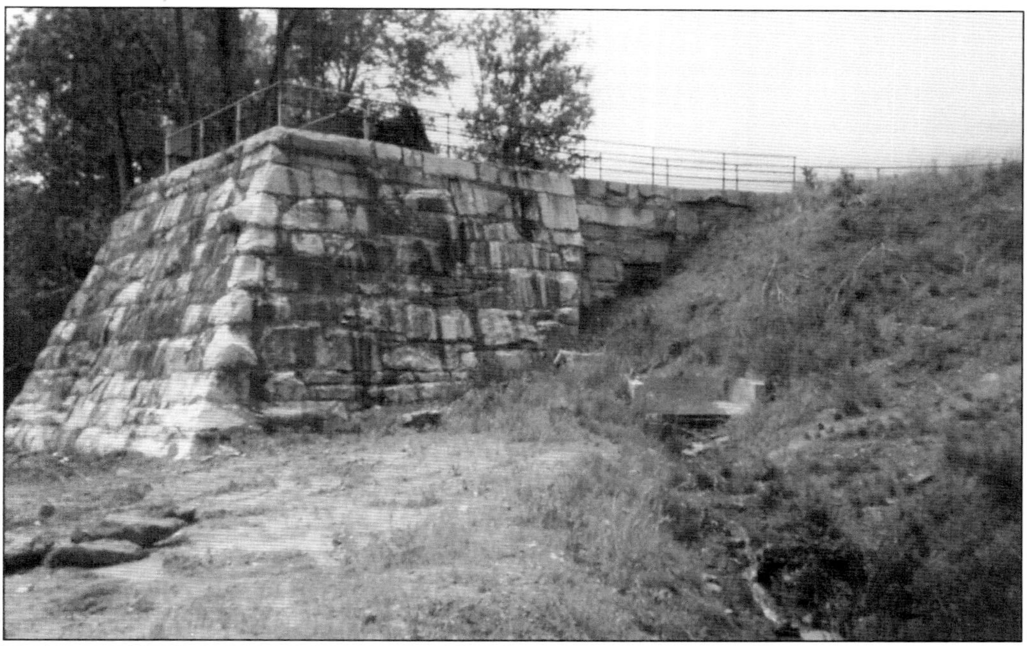

Undamaged by fire or time, the stone bulkhead is where the canal water drained under the mill and went into the power building. This structure is as awesome and attractive now as it was to Booner Meyers and his friends in 1910. (Photograph by Piper Aheron, Belmont, NC.)

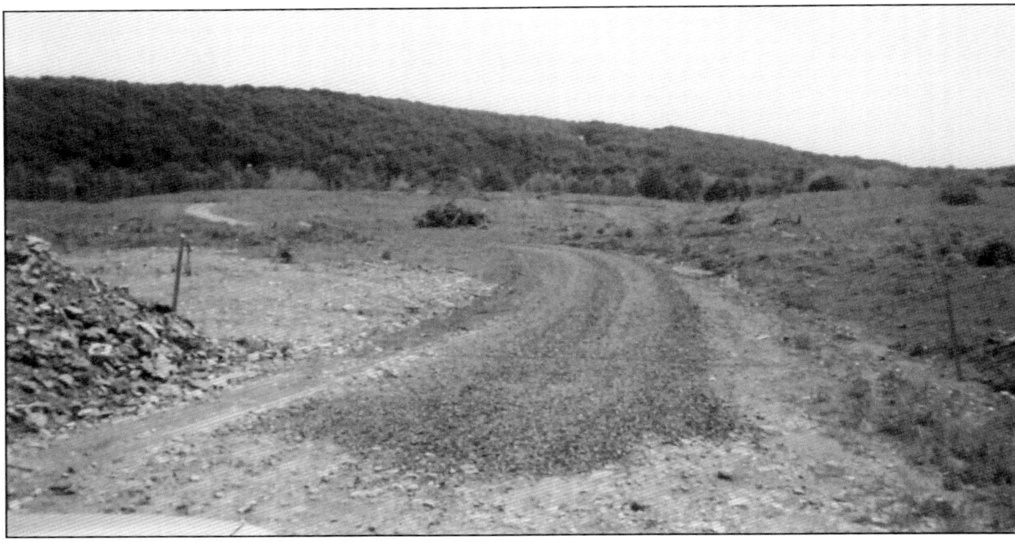

The rolling hills (approximately 135 acres) of Avalon are now for sale today. Once Avalon burned, the mill-owned houses, about sixty total, were hauled southward to Mayodan. The folks used horses and mules and logs and tediously rolled the structures to their new location. These houses still stand in Mayodan today. Most of the Avalon villagers gained employment at the Mayo or Washington Mills, also owned by F.H. Fries. Some folks relocated north to Stoneville, a town incorporated in 1877, about twenty-one years earlier than Avalon or Mayodan. (Photograph by Piper Aheron, Belmont, NC.)

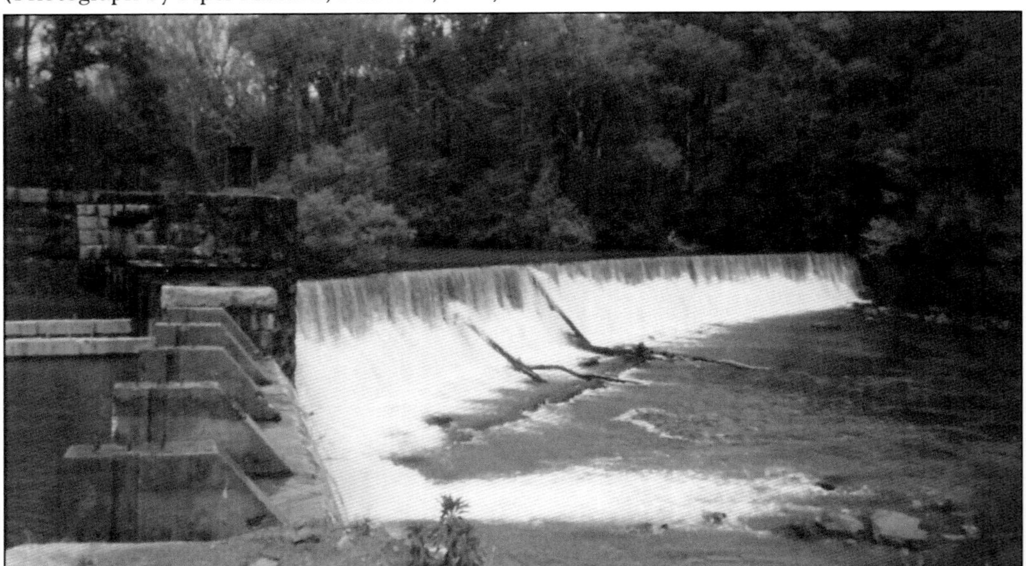

The waters of the Mayo are as picturesque today as the were in the early 1900s. This is a 1997 snapshot showing the Avalon dam, taken near the same point on the canal which was first illustrated in the 1899 postcard on page 10. Remarkably, Mayo Mills (eventually called Washington Mills, now Tultex Corporation) kept the property functional and safe for over eighty-five years. The land and the river are still an excellent location for a family picnic. (Photograph by Piper Aheron, Belmont, NC.)

Two

Stoneville

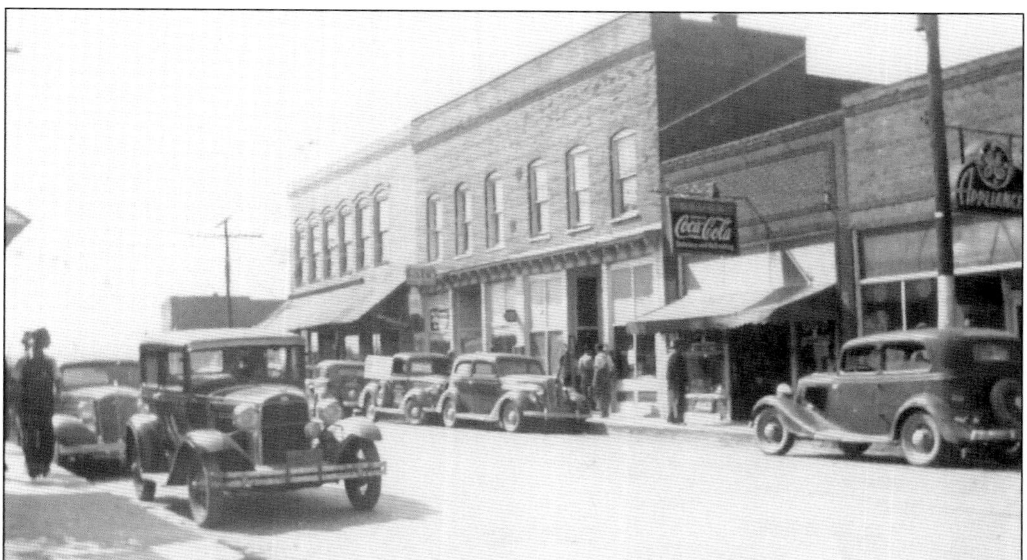

Stoneville became incorporated in 1877. A regular stop for the Norfolk and Western train, Stoneville quickly grew by the waters of the Mayo River. From the start, the town was a trading center for the rural communities of Ayersvile, Price, Groganville, Matrimony, Providence, and Shiloh. Its earliest industries were tobacco farming and gristmilling. In this 1930s image, farmers arrive in town to bargain and get the best prices possible for their tobacco and cotton. (Courtesy of the Zelma Joyce Scott Collection, Stoneville, NC.)

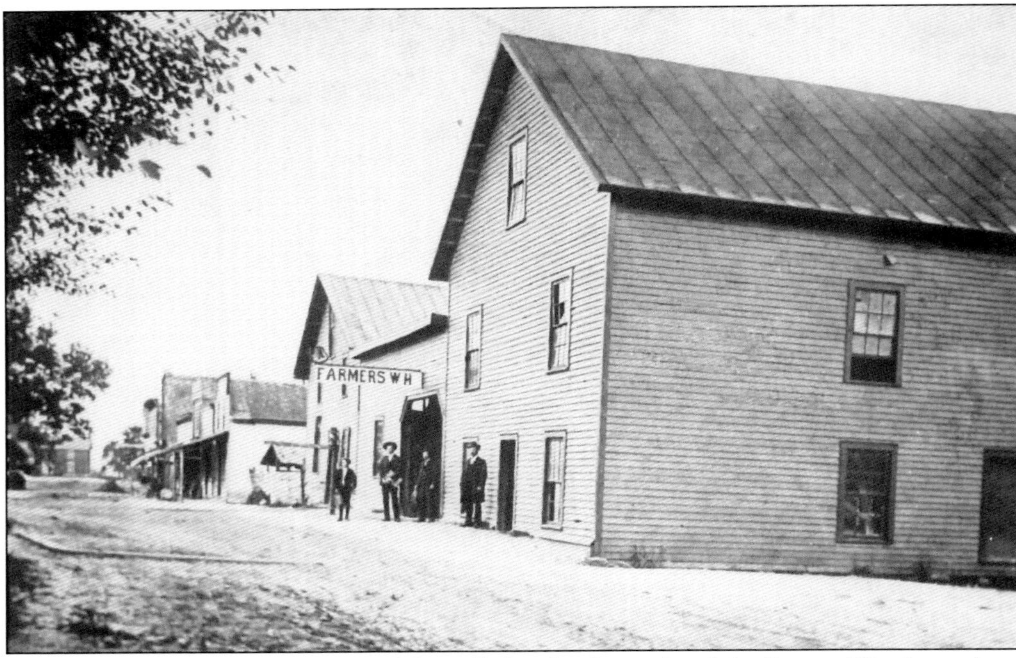

The R.H. Lewis Tobacco Company (also called a plug factory) and the Farmer Warehouse have a history dating back to 1843. This image is from the early 1900s. It was taken on Henry Street. (Courtesy of the Zelma Joyce Scott Collection, Stoneville, NC.)

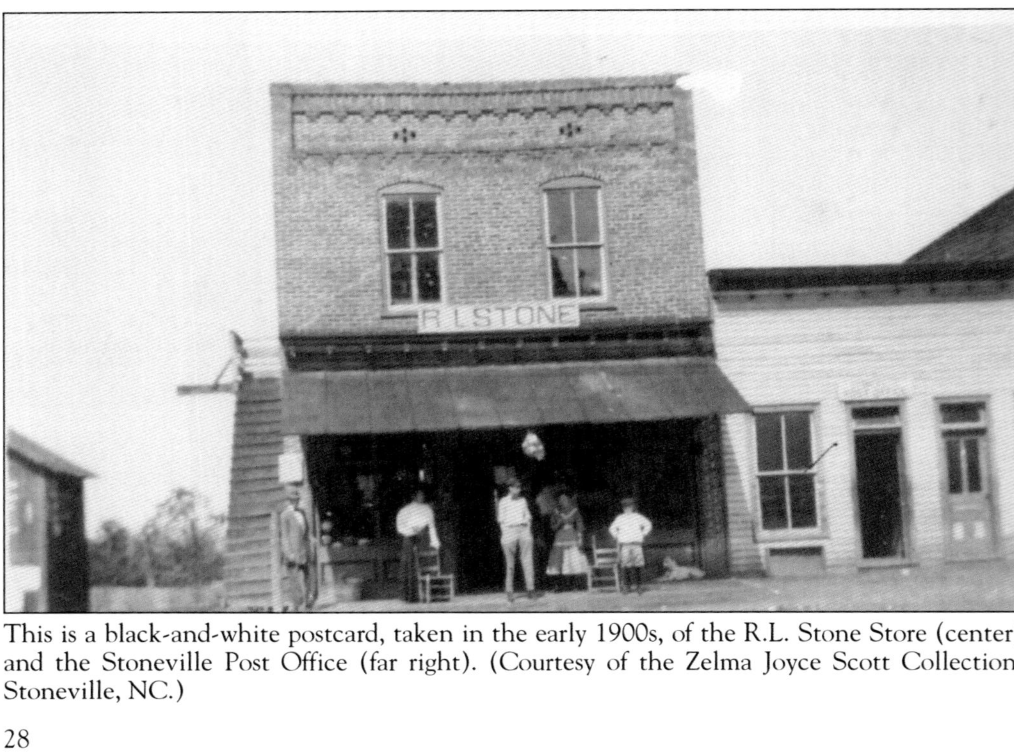

This is a black-and-white postcard, taken in the early 1900s, of the R.L. Stone Store (center) and the Stoneville Post Office (far right). (Courtesy of the Zelma Joyce Scott Collection, Stoneville, NC.)

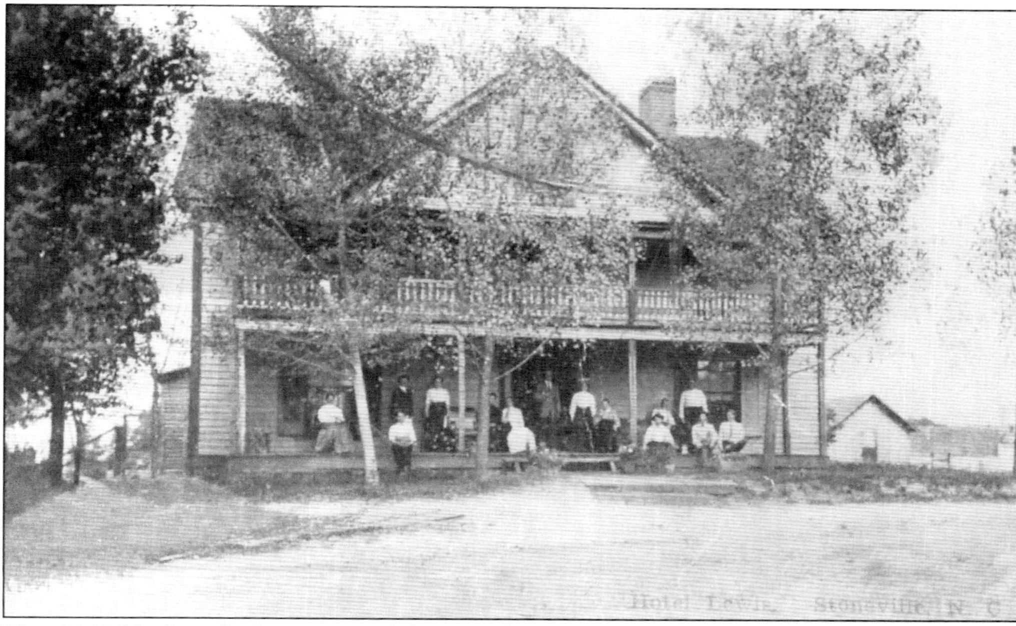

This 1910 black-and-white postcard features the Hotel Lewis, a two-story house that was the picture of Southern hospitality in Stoneville. Until it burned in 1921, the hotel was located across the street from the Norfolk and Western Railroad station. (Courtesy of the Zelma Joyce Scott Collection, Stoneville, NC.)

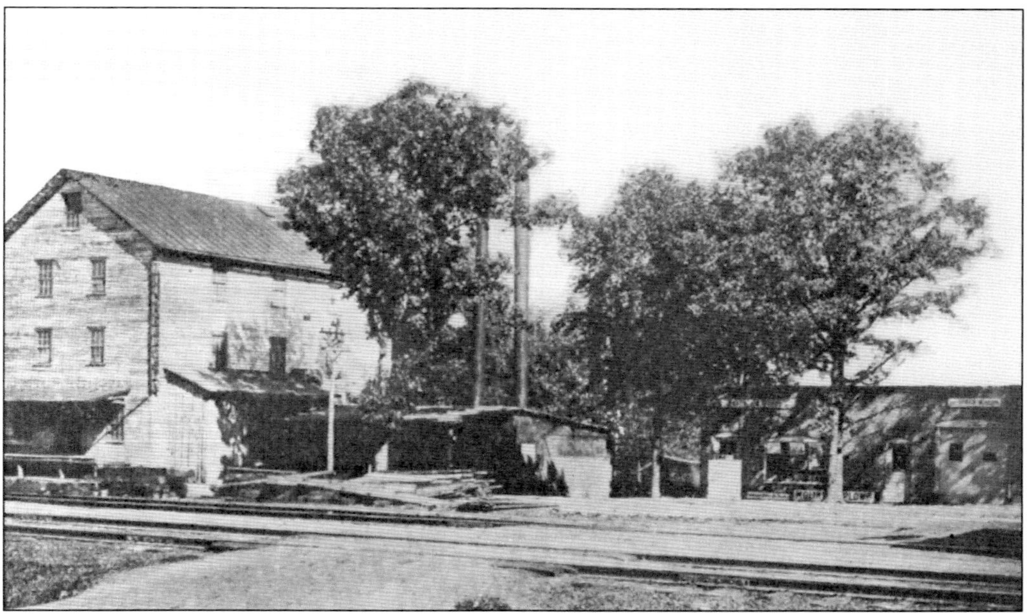

The flour roller mill and powerhouse was owned by George M. Mitchell. This sepia postcard dates back to the 1910s. (Courtesy of the Zelma Joyce Scott Collection, Stoneville, NC.)

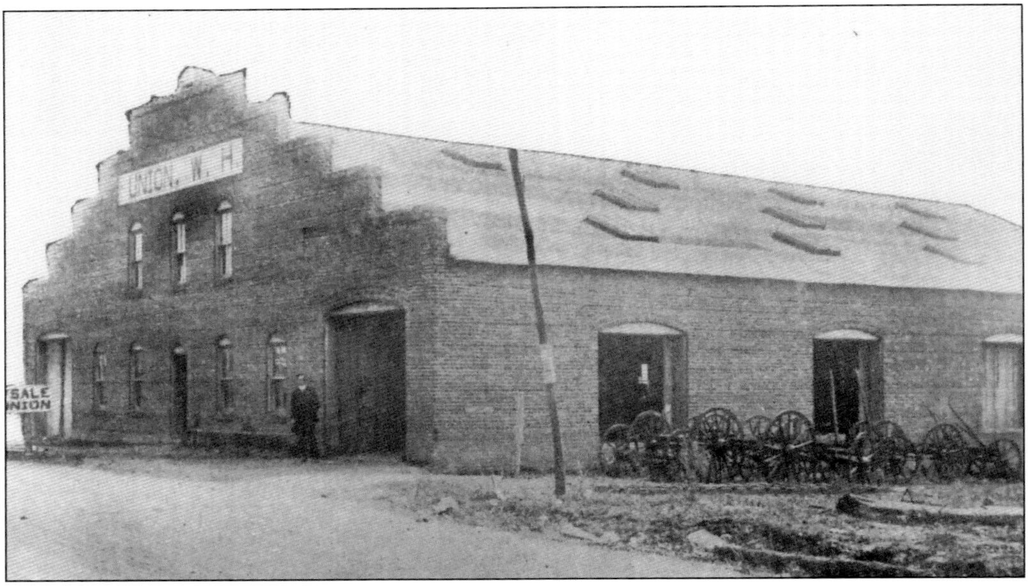

This postcard features the Union Warehouse, which was built on Main Street by J.M. Taylor and Nat Lewis. The Union Warehouse was operated by several owners, including Otis Joyce. Now referred to as the Joyce Warehouse, this brick-and-frame structure still stands, seemingly unchanged by time or technology. (Courtesy of the Zelma Joyce Scott Collection, Stoneville, NC.)

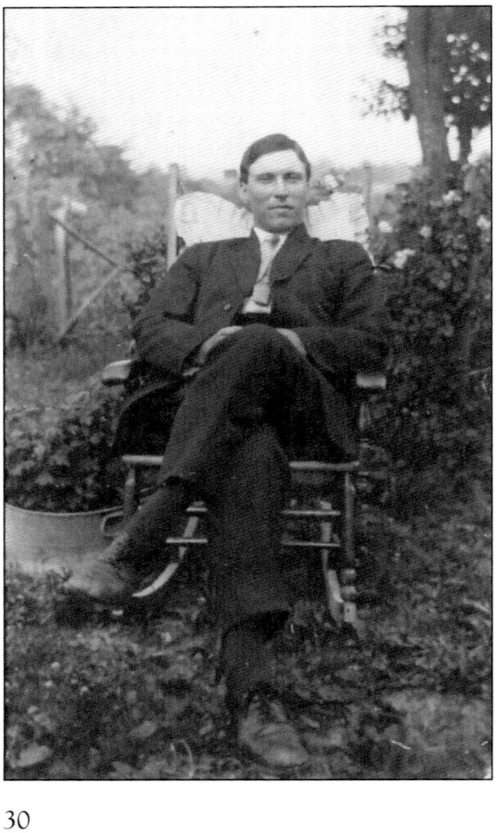

This black-and-white postcard was taken near the Mayo River not far from Stoneville. Seated is Jesse Joyce, a gentleman noted for good humor as well as his good looks. This family card is dated around the early 1900s. (Courtesy of the Zelma Joyce Scott Collection, Stoneville, NC.)

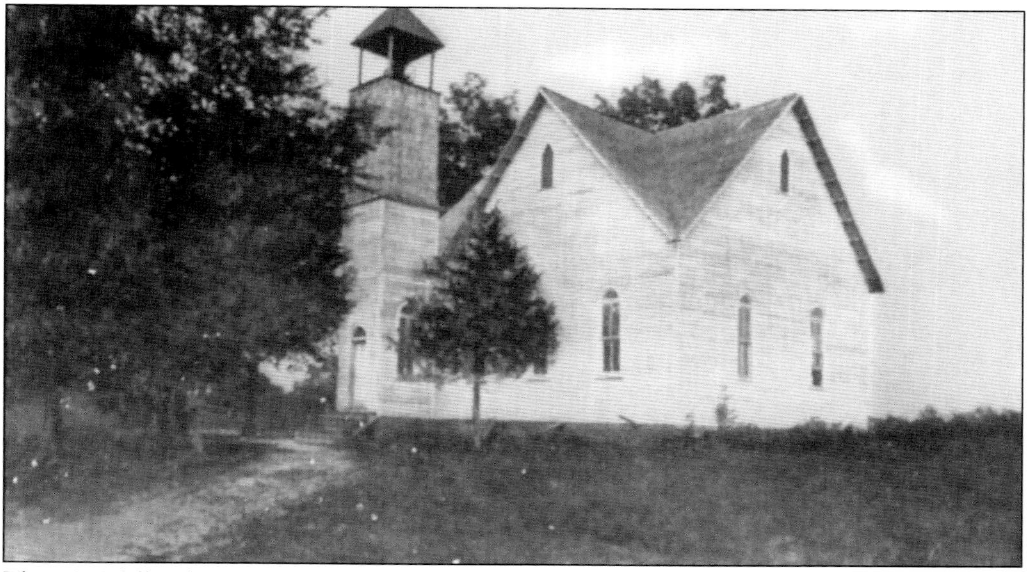

This 1910 full-color postcard shows the Christian Church on Glenn Street, which was organized in 1892. The Church of the Living God presently uses the building today. (Courtesy of the Zelma Joyce Scott Collection, Stoneville, NC.)

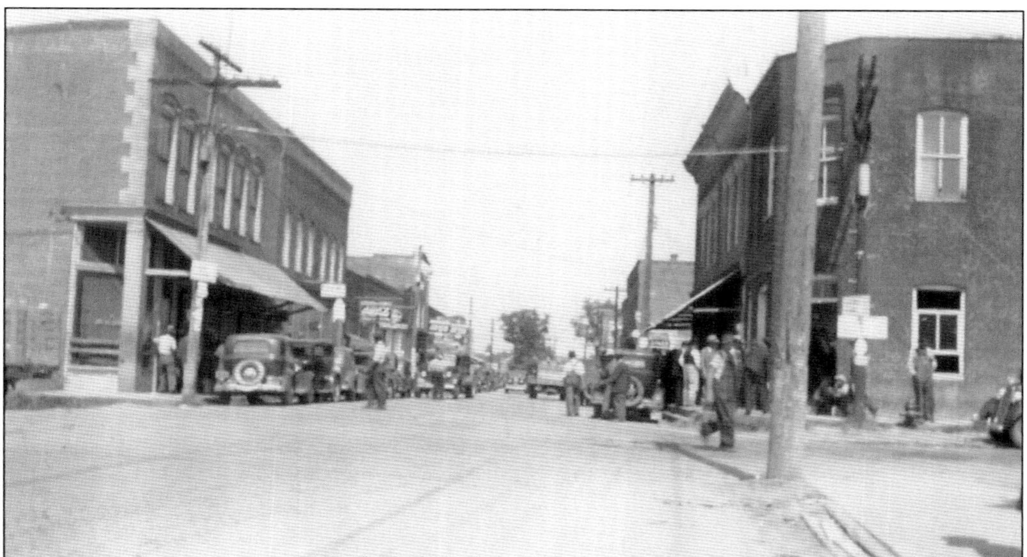

The junction of Highway 770 and Business 220 is still a thriving shopping area for visitors and townspeople. Pictured here is the business district in 1935. (Courtesy of the Zelma Joyce Scott Collection, Stoneville, NC.)

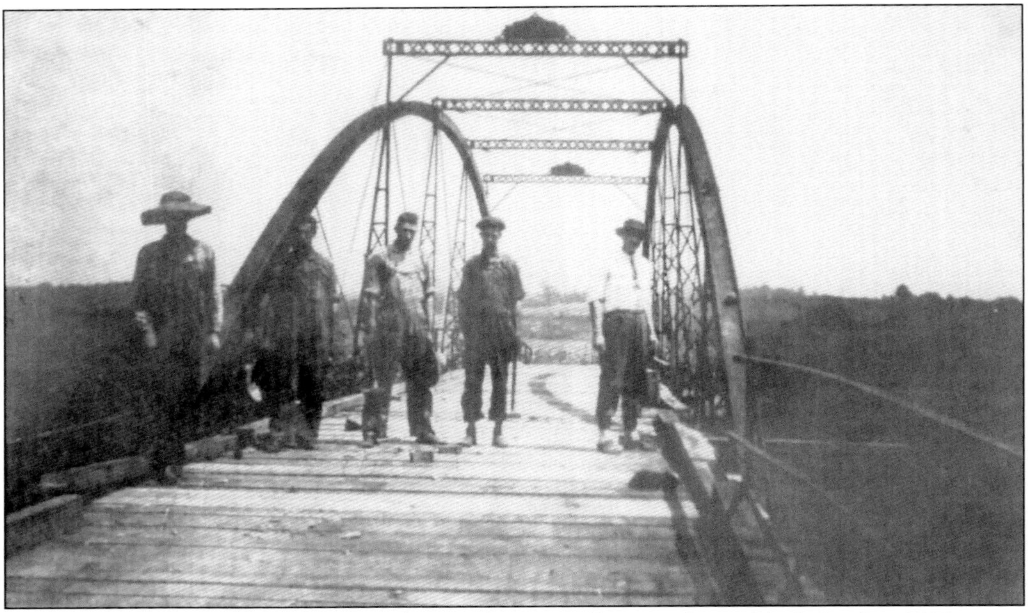

In 1884, the Iron Bridge was erected over the Mayo River at Joyce Ford. In this 1920s sepia postcard, five men with tools in their hands are ready to repair some structural damage. Today, a road bearing the name of the bridge is all that is left of this particular span. (Courtesy of the Zelma Joyce Scott Collection, Stoneville, NC.)

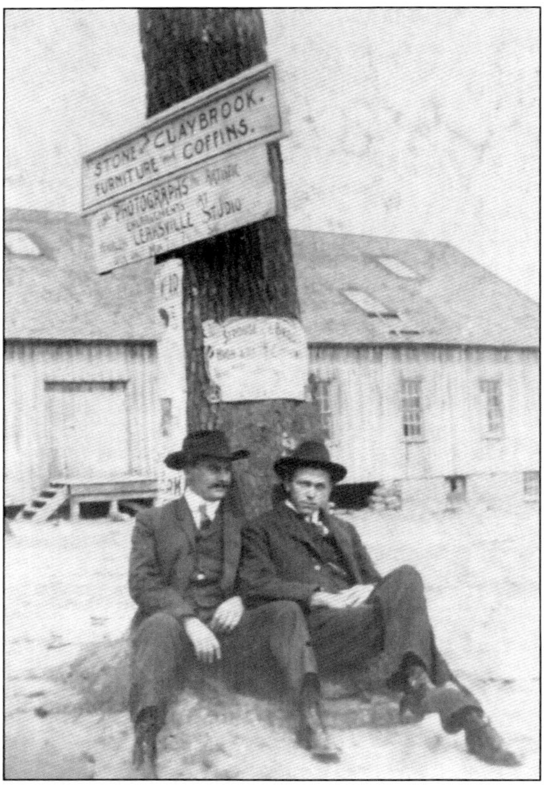

While the men pictured here are no longer identifiable, the tree is consistently mentioned throughout documentation concerning land grants and property lines. It was located on Henry Street. (Courtesy of the Zelma Joyce Scott Collection, Stoneville, NC.)

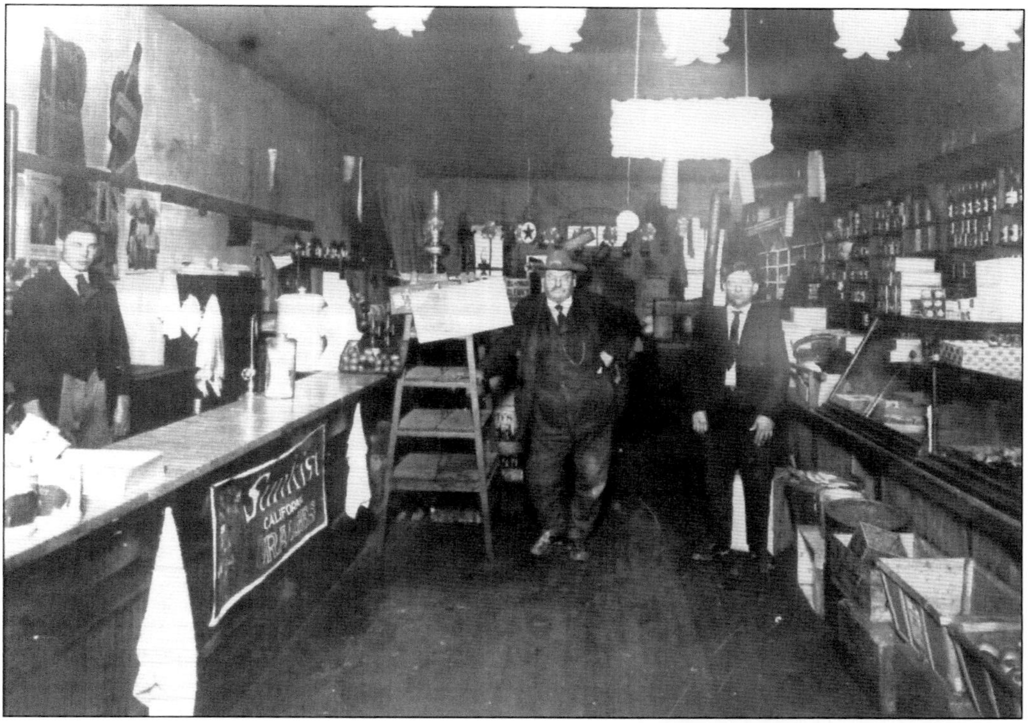

This is an interior shot of the Thomas Store on Henry Street. The building is featured in several postcards and still exists as an auto parts store. From left to right are as follows: Tom Orlander, Robert "Bob" Thomas, and John D. Matthews. The image dates to the early 1900s. (Courtesy of the Zelma Joyce Scott Collection, Stoneville, NC.)

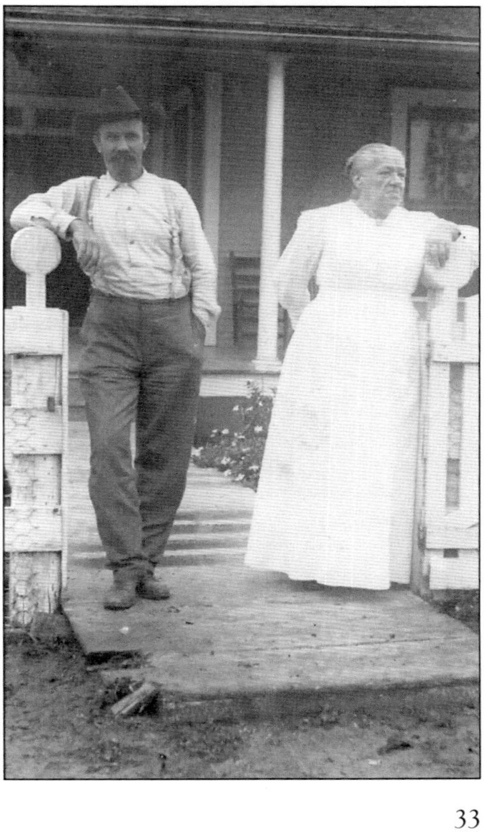

Rubin Hensley Joyce and his wife are the subjects of this postcard dating around the 1870s. The exact location in Stoneville is not known. (Courtesy of the Zelma Joyce Scott Collection, Stoneville, NC.)

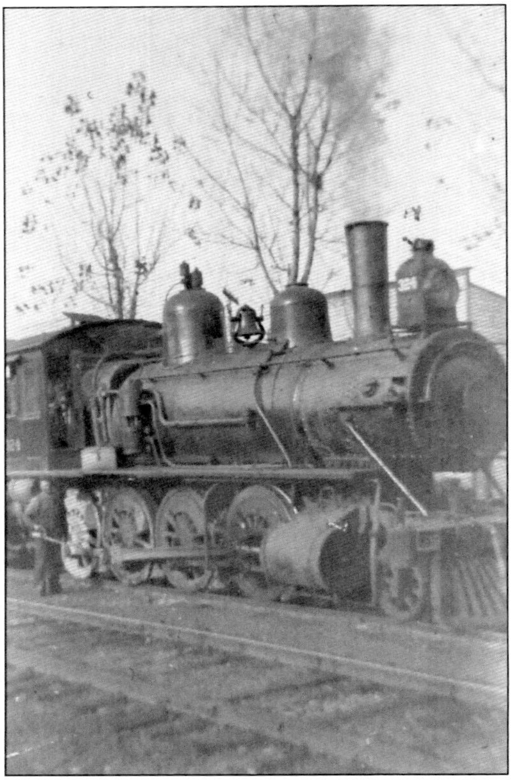

The Norfolk and Western passenger trains stopped at the Stoneville Depot en route to Roanoke, Virginia. The train's stops south of Stoneville included Avalon, Mayodan, and Madison. Below is a sepia image of the depot in 1910. (Postcards courtesy of the Zelma Joyce Scott Collection, Stoneville, NC.)

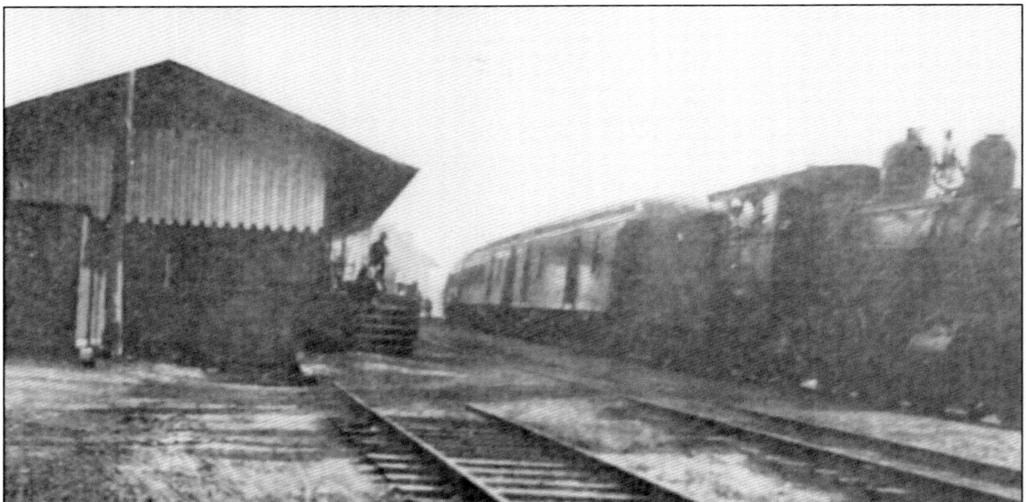

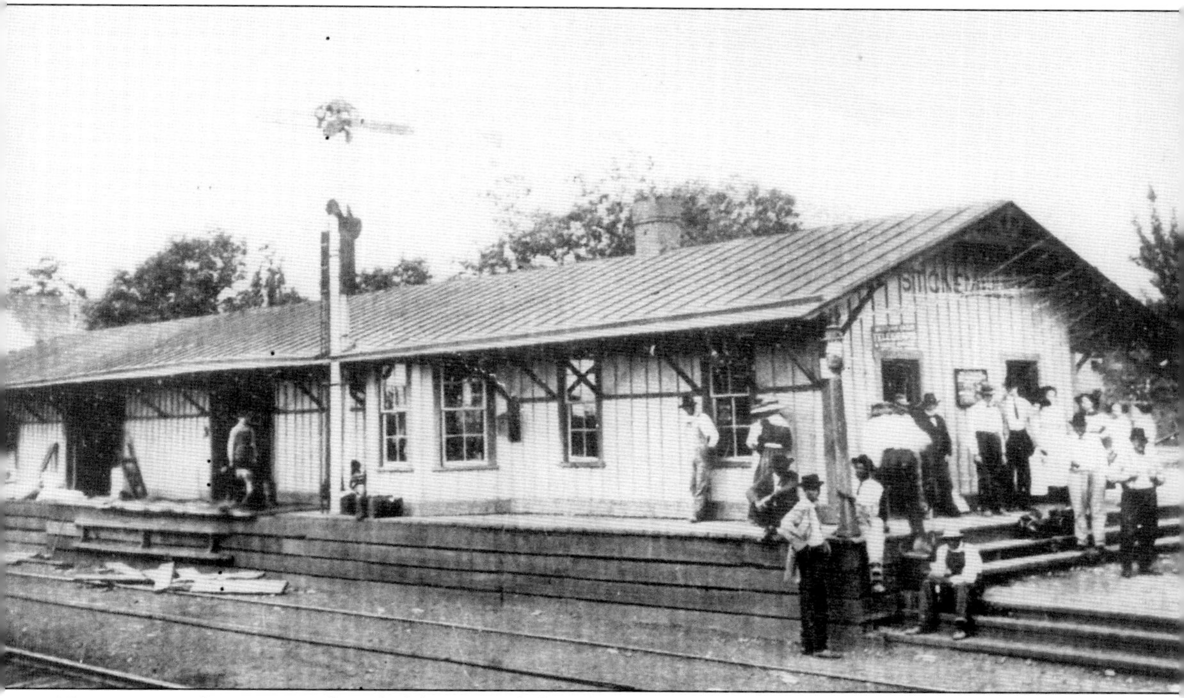

Above is another postcard probably created shortly after the facility was erected in 1892. The depot was closed in 1973 and used for storage, as seen in the 1979 photo below. (Photograph by Guy Lewis. Postcard courtesy of the Zelma Joyce Scott Collection, Stoneville, NC.)

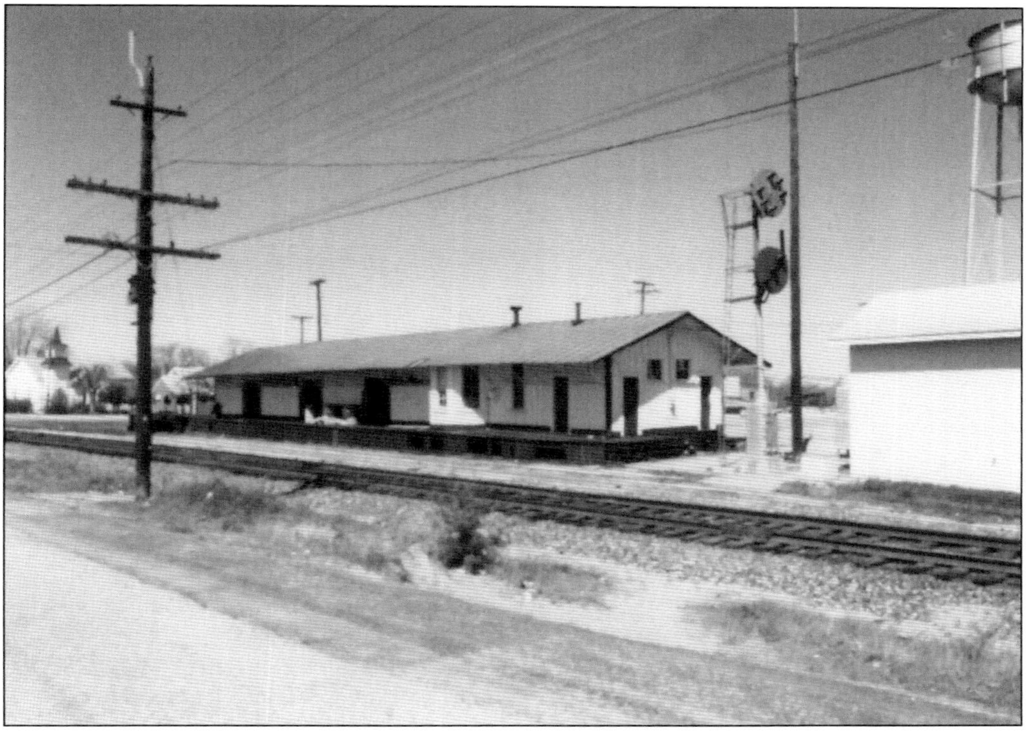

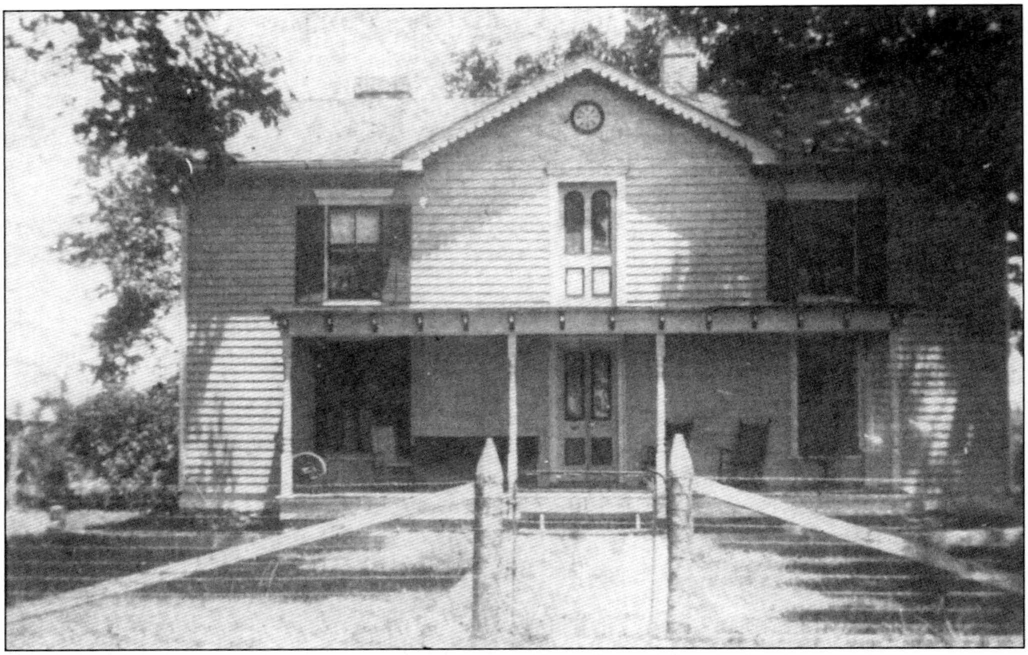

Many villagers sent postcards of their homes to friends and family. Robert L. Stone was one of these folks. Here is a black-and-white postcard of his house, which was built at the time of his marriage in 1892; it burned in 1920. (Courtesy of the Zelma Joyce Scott Collection, Stoneville, NC.)

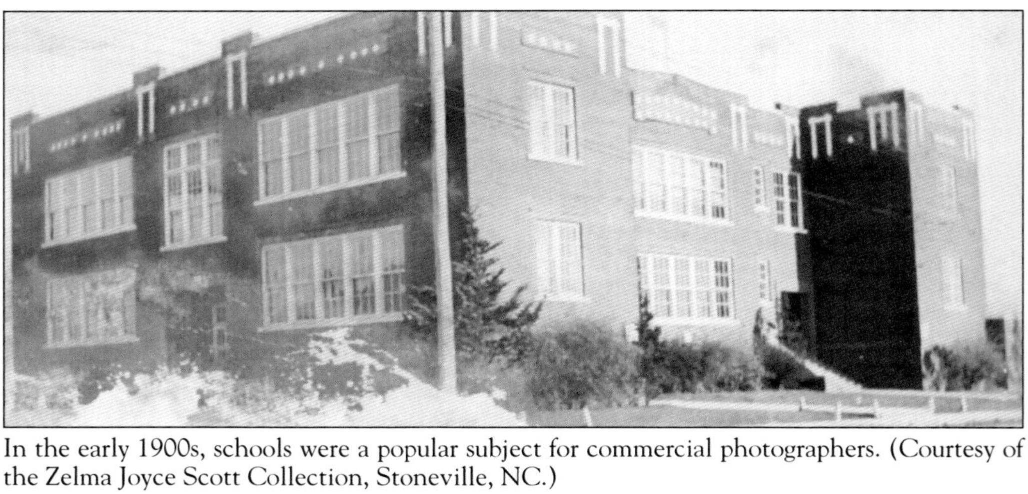

In the early 1900s, schools were a popular subject for commercial photographers. (Courtesy of the Zelma Joyce Scott Collection, Stoneville, NC.)

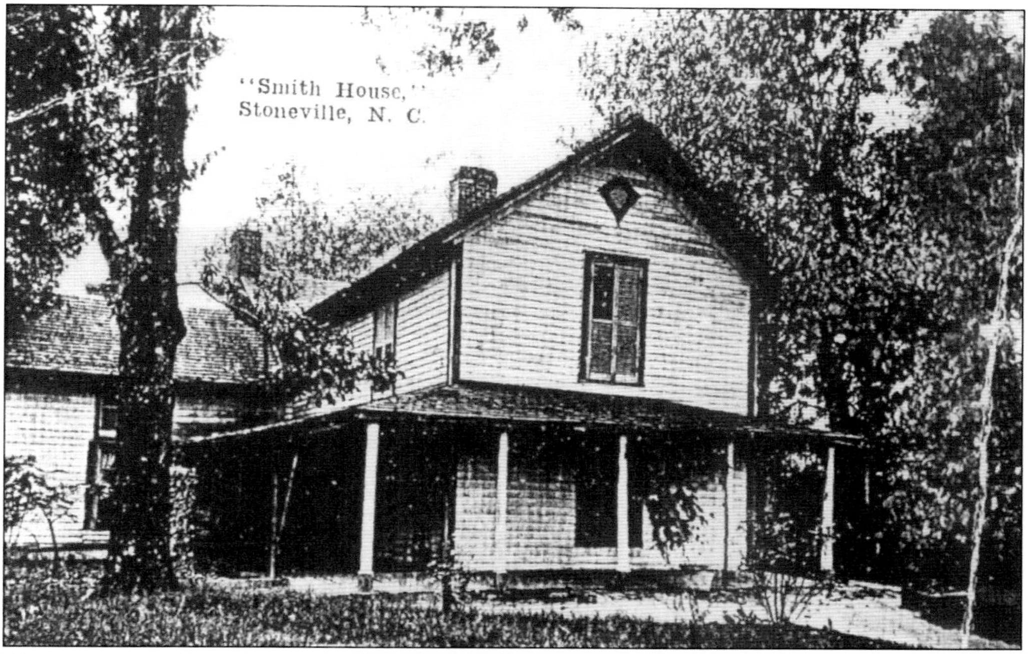

This is a copy of a color postcard marked 1912. It features the home of Dr. Joshua R. Smith, which still stands on Main Street today. (Courtesy of the Zelma Joyce Scott Collection, Stoneville, NC.)

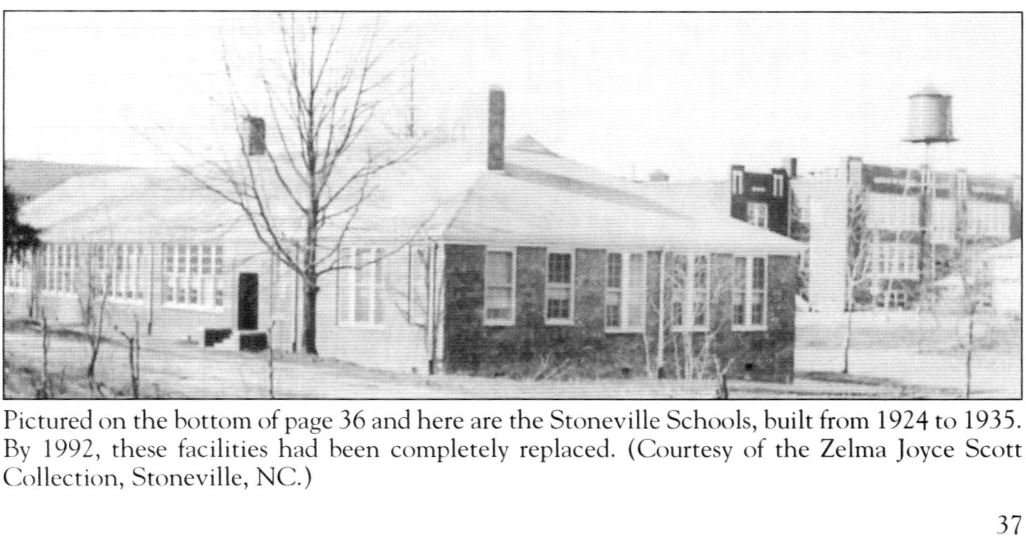

Pictured on the bottom of page 36 and here are the Stoneville Schools, built from 1924 to 1935. By 1992, these facilities had been completely replaced. (Courtesy of the Zelma Joyce Scott Collection, Stoneville, NC.)

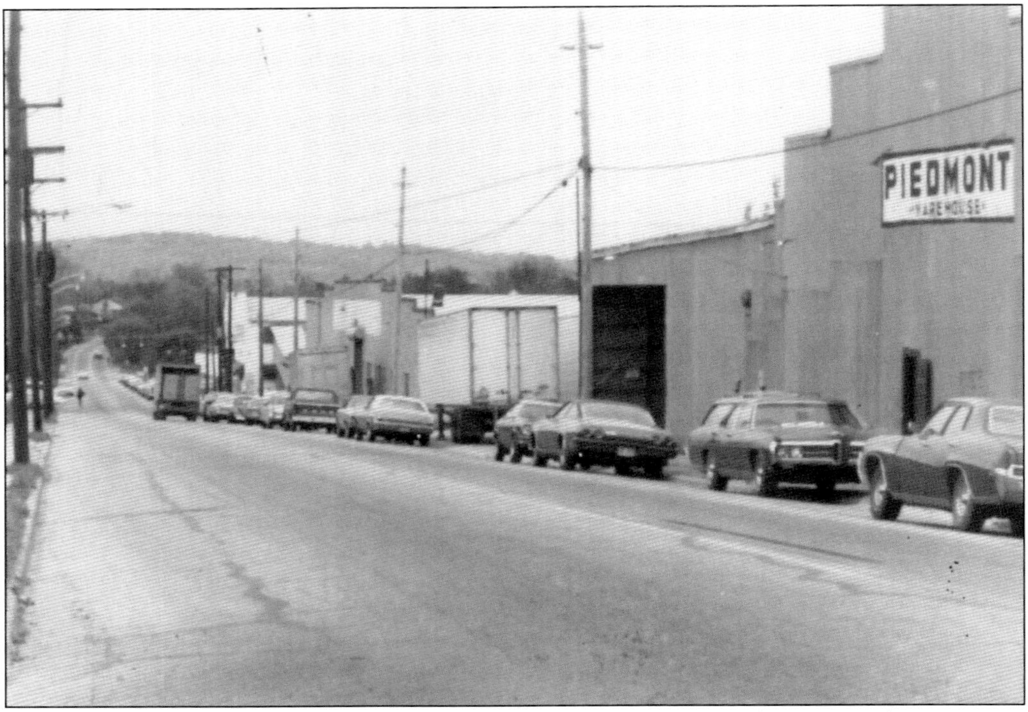

Postcards of the Piedmont Warehouse date back to 1910. Built around 1901, the Piedmont was the property of John H. Glenn and Robert Price. This 1970s photograph looks down Henry Street where the warehouse sat until Stoneville Furniture Company built its facilities along the left and right of the road. (Courtesy of the Zelma Joyce Scott Collection, Stoneville, NC.)

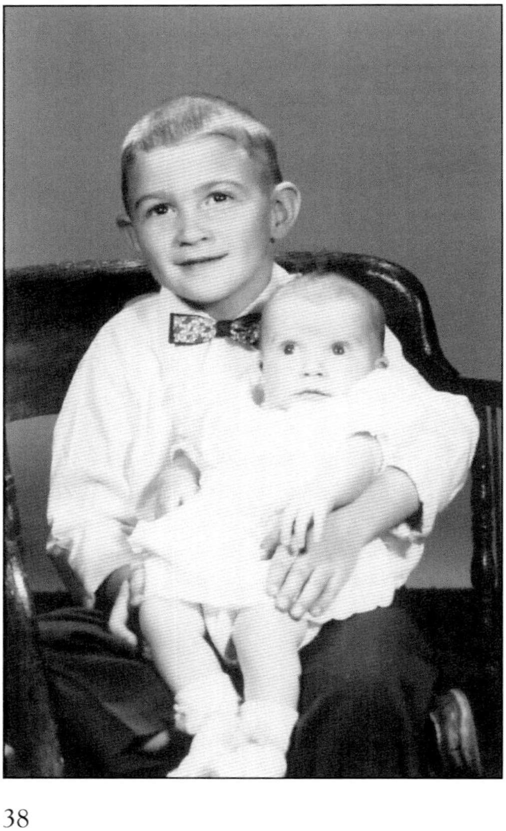

By 1955, postcards of families were increasingly rare. Commercial subjects had taken over the market due to tourism. In this vintage black-and-white postcard, John D. Shumate and Jo D. Shumate, children of Jack G. Shumate and Mrs. Zelma Joyce Scott, are seated in a wooden office chair known as the Americana Classic. Mrs. Scott is the city historian of Stoneville. (Courtesy of the Zelma Joyce Scott Collection, Stoneville, NC.)

Three

MAYODAN

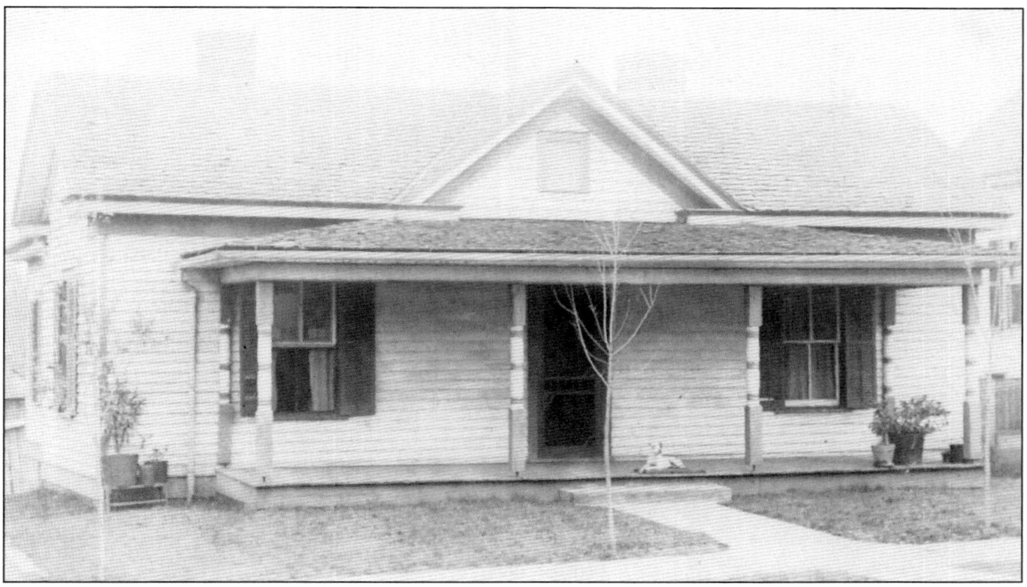

After Avalon Mills burned to the ground, its principals decided not to reconstruct. Instead, the townspeople and the houses were physically relocated to Mayodan. Structures like this simple plank unit were loaded onto logs and slowly towed by mules and horses 2 miles farther south along the Mayo River to the city limits of Mayodan. The postcard above is from the early 1900s and was shot by Mayodan commercial photographer Allen Benton. (Courtesy of the Jeff Bullins Collection, Mayodan, NC.)

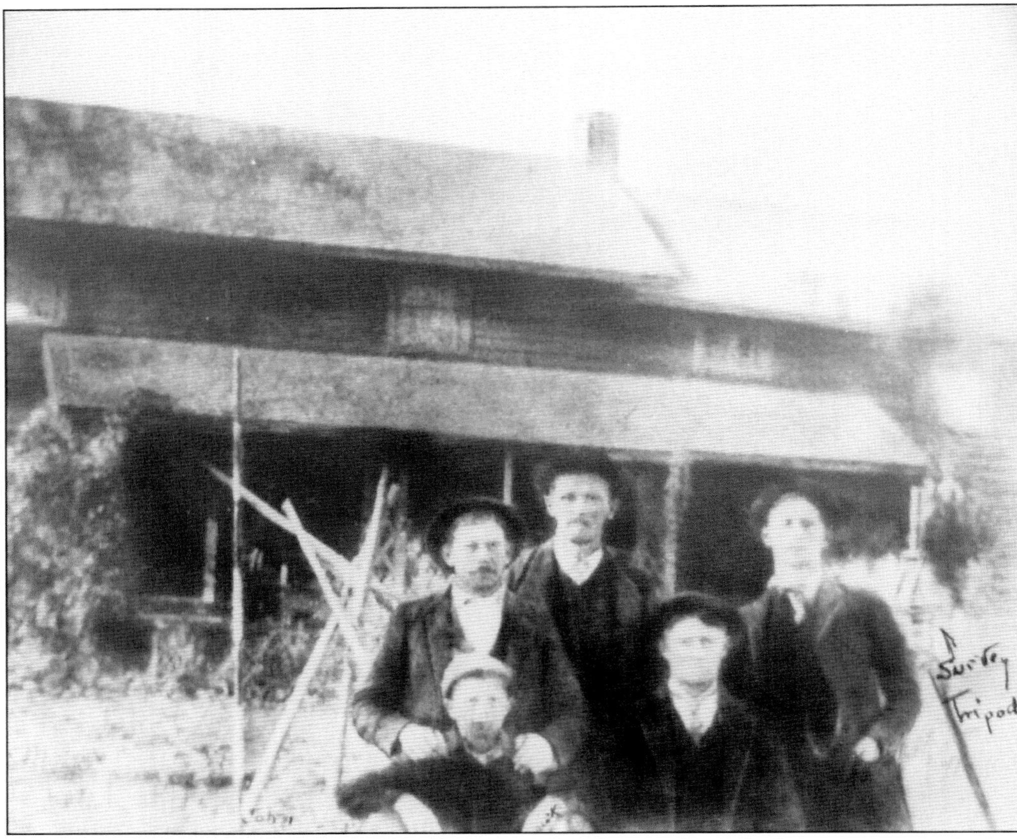

Mayodan was created around 1885 when surveyors searched the Mayo River flats for the best railroad route through the hills to Roanoke, Virginia. Surveyors stand before the home of Robert Lewis. Later, the house became the Mayodan Hotel. This image was produced around 1890. In 1896 Mayo Mills (Washington Mills, now Tultex) was completed 2 miles south of Avalon. (Courtesy of the Jeff Bullins Collection, Mayodan, NC.)

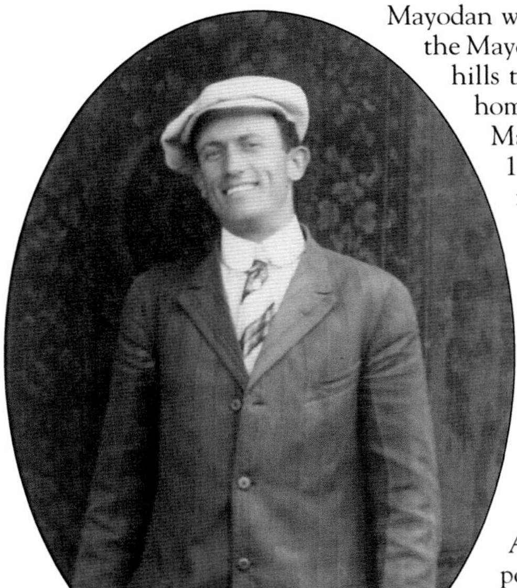

Allen Benton is featured on this self-promotional postcard. He was born and raised in Mayodan and cataloged life in the villages of Madison and Mayodan. This black and white is dated around 1900. (Courtesy of the Jeff Bullins Collection, Mayodan, NC, and the Jerri Griffin Collection, Madison, NC.)

Ed Johnson, a cutting room foreman at Mayo Mills, is seated on a roll of cloth inside his department. This image is from commercial and postcard photographer Allen Benton. (Courtesy of the Jeff Bullins Collection, Mayodan, NC.)

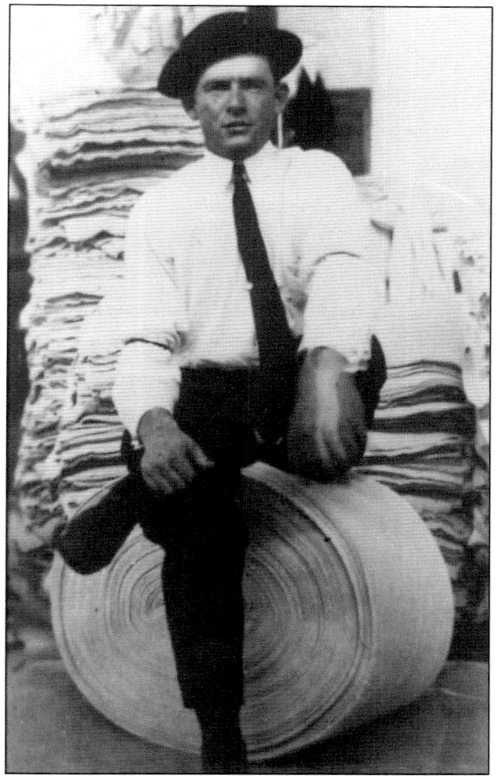

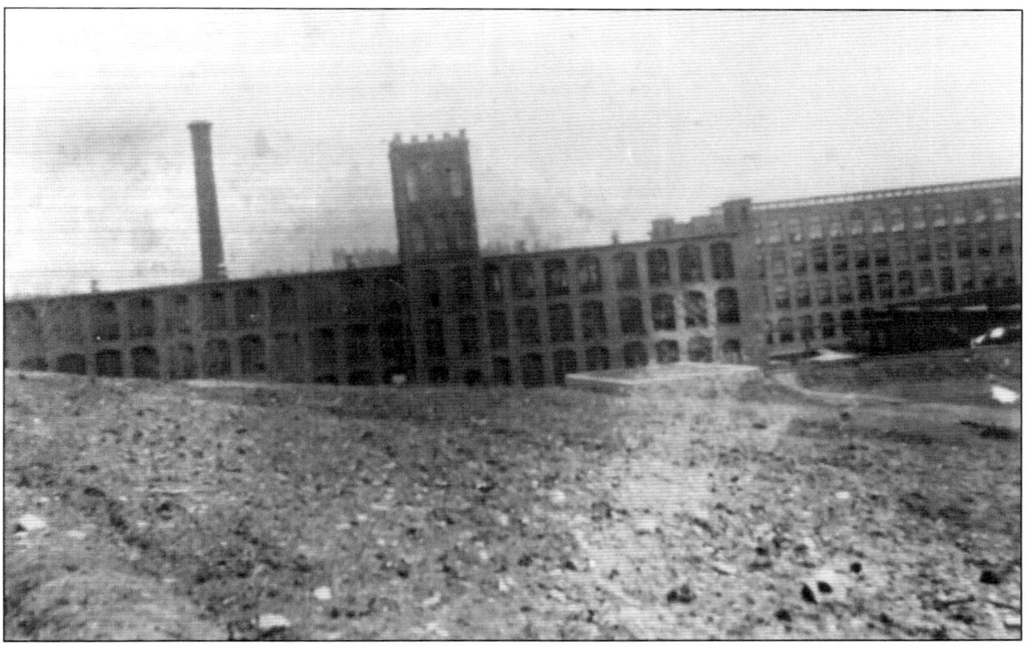

Probably for a postcard, this shot features the new Mayo Mills as seen by Allen Benton through his camera lens. Construction was completed on this factory three years prior to Colonel Fries' Avalon Mills. (Courtesy of the Jeff Bullins Collection, Mayodan, NC.)

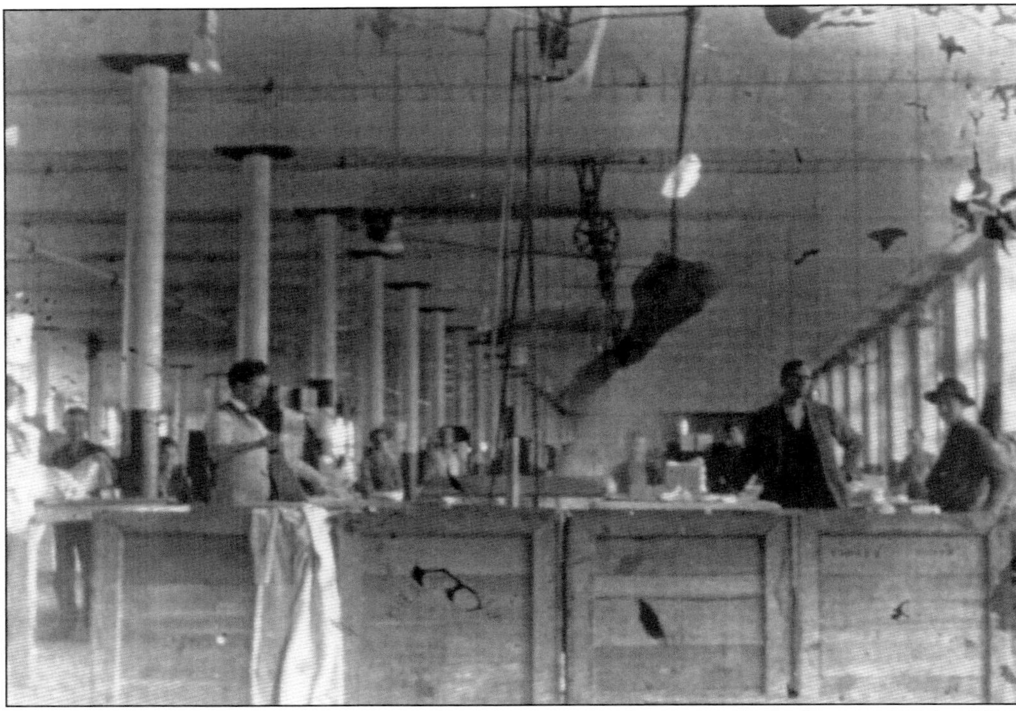

The crates identify this interior shot as the sewing room of Mayo Mills. Taken *c.* 1900 by Allen Benton, the postcard was trimmed for a frame. Allen Benton's postcards and pictures are noted for great clarity and composition. (Courtesy of the Jeff Bullins Collection, Mayodan, NC.)

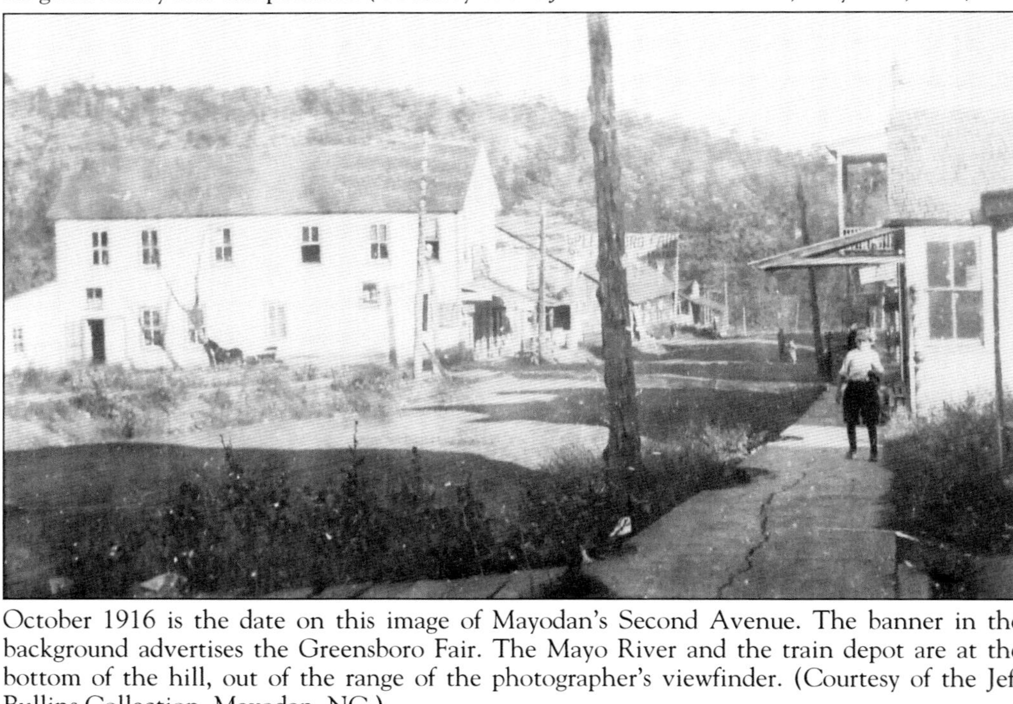

October 1916 is the date on this image of Mayodan's Second Avenue. The banner in the background advertises the Greensboro Fair. The Mayo River and the train depot are at the bottom of the hill, out of the range of the photographer's viewfinder. (Courtesy of the Jeff Bullins Collection, Mayodan, NC.)

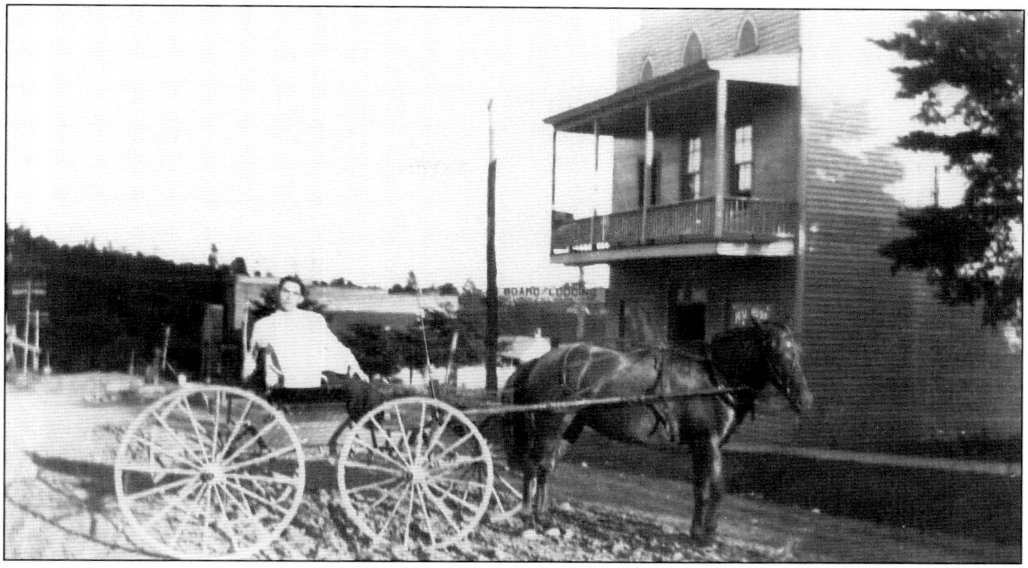

The R.J. Ross Store is pictured here on Main Street. It was bought out by C.P. Baughn in 1906. The identity of the man in the carriage is not known. (Courtesy of the Jeff Bullins Collection, Mayodan, NC.)

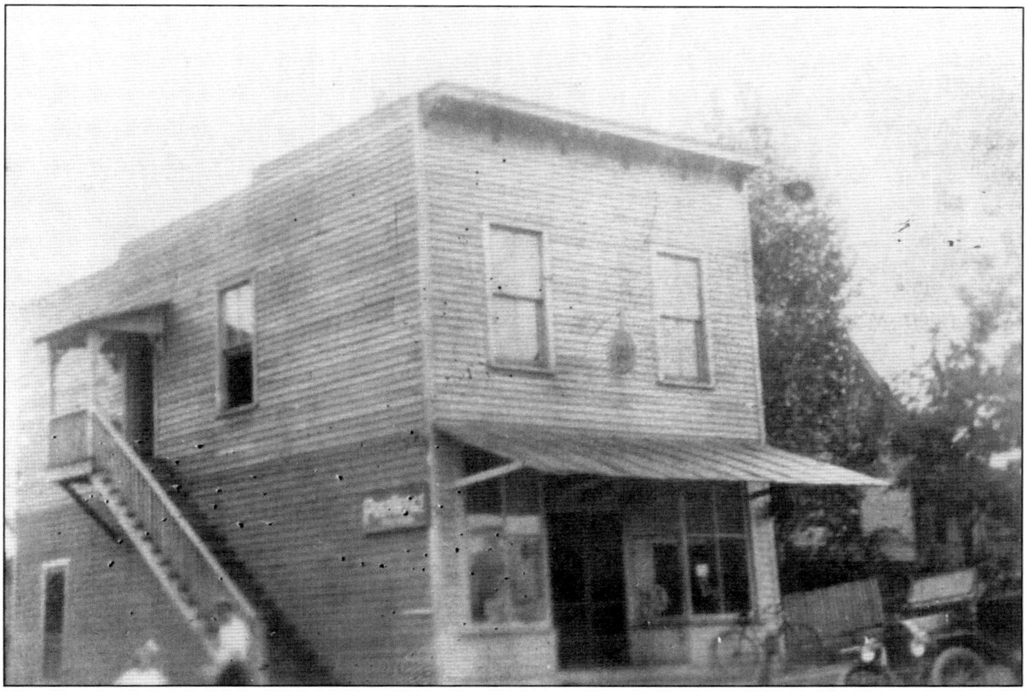

Roy Martin's Store housed the post office. Roy Martin was the subject of postcards and his store sold them in quantity. A 1915 Ford Model D is parked in front of the plank structure. (Courtesy of the Jeff Bullins Collection, Mayodan, NC.)

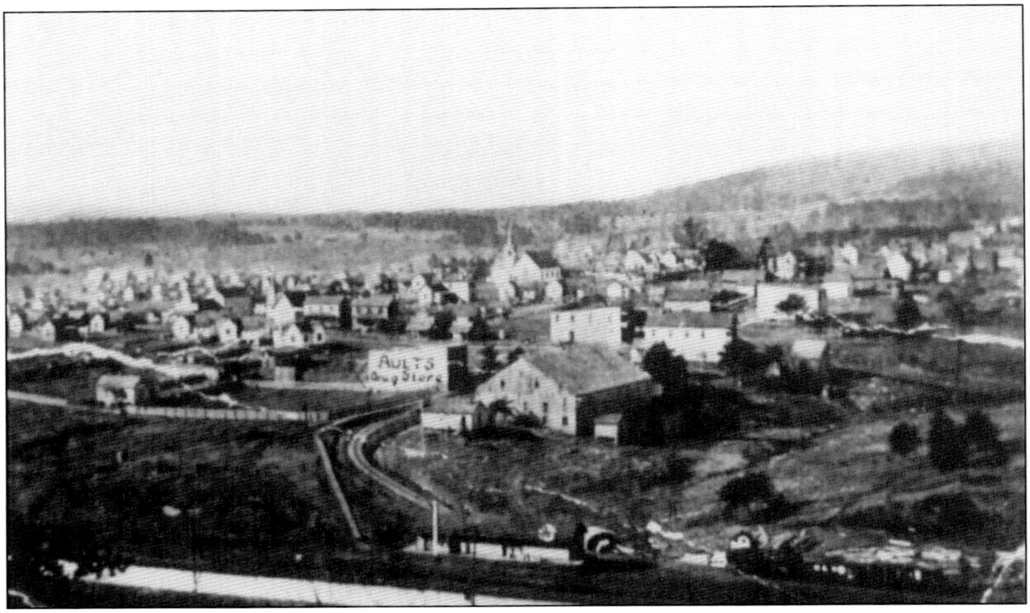

Mayodan is the subject of this 1907 postcard. At the bottom of the image is the railroad depot. In the mid-ground is Aults Drug Store. Across the street (center) from Aults is a huge structure that was the Mayodan Lumber Company. Mayodan needed the wood. The town nearly doubled in size when the Avalon villagers relocated to the area in 1911. (Courtesy of the Jeff Bullins Collection, Mayodan, NC.)

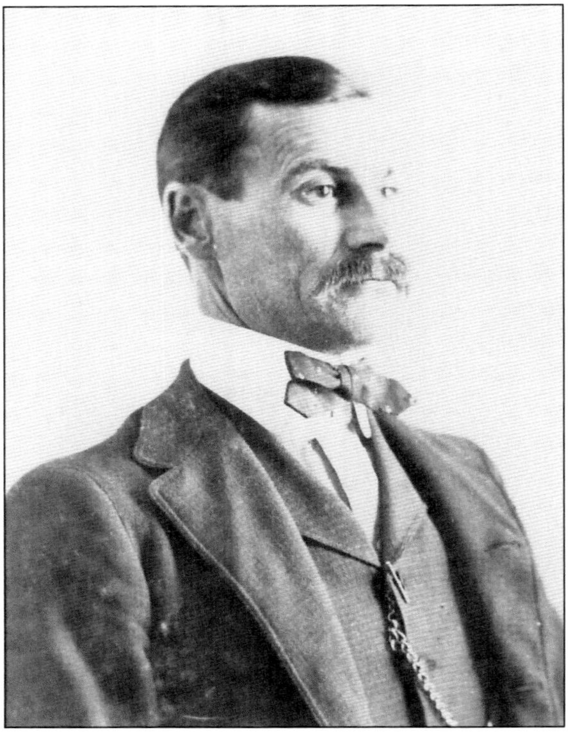

This is a portrait of T.C. Black. On the facing page is his store. It was on Main Street where the Lefty's Restaurant parking lot now exists. (Courtesy of the Jeff Bullins Collection, Mayodan, NC.)

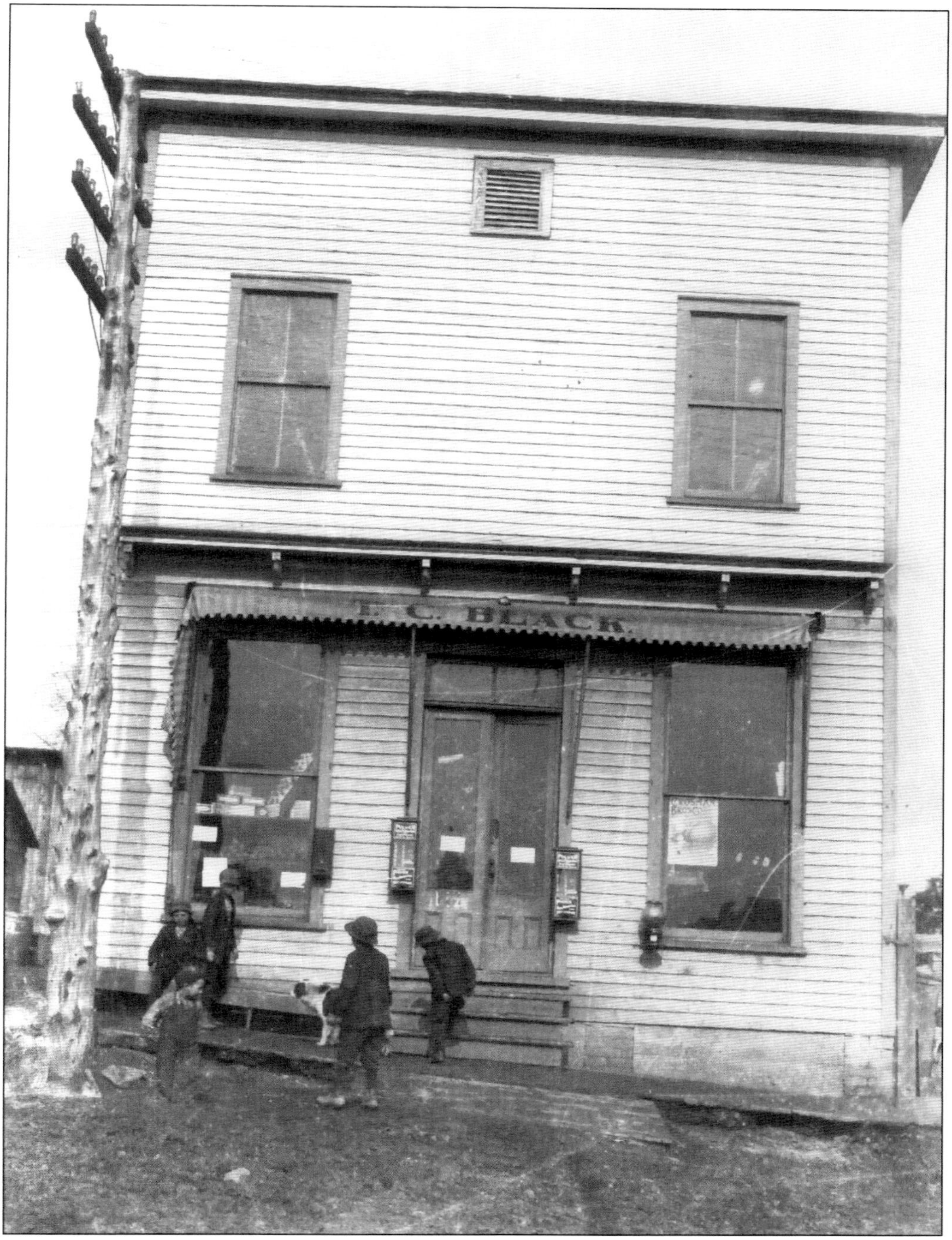

T.C. Black's was especially popular among farm children. Notice the gumball machine to the right of the door, a nifty device in the early 1900s. (Courtesy of the Jeff Bullins Collection, Mayodan, NC.)

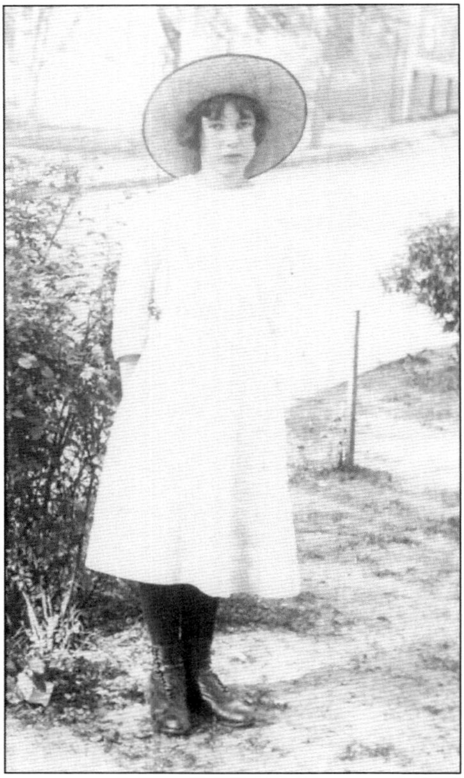

Here is another 1900s portrait taken by Allen Benton. In the background is the business district of Mayodan; the identity of the girl is not known. Allen Benton sometimes stamped his work with his name. He was an agent for A.W. Jones Photographers in Greensboro, North Carolina. (Courtesy of the Jeff Bullins Collection, Mayodan, NC.)

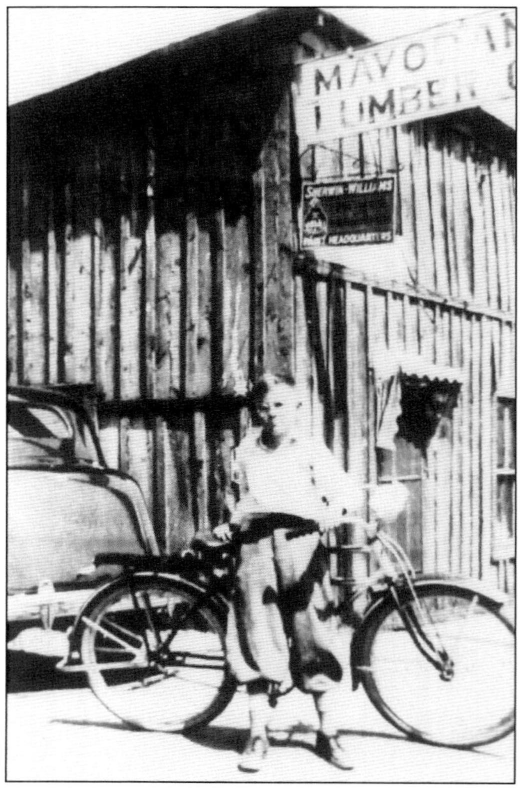

Vernon Highfill stands in front of the Mayodan Lumber Company on East Main. The lumberyard was across the street from the livery stables that provided mules and horses so that the Avalon villagers could move their houses into Mayodan. (Original photograph owned by Violet Young. Courtesy of the Jeff Bullins Collection, Mayodan, NC.)

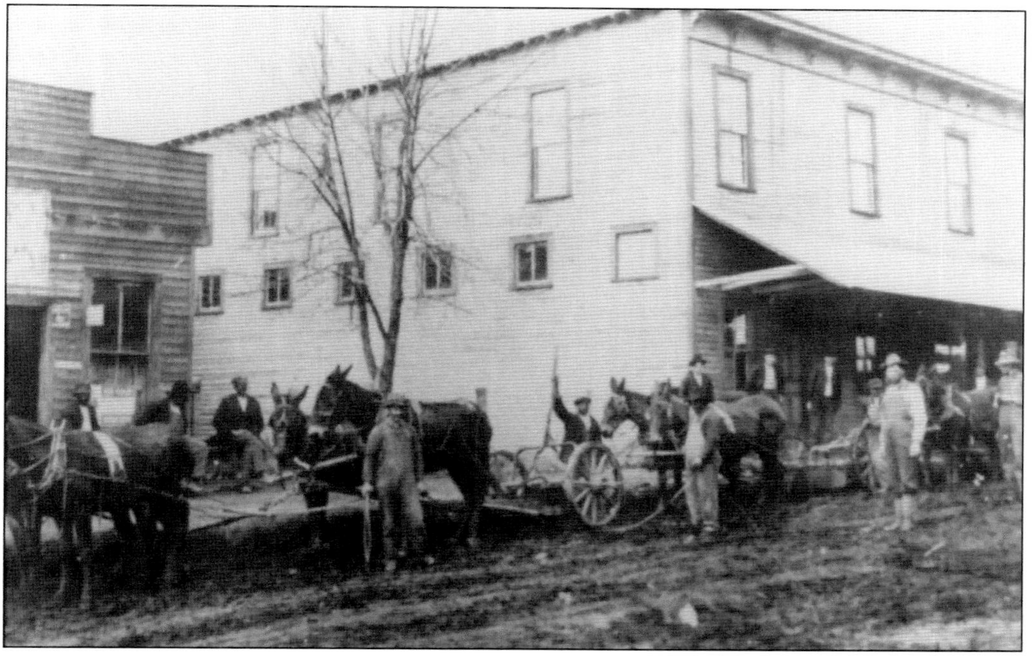

S.P. Tesh (pictured below) owned a store on the southwest corner of Second and Adams. Taken in the early 1900s, this image (above) shows street pavers working in front of Tesh's store. (Courtesy of the Jeff Bullins Collection, Mayodan, NC.)

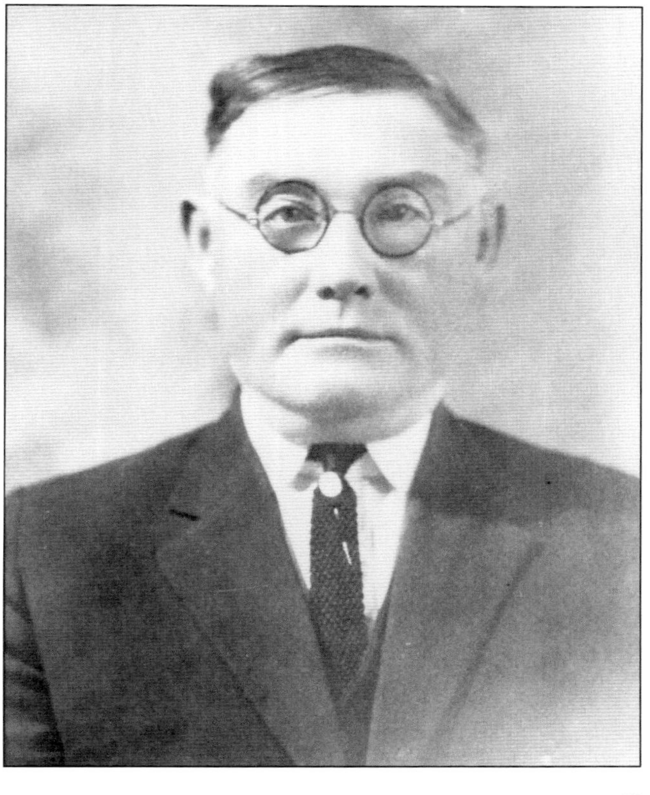

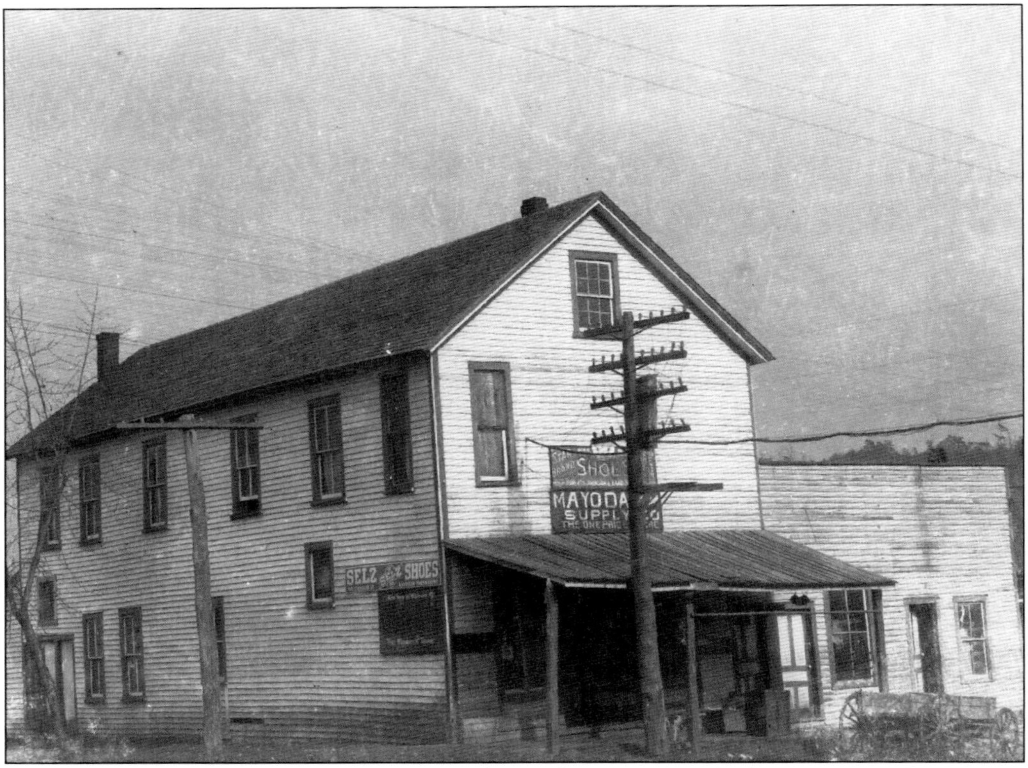

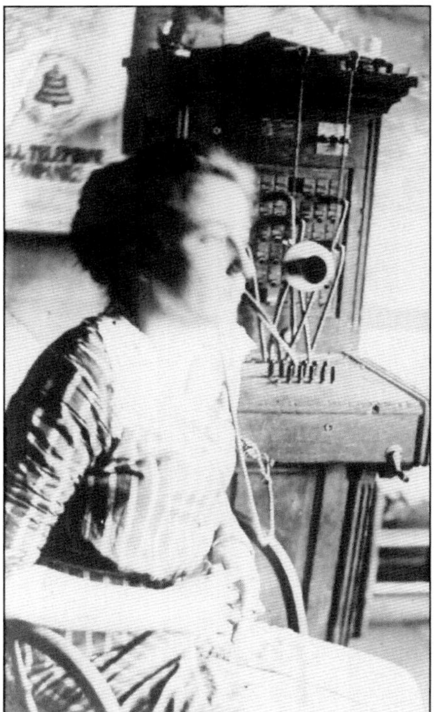

Above, the Mayo Supply Company was the site of the first telephone exchange in Mayodan in the early 1900s. (Courtesy of the Jeff Bullins Collection, Mayodan, NC.)

On the left is Lelia Redman Martin, Mayodan's first operator at the Bell Telephone Company exchange. This exchange notified Washington Mills that Avalon had indeed caught fire and was rapidly burning to the ground. (Courtesy of the Jeff Bullins Collection, Mayodan, NC.)

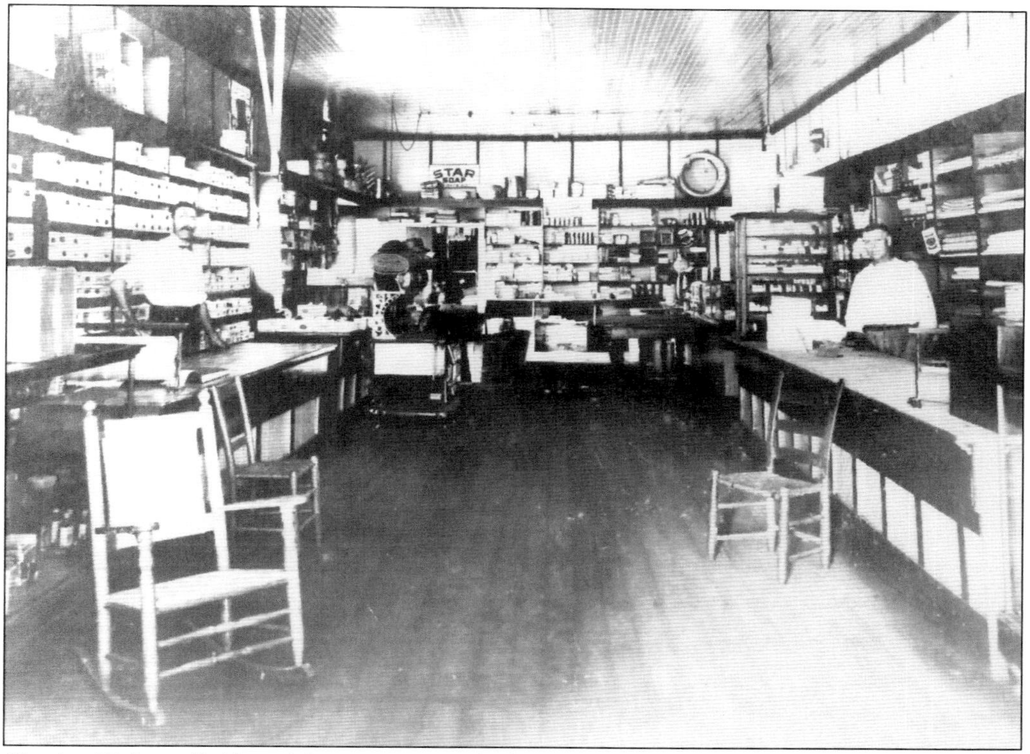

Charlie Walters (left) and Jasper Lemons (right) are inside the Mayodan Supply. Later this store became known as Nu-Supply. (Courtesy of the Jeff Bullins Collection, Mayodan, NC.)

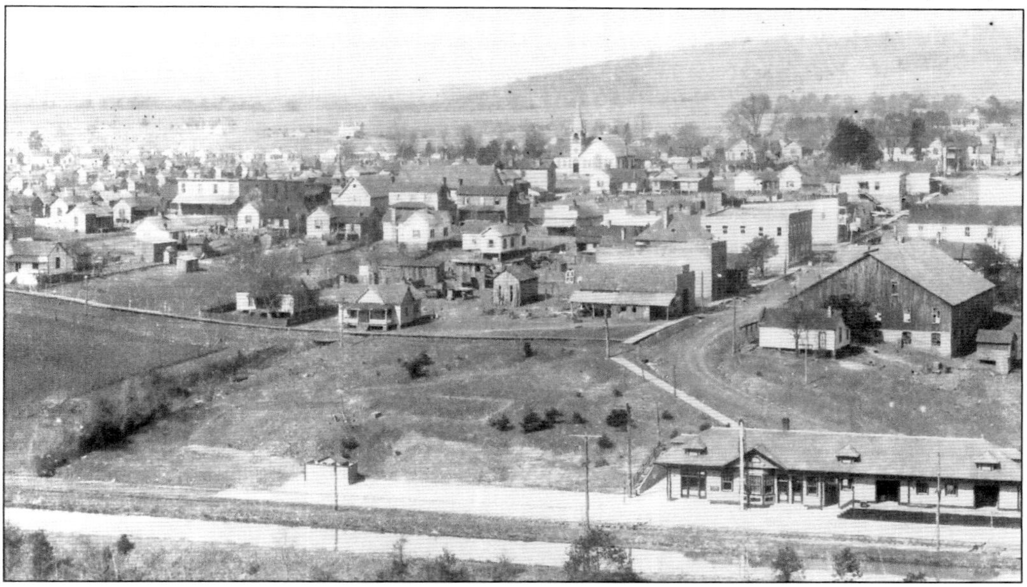

Mayodan is named for the Mayo River and the Dan River which merge near the town. Originally known as Mayo Falls, beautiful Mayodan is just north of the equally charming village of Madison. In 1916 this is how the town appeared from a hillside. In the lower right hand corner is the new depot. (Courtesy of the Jeff Bullins Collection, Mayodan, NC.)

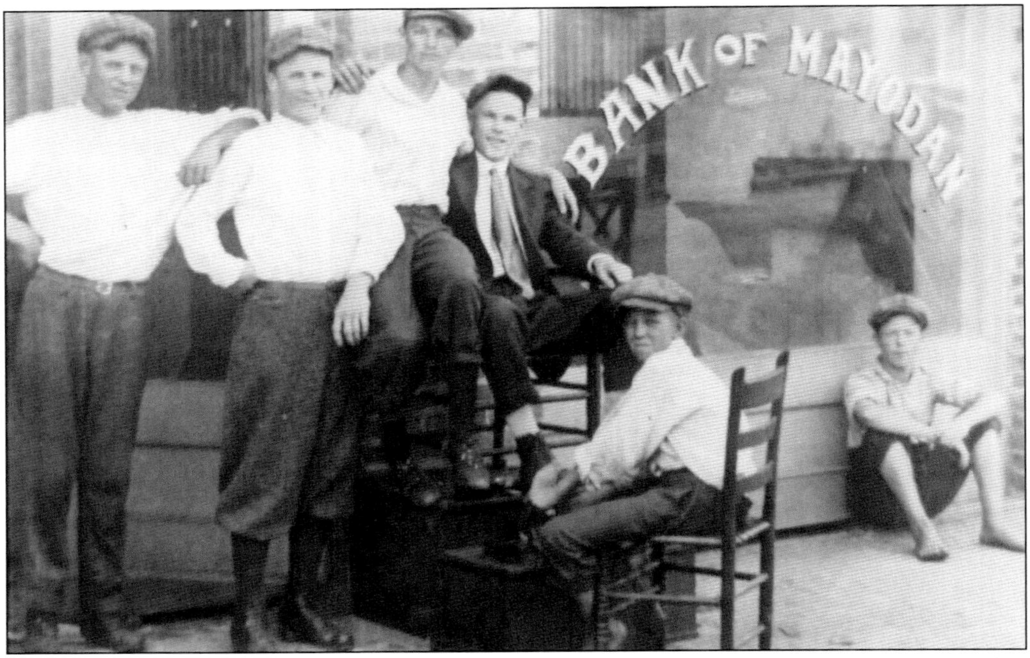

Andrew Thacker, Earnest Reynolds, and friend wait while Mr. Robertson gets his shoes shined. The identity of the shoeshine boy and the youth on the far right is not known. These young men posed for Allen Benton in the early 1900s. (Names of the boys are courtesy Daisy Hurd. Postcard courtesy of the Jeff Bullins Collection, Mayodan, NC.)

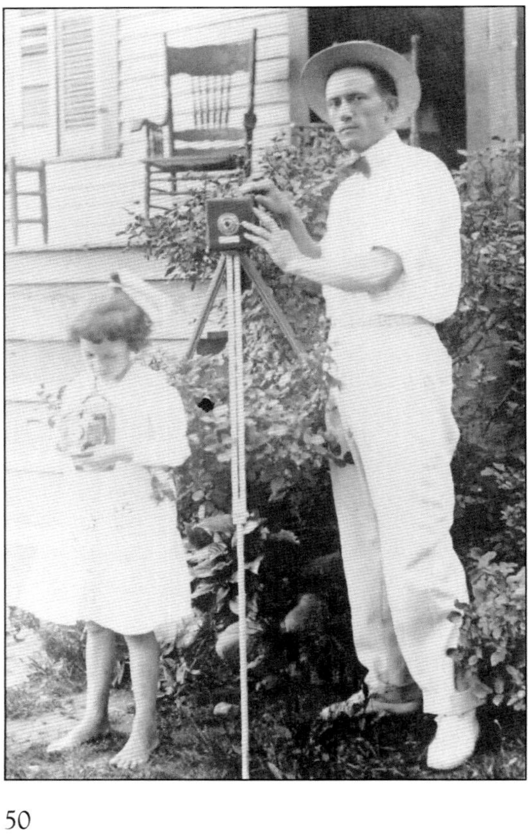

Allen Benton advertised his services in postcards. This is one of his finer self-portraits. The little girl is unknown. Benton was not married and fathered no children. He perished in World War I the night prior to surrender. He is buried in Madison, a town that named its V.F.W. after him. (Postcard courtesy of the Jeff Bullins Collection, Mayodan, NC. Courtesy of the Jerri B. Griffin Collection, Madison, NC.)

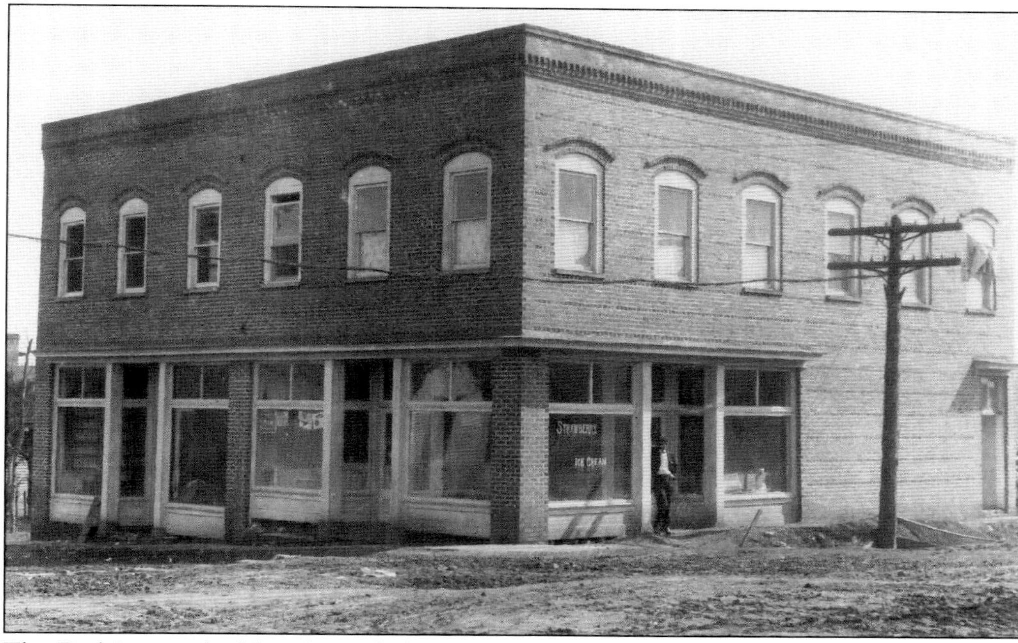

The Red Lauten building housed the Mayodan Bank in 1915. It also housed Nu-Supply Company on the corner of Second and Main. This is the store's brick building when it was brand new. (Courtesy of the Jeff Bullins Collection, Mayodan, NC.)

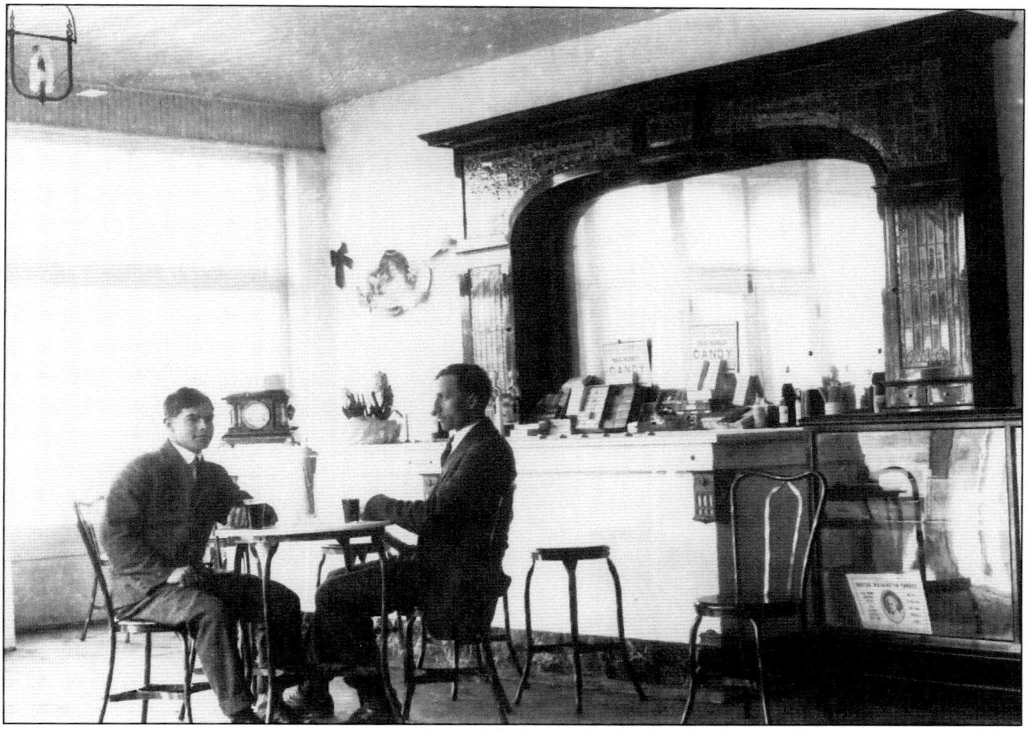

The soda shop at Red Lauten's was a wonderful meeting place for people like Roy Farmer (left) and his friends. (Courtesy of the Jeff Bullins Collection, Mayodan, NC.)

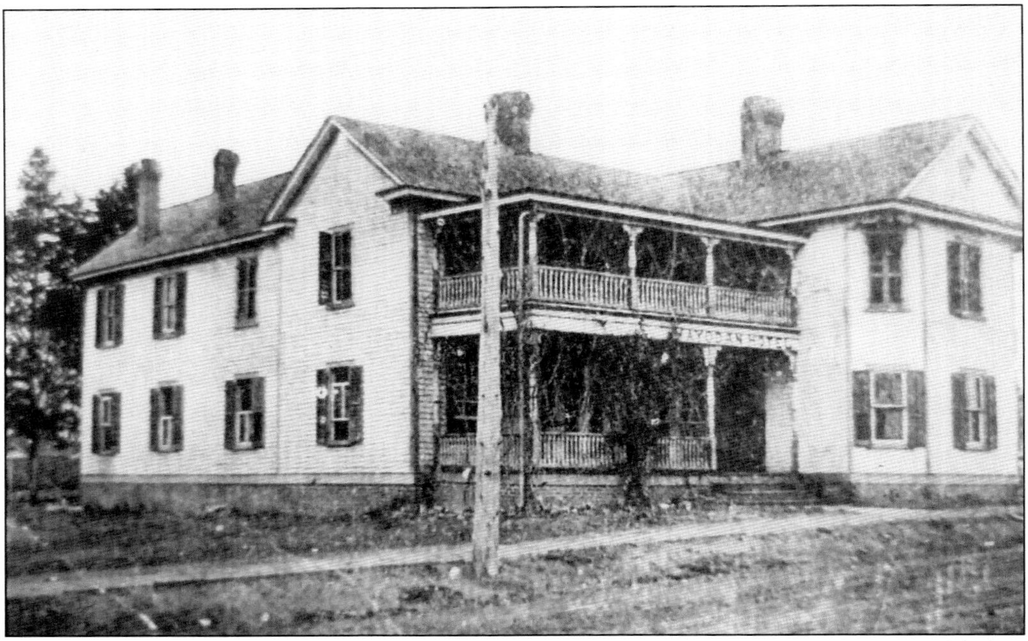

This rare postcard (above) features the Mayodan Hotel on Second Avenue. Pictured below is the same structure with its third-story addition. By 1920, the hotel was home to many area schoolteachers. The facility still stands today as one of the older structures of Mayodan. (Courtesy of the Jeff Bullins Collection, Mayodan, NC.)

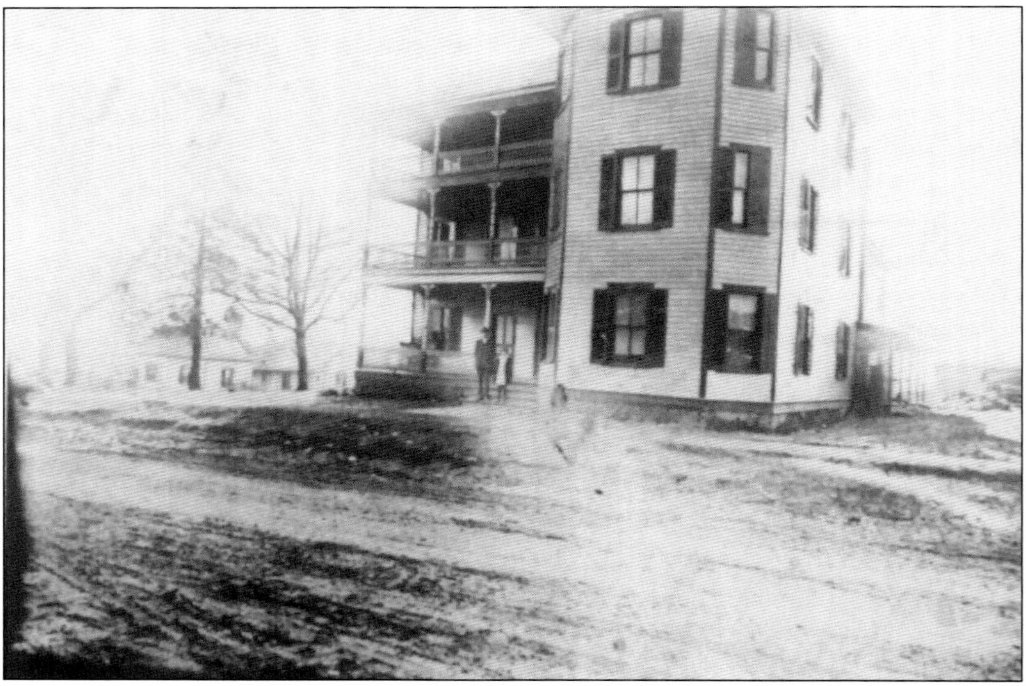

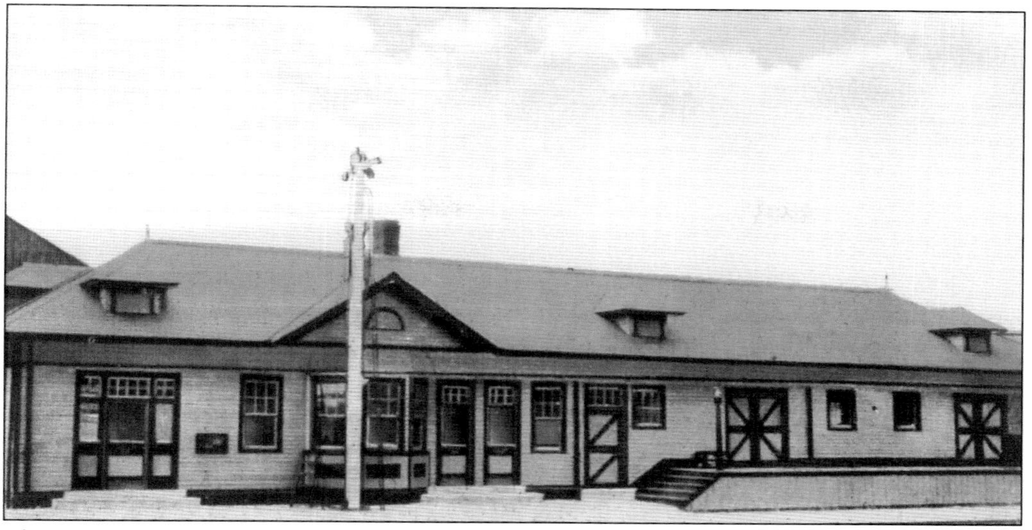

This Norfolk and Western Depot was the second depot built in Mayodan. A colorful postcard from the 1920s, the image features the east elevation, the side that the passengers saw when they got off the train. (Courtesy of the Jeff Bullins Collection, Mayodan, NC, and the Jerri B. Griffin Collection, Madison, NC.)

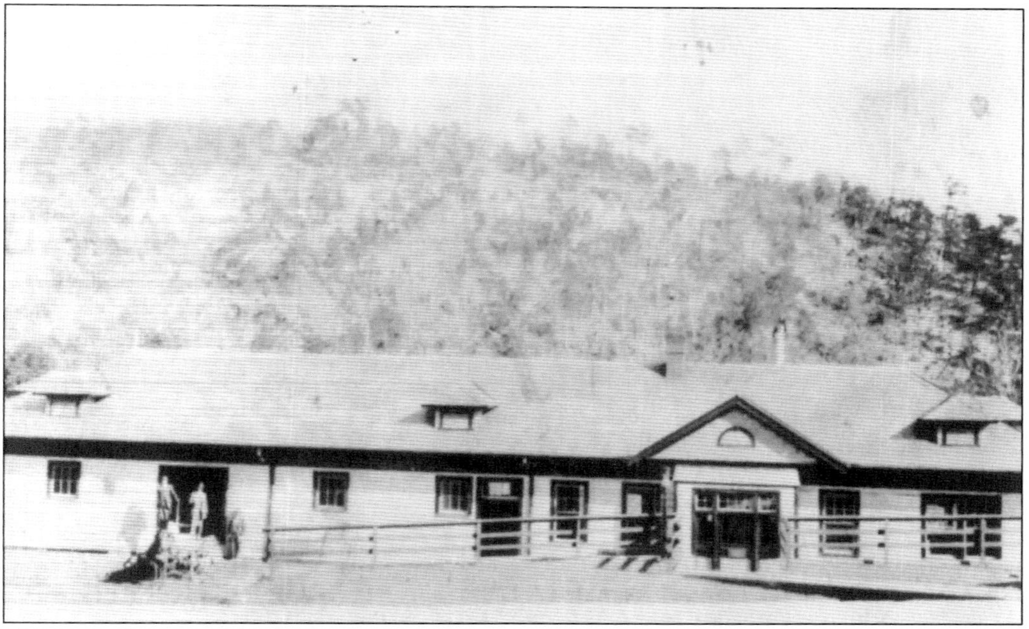

The west elevation (the back of the depot) was not prominent in postcards. Yet, it is the side that the villagers best remember since it faced the town. Postcards of the depot were an item at Roy Martin's store. Unfortunately, this charming, historical structure had to be demolished in 1971. (Courtesy of the Jeff Bullins Collection, Mayodan, NC.)

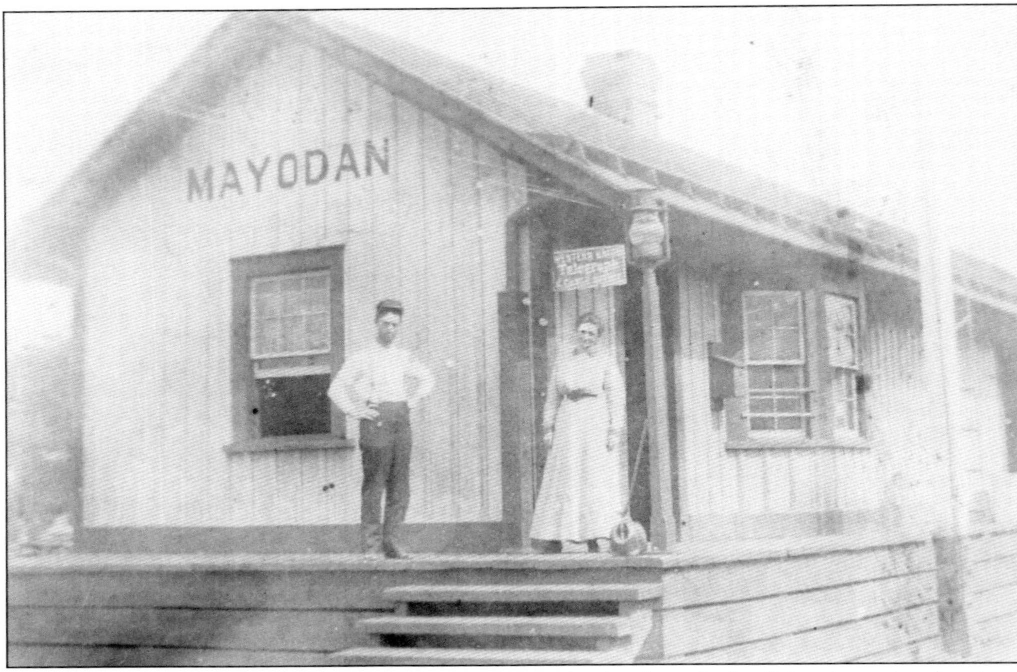

Depot agents John E. and Mary Dempster pose on the loading dock of the depot by the river. (Courtesy of the Jeff Bullins Collection, Mayodan, NC.)

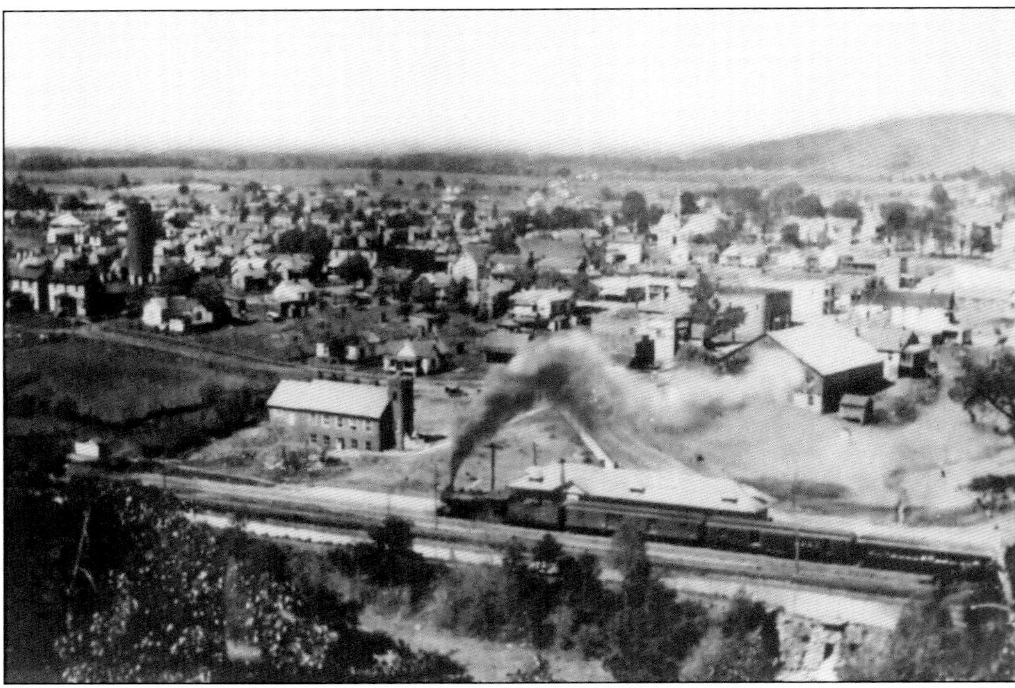

Mr. Portis reportedly snapped this photograph on a Sunday morning in 1919. To the left of the train is the Baptist church. Houses from Avalon have been added to the town's landscape by this time. (Courtesy of the Jeff Bullins Collection, Mayodan, NC.)

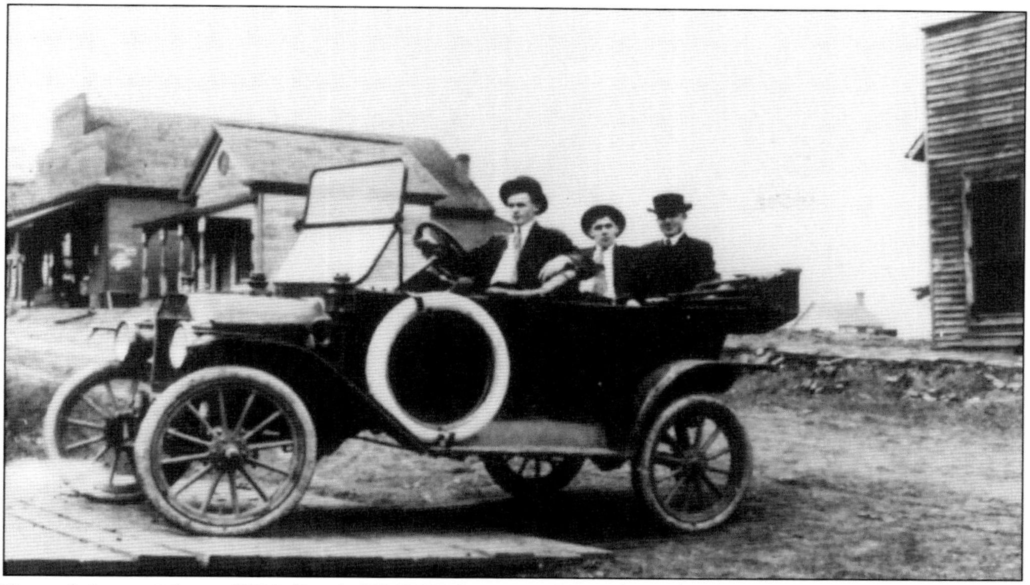

From left to right is K.V. Reid, Will Walters, and Frank Tullock in a jalopy that is exiting Second Avenue. Behind them are some of the town businesses. Allen Benton probably took this picture. (Courtesy of the Jeff Bullins Collection, Mayodan, NC.)

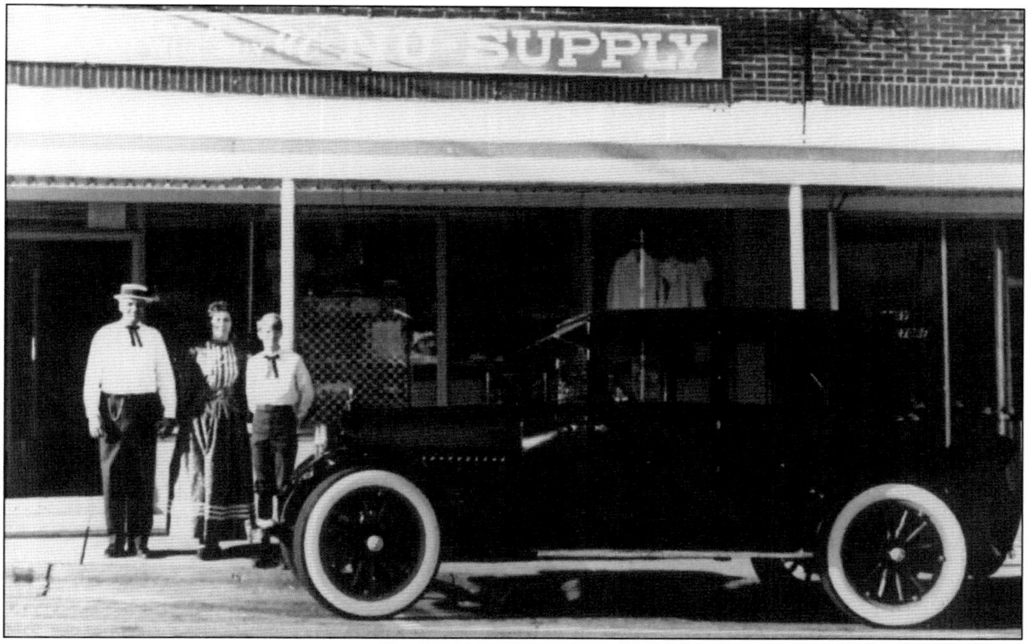

Here is Nu-Supply Company in a store anniversary photograph from the 1970s. From left to right are the store owners, C.G. Bullins, Katherine Bullins, and their son Jeff Bullins. The family stands before a 1929 Nash as if they're the subjects of a postcard. From working in this store, Jeff Bullins met many people connected with the development of Rockingham County. He collected copies of postcards and photographs. His passion for history, its documentation, and its preservation are a blessing to those interested in the county's past. (Courtesy of the Jeff Bullins Collection, Mayodan, NC.)

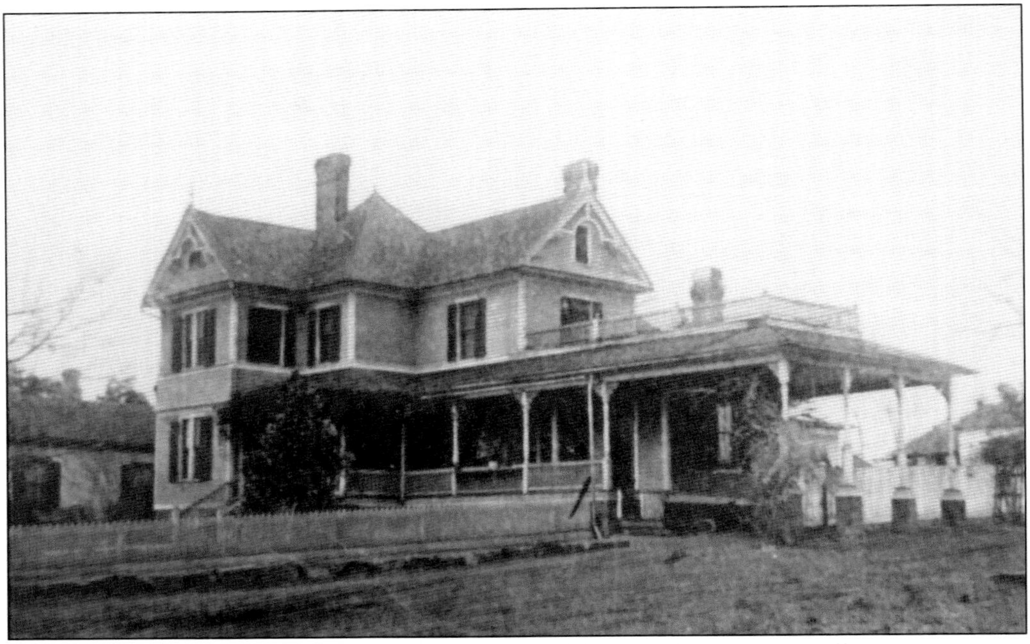

This is a 1919 postcard of W.C. Ruffin's home. Ruffin, a Washington Mills executive, was Mayodan's first mayor and the man that named Avalon. The two-story Victorian home was at the corner of Second Avenue and West Roosevelt. (Courtesy of the Jeff Bullins Collection, Mayodan, NC.)

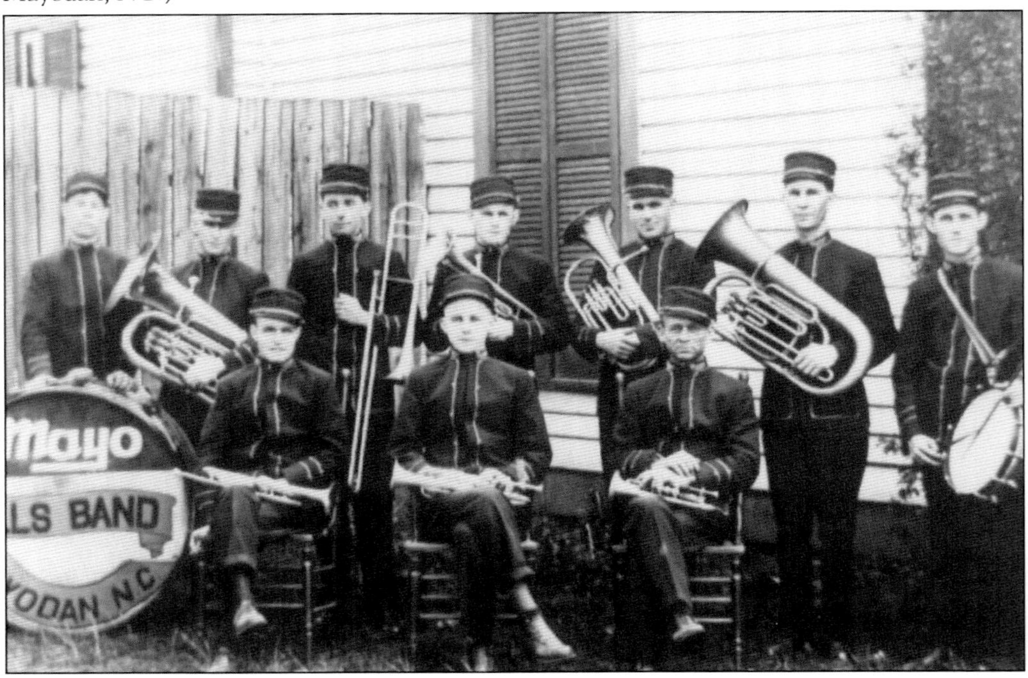

This is a postcard copy of the Mayo Mills Band. Mill bands provided local entertainment at special events and parades in the early 1900s. (Courtesy of the Jeff Bullins Collection, Mayodan, NC.)

Allen Benton's homeplace had its own charm. Benton was not married, so the children in the photograph were brothers, sisters, and cousins. Benton took this photograph around the early 1900s. Reportedly, Benton grew up in the countryside near the Mayo River. (Courtesy of the Jeff Bullins Collection, Mayodan, NC.)

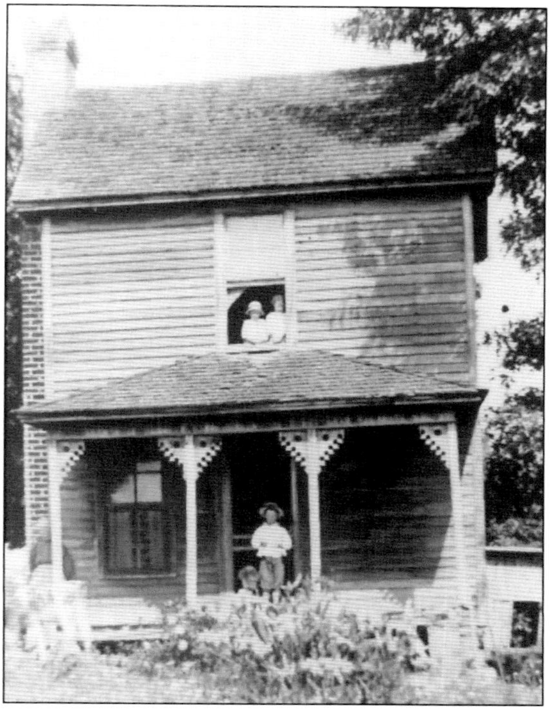

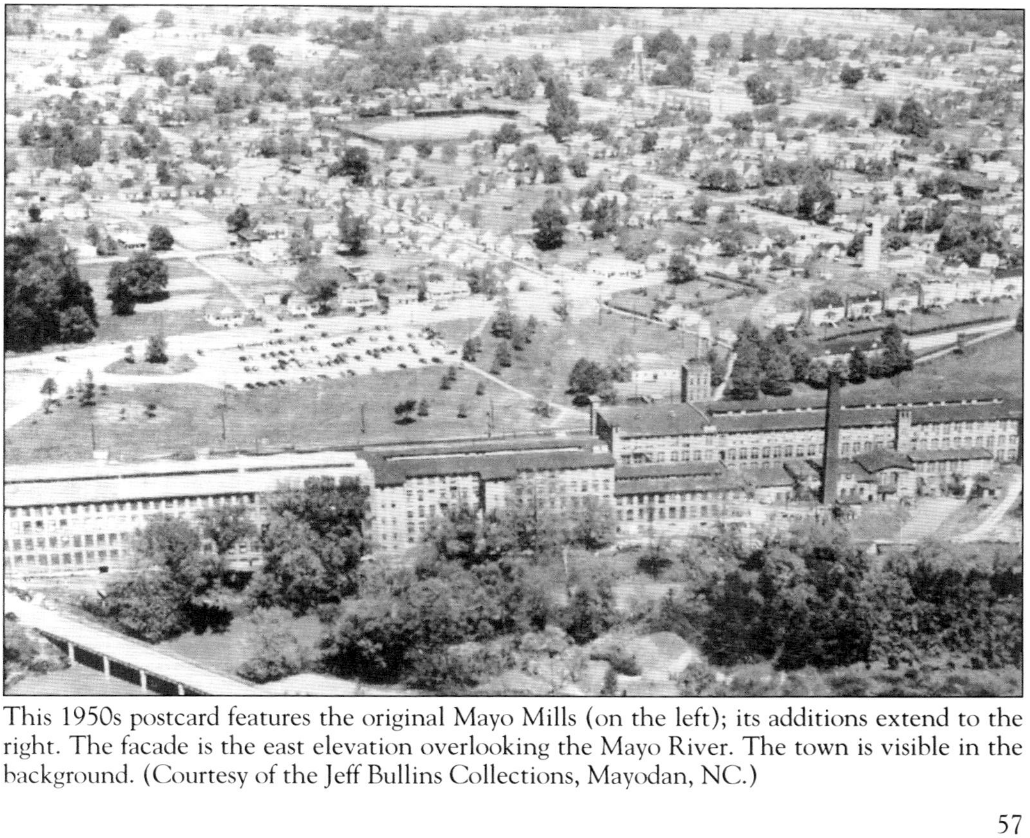

This 1950s postcard features the original Mayo Mills (on the left); its additions extend to the right. The facade is the east elevation overlooking the Mayo River. The town is visible in the background. (Courtesy of the Jeff Bullins Collections, Mayodan, NC.)

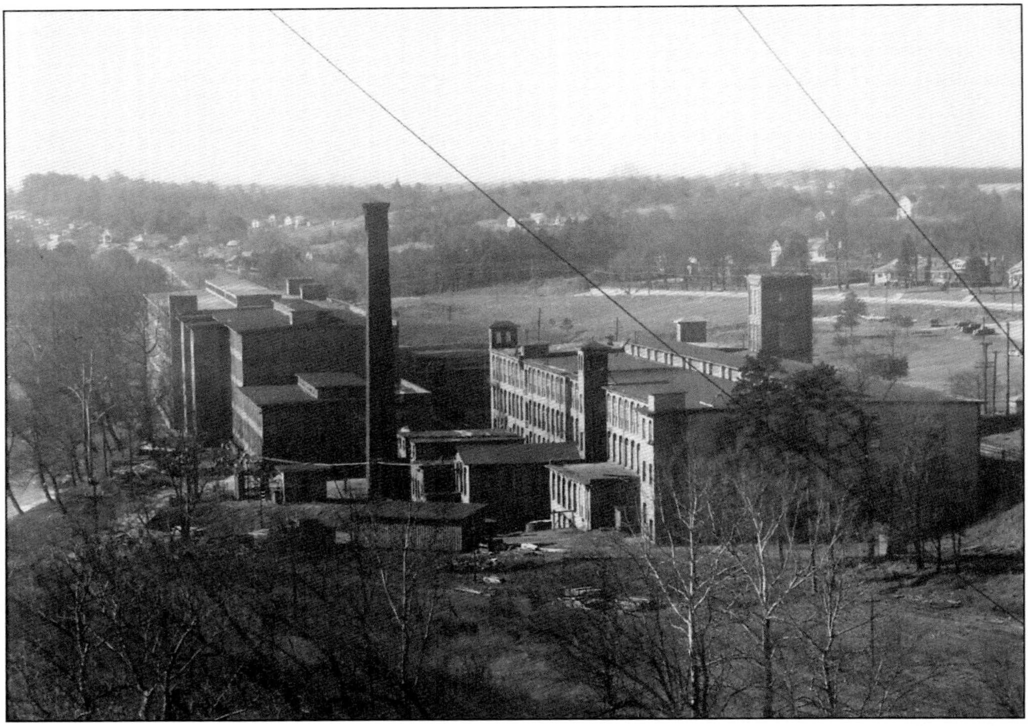

Once Avalon and Mayo Mills combined, Mayo Mills became Washington Mills. Today, Washington Mills is owned and operated by Tultex. (Courtesy of the Jeff Bullins Collection, Mayodan, NC.)

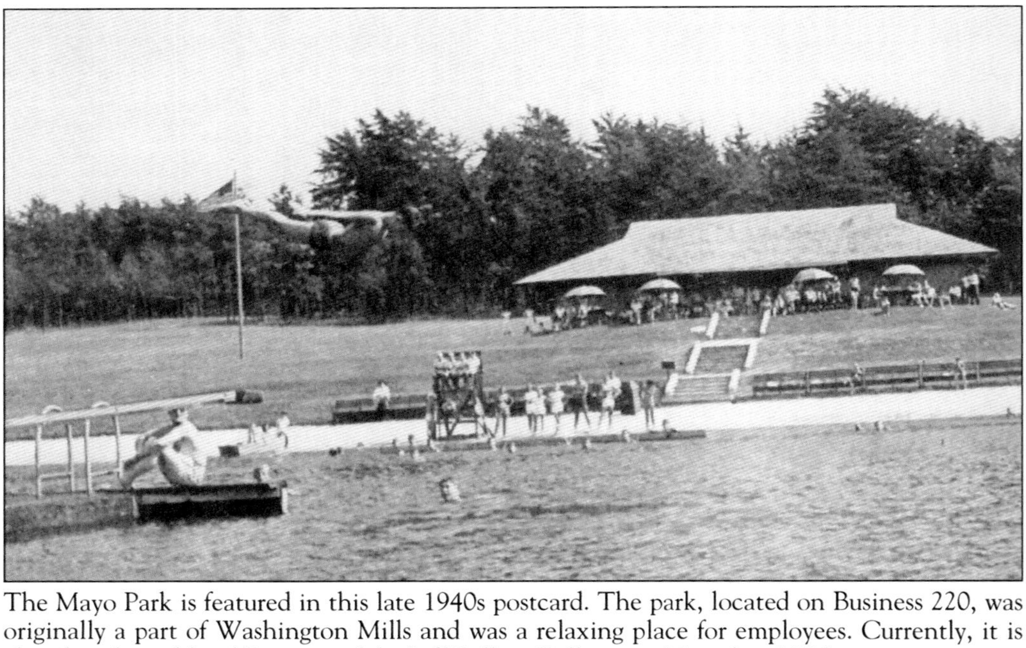

The Mayo Park is featured in this late 1940s postcard. The park, located on Business 220, was originally a part of Washington Mills and was a relaxing place for employees. Currently, it is closed to the public. (Courtesy of the Jeff Bullins Collection, Mayodan, NC.)

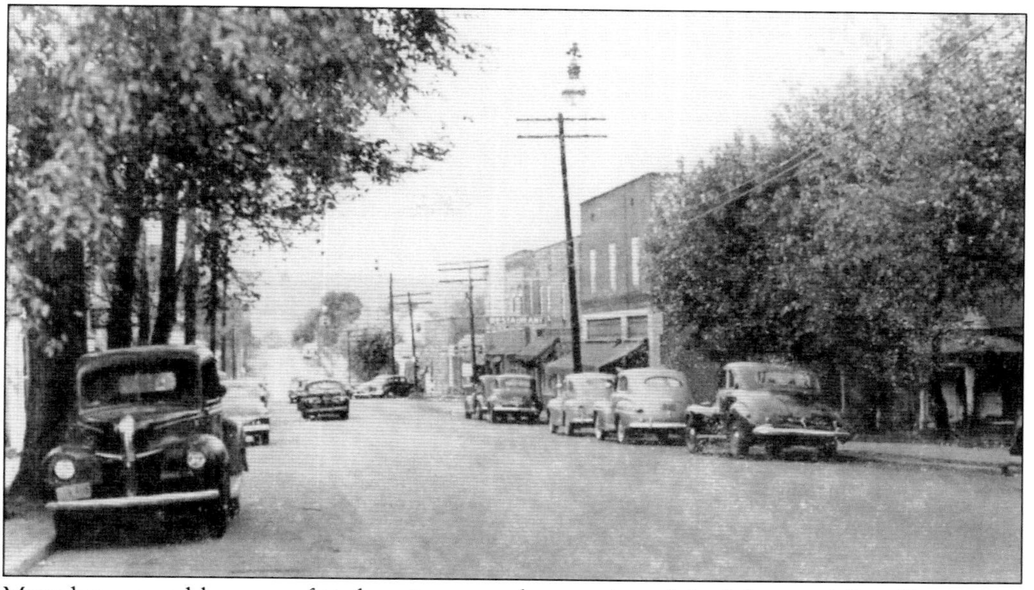

Mayodan, named because of its location near the merging of the Mayo and Dan Rivers, was founded in 1899 as a company town for the workers of Washington (now Tultex) Mills. It has always had a productive downtown district, located along Second Avenue and Main. This postcard is from the 1950s. (Courtesy of the Jeff Bullins Collection, Mayodan, NC.)

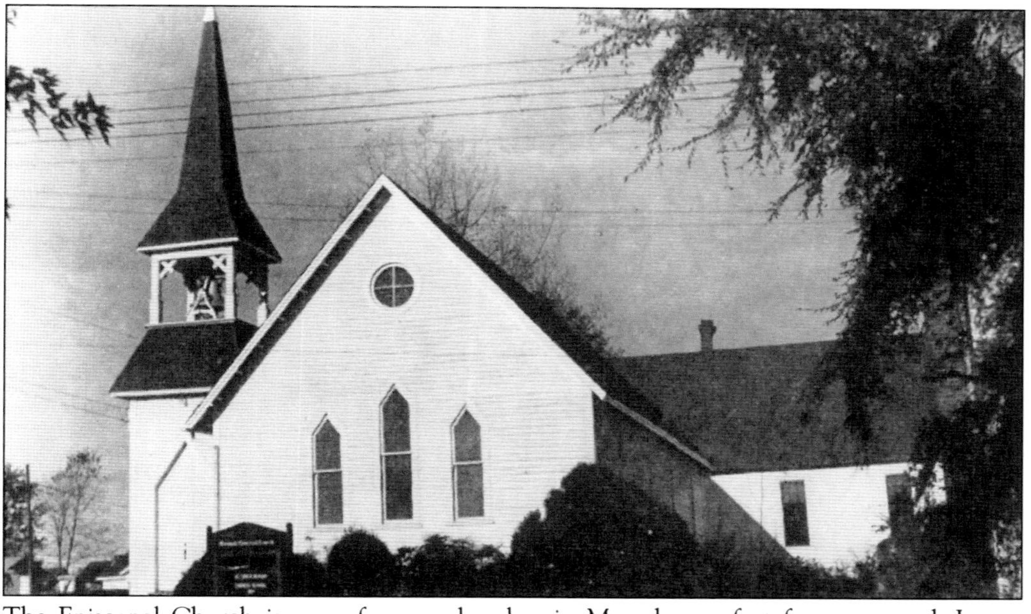

The Episcopal Church is one of many churches in Mayodan perfect for a postcard. It was erected in 1897 and was the second church built in the town. The church has been the subject of commercial photography since the 1910s. (Courtesy of the Jeff Bullins Collection, Mayodan, NC.)

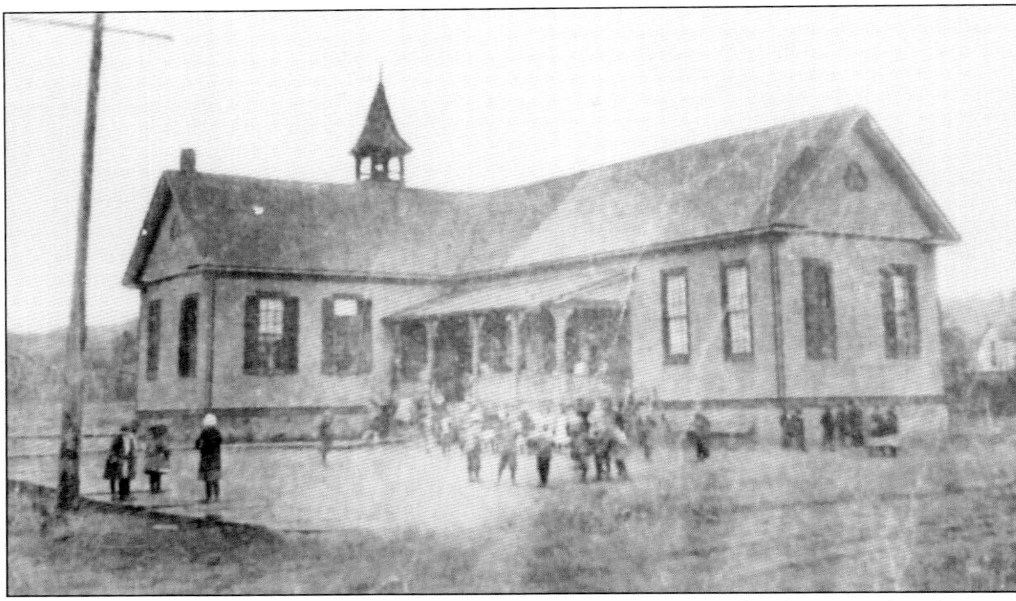

The Mayodan School was built about 1901. This postcard of the school was produced around 1919. In 1924 a modern brick structure was erected on Second Avenue, which replaced this little building. (Courtesy of the Jeff Bullins Collection, Mayodan, NC.)

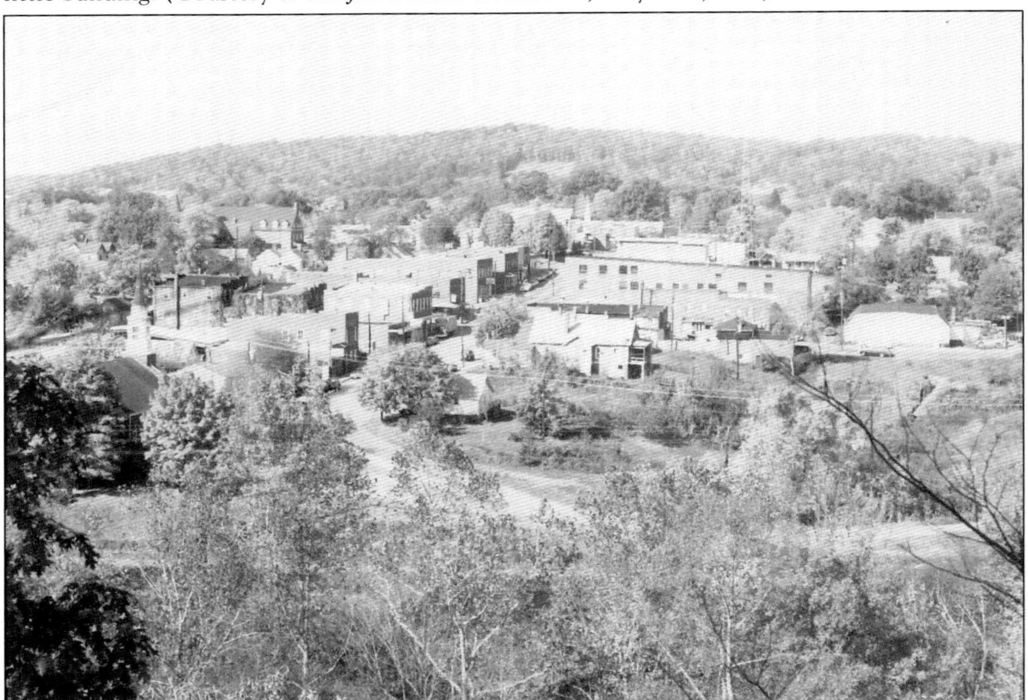

Mayodan is as charming now as it was in the early 1900s. In this 1979 photograph, the photographer is situated on Mayo Mountain and faces west. Many historical buildings along Second Avenue and Main are still intact for visitors and residents to enjoy. (Courtesy of the Jeff Bullins Collection, Mayodan, NC.)

Four

MADISON

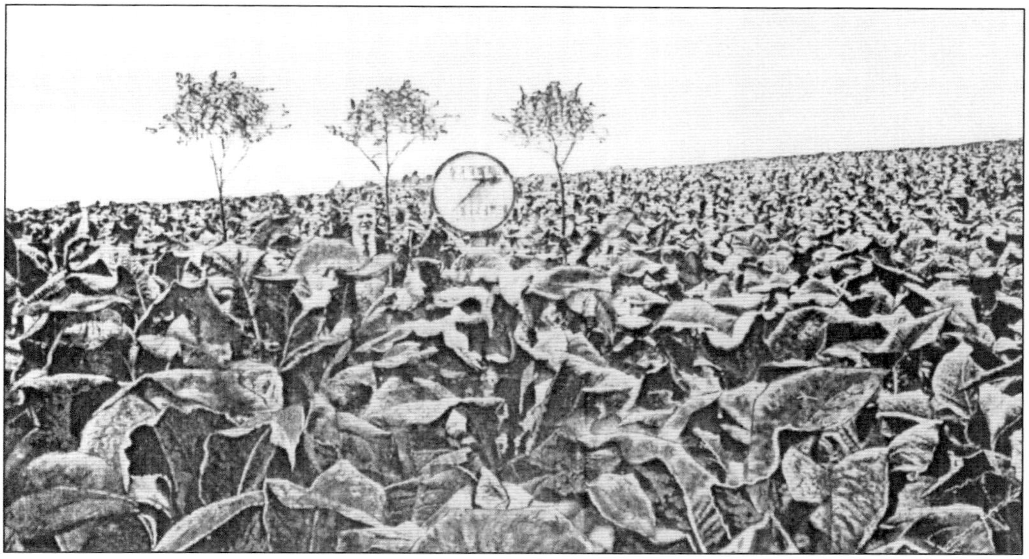

John M. Gallaway Jr. was the owner of the largest flue-cured tobacco operation in Stokes County. (Stoke County eventually became a part of Rockingham County.) The town of Madison, like many in the South, developed from an agrarian economy. Despite past town fires, the community and its people continue to thrive in the valley of the Mayo and Dan. (Courtesy of the Jerri B. Griffin Collection, Madison, NC.)

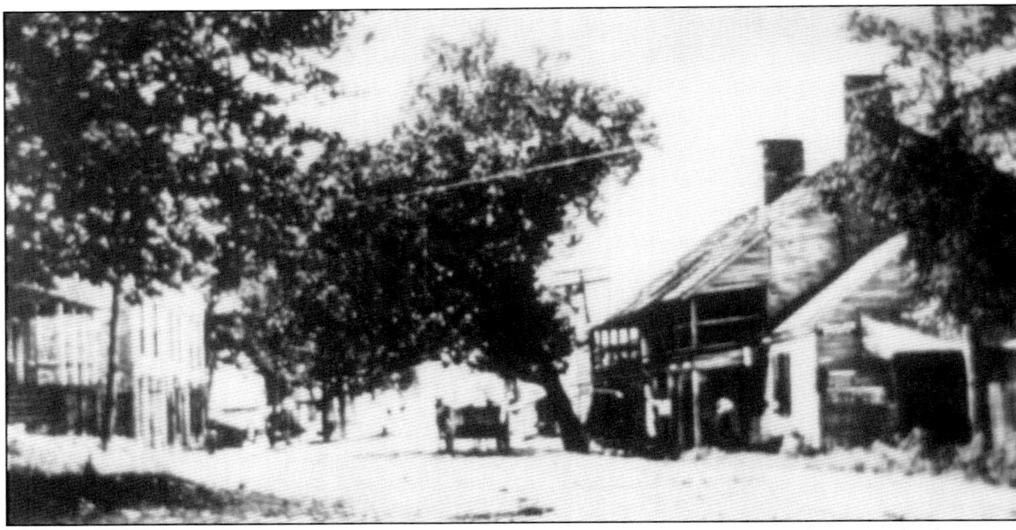

This tinted card, postmarked 1908, is a street scene that was probably photographed around 1889. The image depicts the intersection of Murphy and Market. Pictured is Captain Thomas Woodburn's House (foreground, left), the Long Hotel for Drovers, and the Woodburn Store, which later would be McGee Store. Madison was established in 1815. (Courtesy of the Jerri B. Griffin Collection, Madison, NC.)

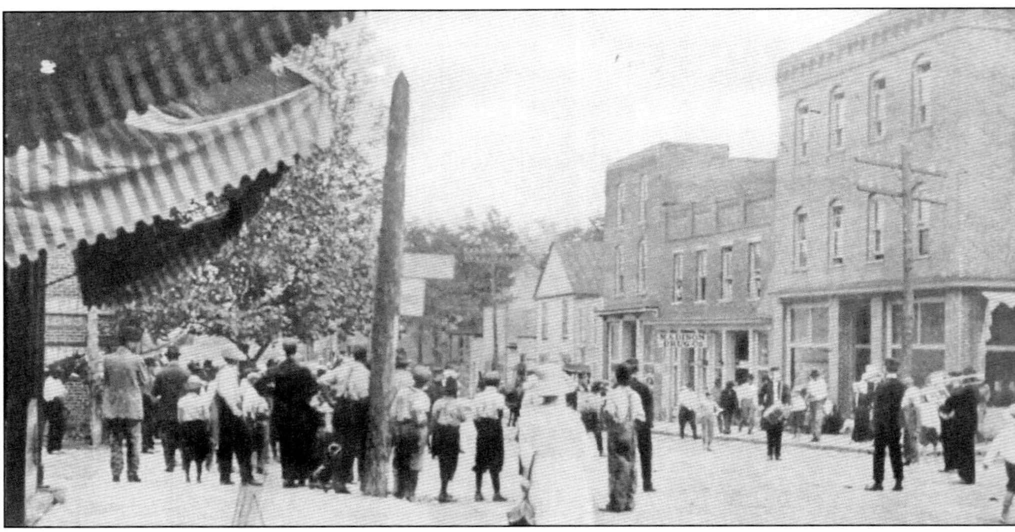

Postmarked 1912, this image captures townspeople viewing a parade at East Murphy and Market Streets. On the right side, sandwiched between two tall brick buildings and nearly centered in the photograph, is the Madison Drug Company. Its hand-painted sign is above the entrance to a business which frequently utilized postcards as a means to promote its many goods and services. (Courtesy of the Jerri B. Griffin Collection, Madison, NC.)

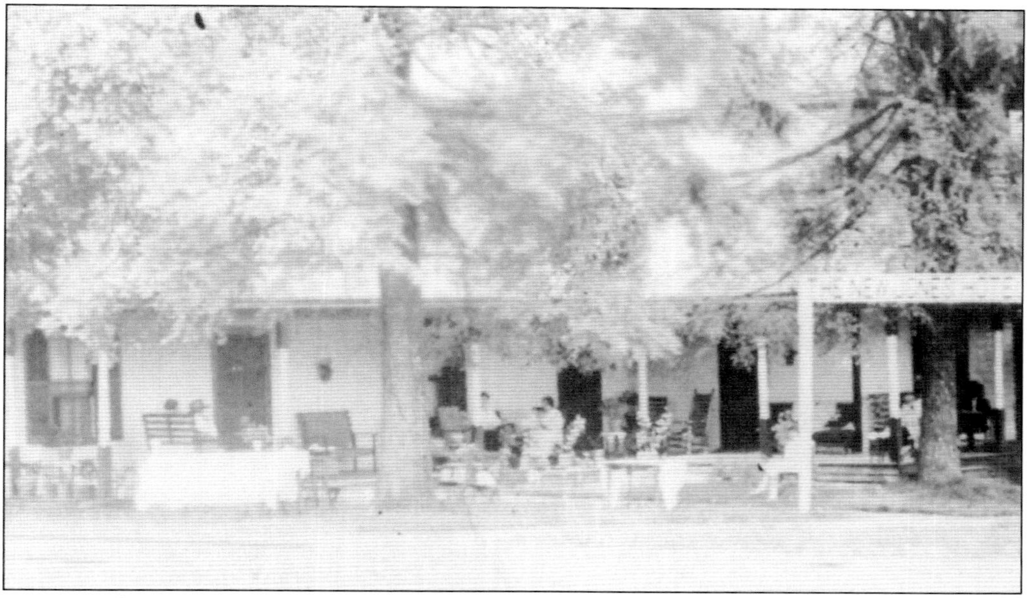

By 1919, the New Jones Hotel was in operation and was the place to stay when visiting the area. It was located on East Murphy Street between the A & Y and the N & W Railroads. As seen in this sepia image, people relished the comfortable accommodations, the big swings, the shaded porches, and the long tables of fine food, for which the hotel was noted. It was operated by Colonel and Mrs. Ed Jones, but in 1965 time and age had taken its toil on the two-story structure and it was demolished. The original postcard was used to promote the hotel as well as provide a small letterhead for the folks that stayed in the house. The actual photographer is not known. (Courtesy of the Jerri B. Griffin Collection, Madison, NC.)

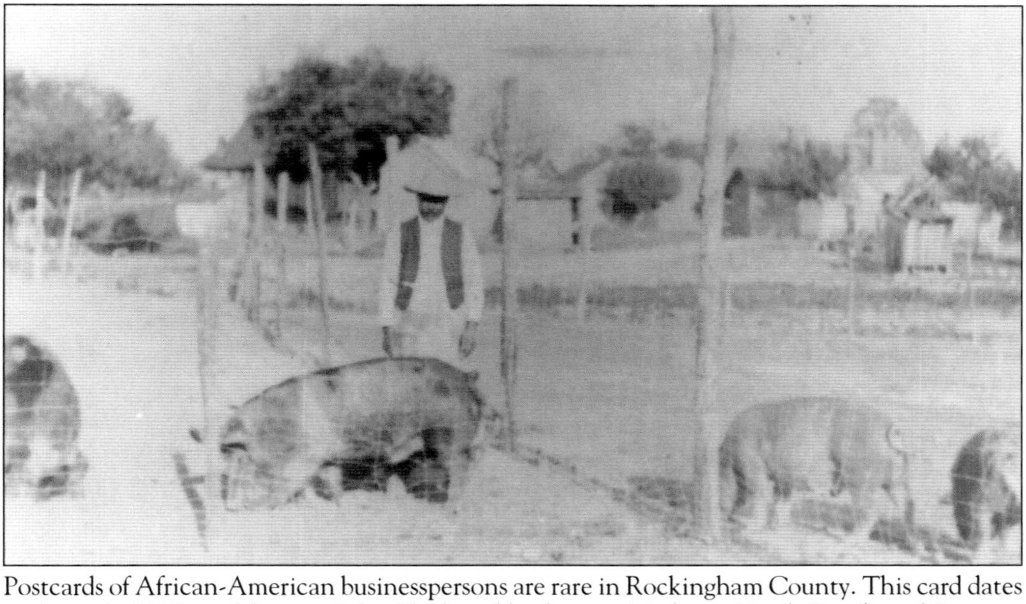

Postcards of African-American businesspersons are rare in Rockingham County. This card dates to the early 1900s and features John Black and his hogs in Madison, North Carolina. (Courtesy of the Jerri B. Griffin Collection, Madison, NC.)

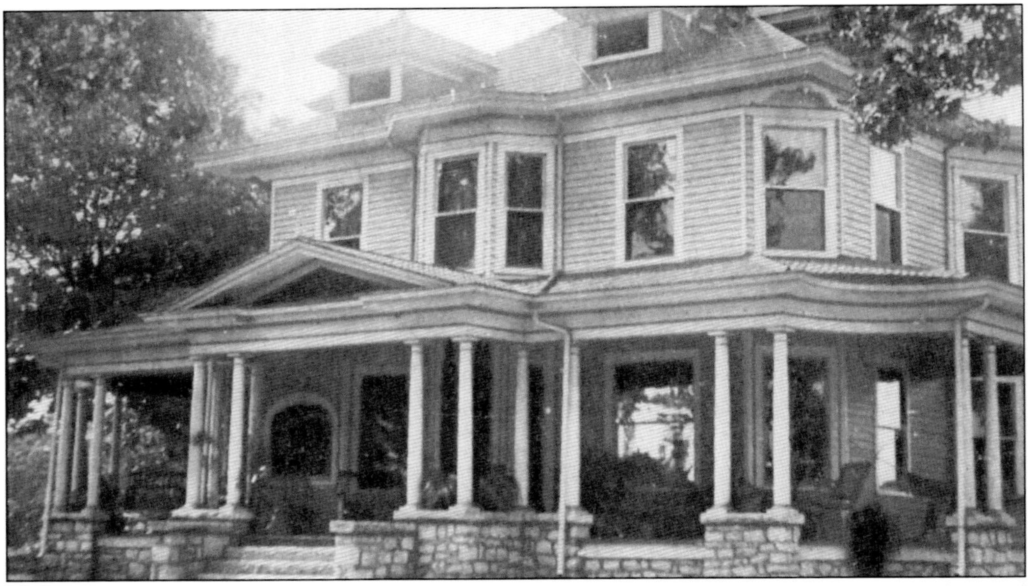

The residence of Dr. John Alexander Roach, D.M.D., was built in the early 1900s. It is featured in many publications and postcards. It is also referred to as the Oak Lawn Guest Home, a grand stay for the weary traveler. The above card is postmarked 1911. About 1970, the estate was demolished and the land is now used as the Madison Throwing Company parking lot. (Courtesy of the Jerri B. Griffin Collection, Madison, NC.)

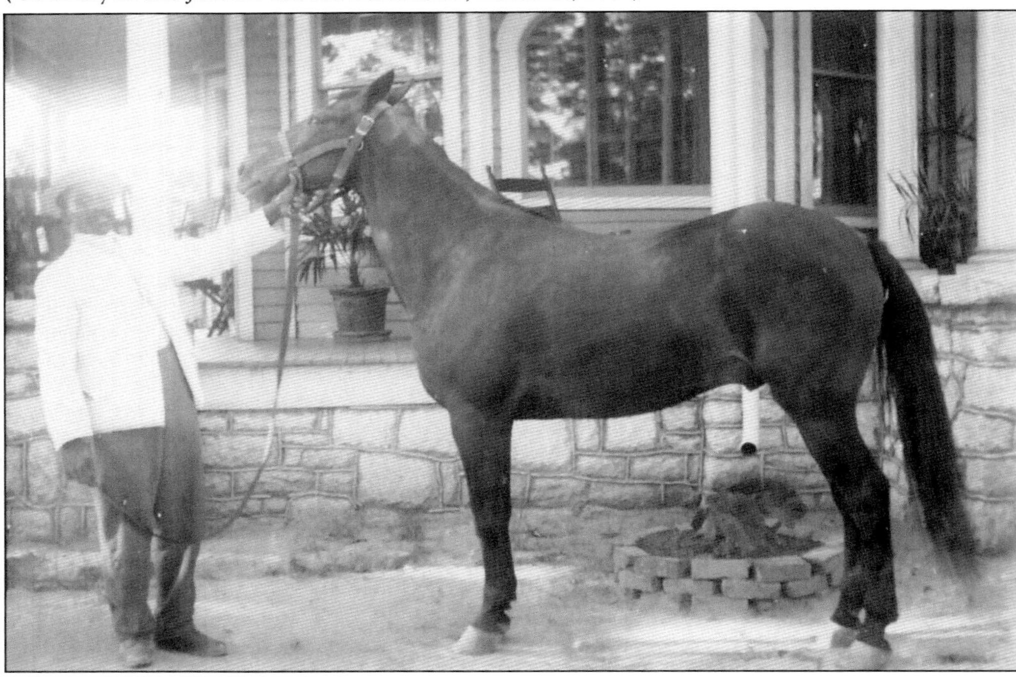

This man's identity is not known, but the nameless horse belonged to Dr. Roach, a successful businessman in Madison. This black-and-white postcard's commercial font style suggests that the informal shoot was snapped by Allen Benton in front of the great wrap-around porch of the three-story structure. (Courtesy of the Jerri B. Griffin Collection, Madison, NC.)

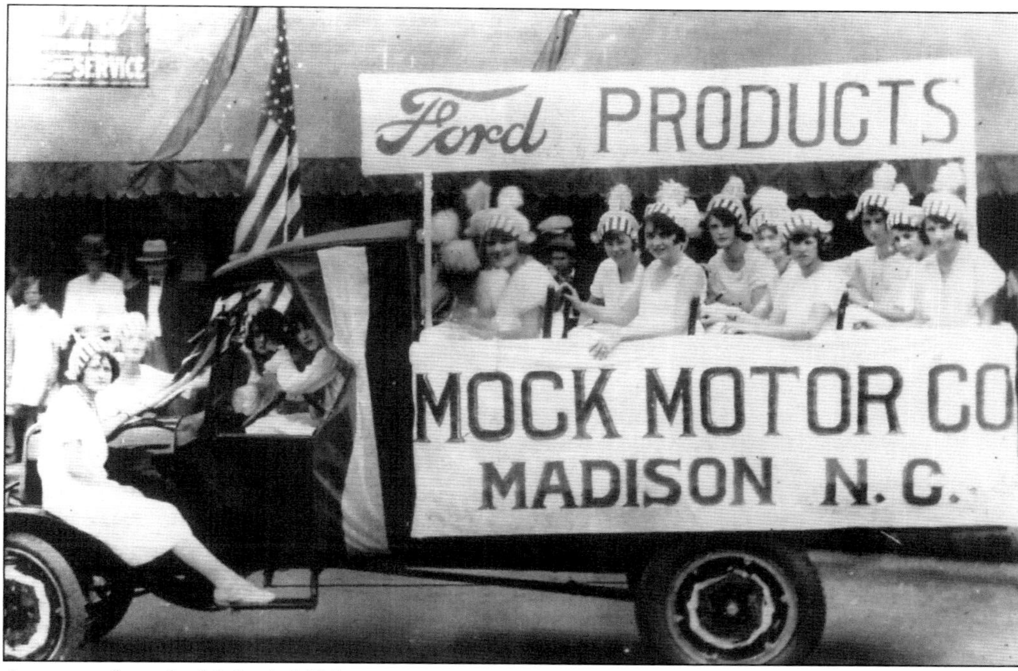

A postcard marked July 4, 1925, advertises the Mock Motor Company and the latest in Ford products. Note that the road and sidewalks are paved. They were heavily used, as seen in this 1927 portrait of Myrtle Hawkins (in the image on the right). She is shown before the Crystal Cafe on Murphy Street where she provided home-cooked meals for businessmen and families in the area. (Courtesy of the Jerri B. Griffin Collection, Madison, NC.)

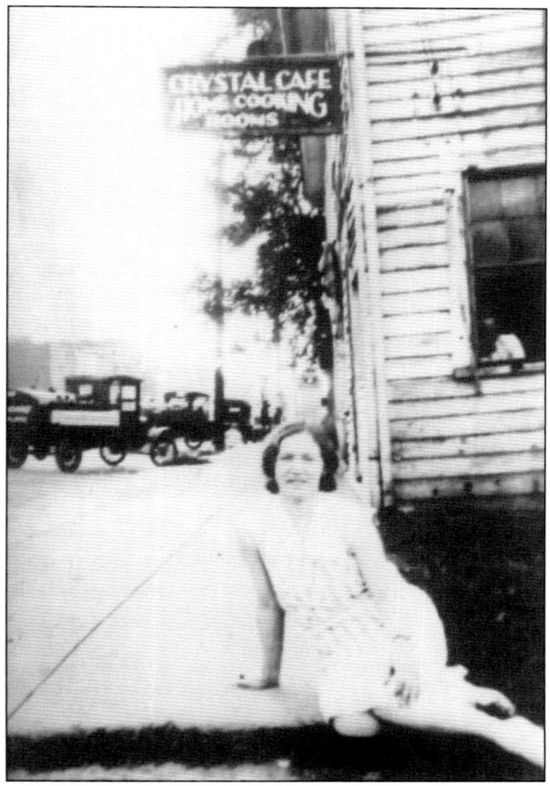

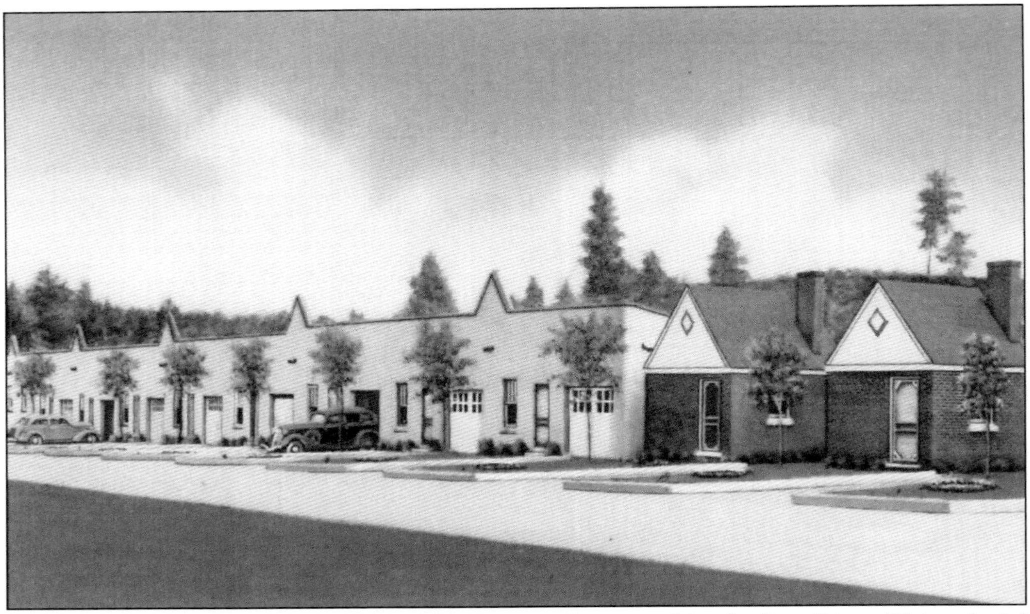

Grogan's Tourist Court on US Route 220 was a modern motel by the Dan River. This colorful postcard dates from around the 1930s and boasts of the motel's city water, steam heat, and free garage for the family car. Today the facility is vacant. (Courtesy of the Jerri B. Griffin Collection, Madison, NC.)

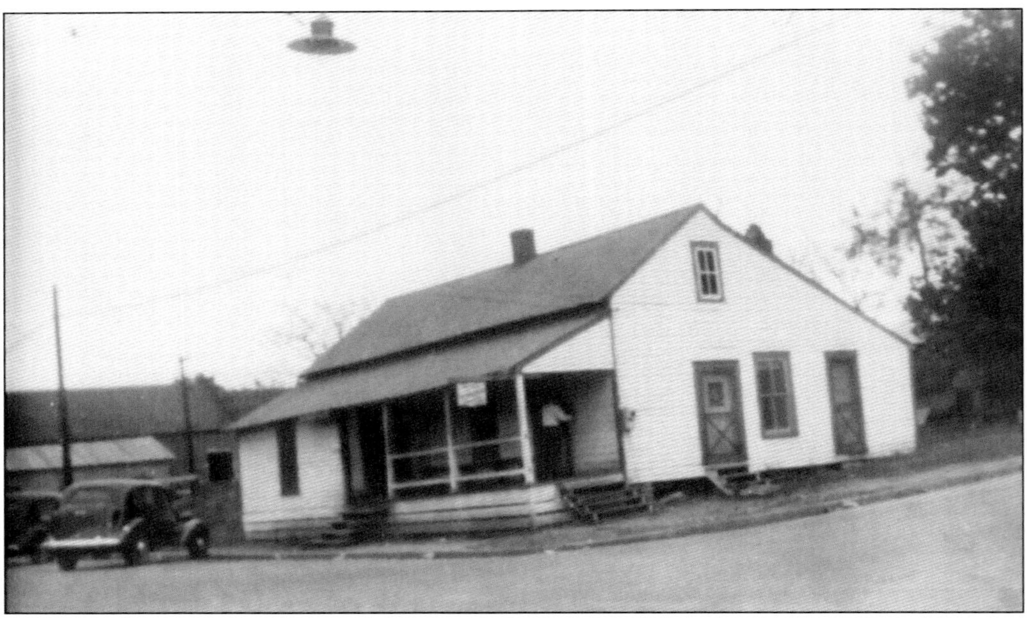

A small African-American establishment called Greasy Bill's used to be located on the corner of Franklin and Murphy Streets. It was a simple white house that was demolished for the post office, which is still in use today. (Courtesy of the Jerri B. Griffin Collection, Madison, NC.)

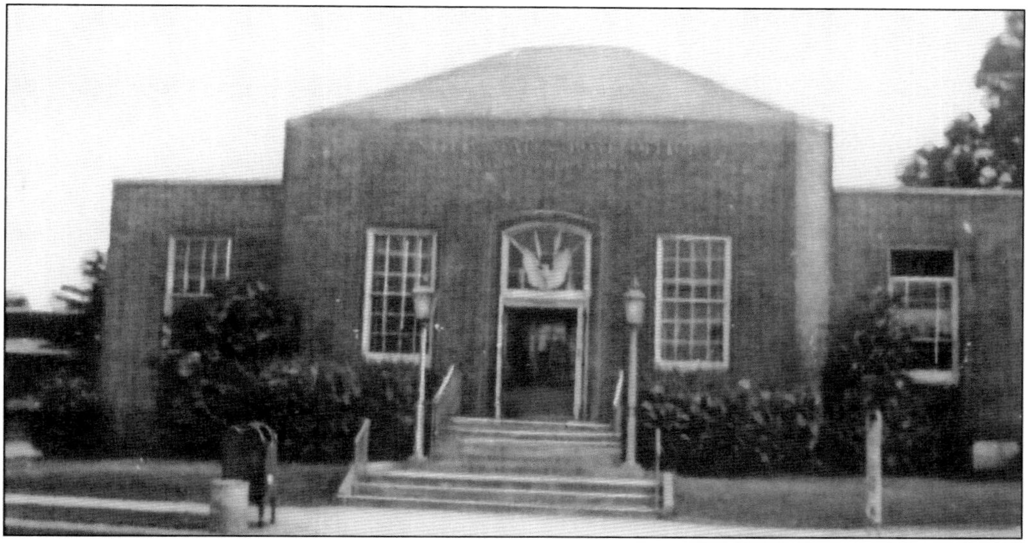

The Madison Post Office, featured in this 1940s black-and-white postcard, sits on the corner of Murphy and Franklin Streets. The facility is still used today and is a good example of the symmetry in post-World War II architecture. (Courtesy of the Jerri B. Griffin Collection, Madison, NC.)

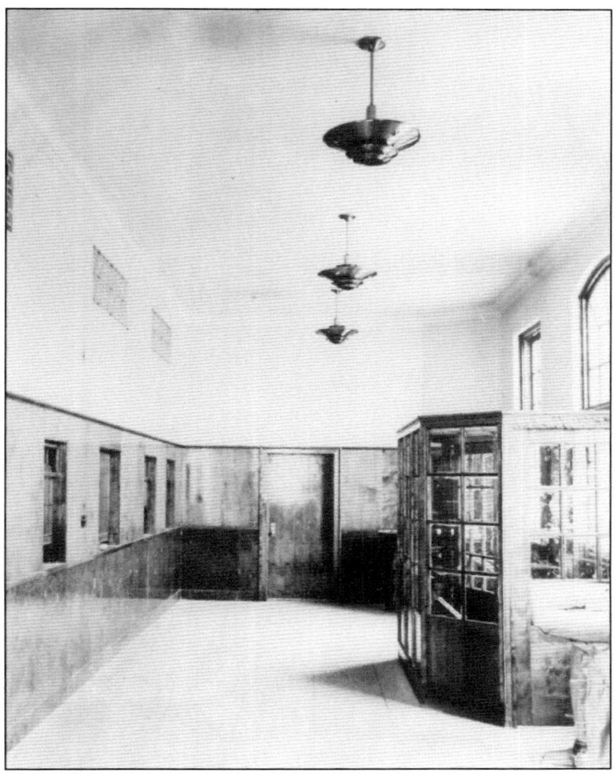

The Madison Post Office once had a stylish interior of marble and wood. (Courtesy of the Jerri B. Griffin Collection, Madison, NC.)

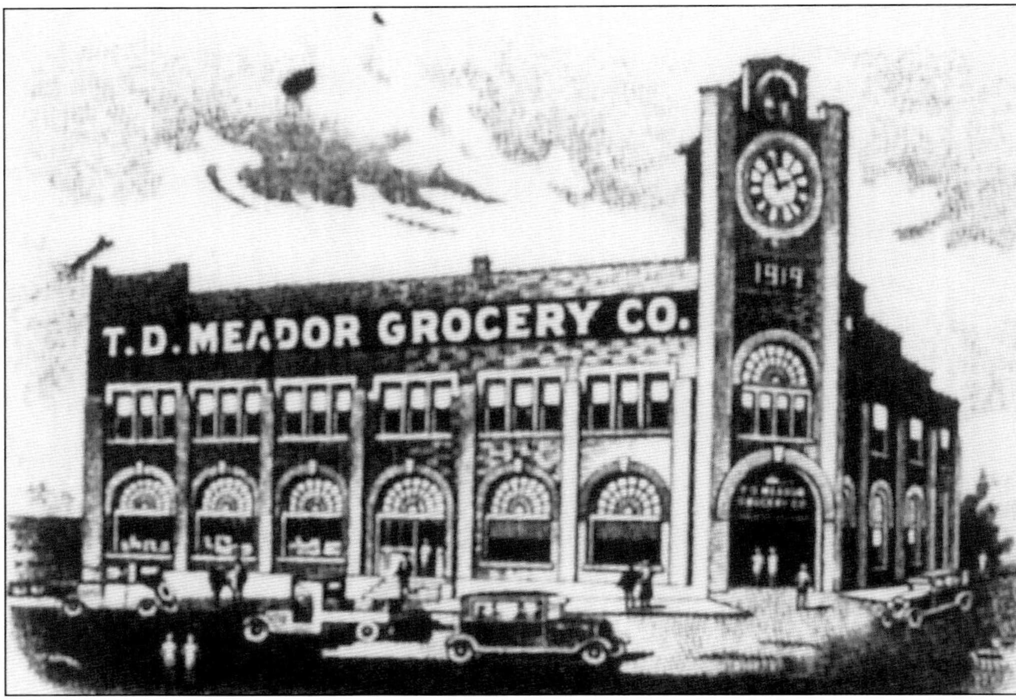

The T.D. Meador Grocery Company, a wholesale grocer, owned the 1919 clock tower, a landmark that dominates Madison's East Main Street to this day. As seen in the 1938 stationary logo, the brick building itself was a handsome series of arches, large windows, and grand doorways. On the second floor, town dances were held. (Courtesy of the Jerri B. Griffin Collection, Madison, NC.)

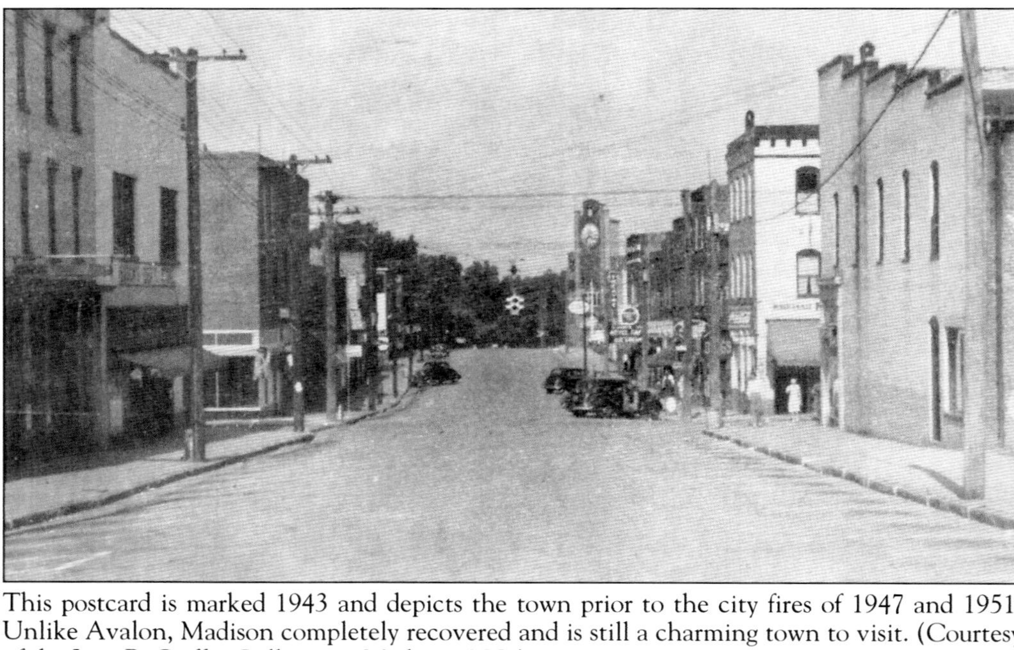

This postcard is marked 1943 and depicts the town prior to the city fires of 1947 and 1951. Unlike Avalon, Madison completely recovered and is still a charming town to visit. (Courtesy of the Jerri B. Griffin Collection, Madison, NC.)

Shown here is a close-up of the tower, a timepiece dedicated to the World War I veterans. It is located just west of the Dan River on East Main. (Courtesy of the Jerri B. Griffin Collection, Madison, NC.)

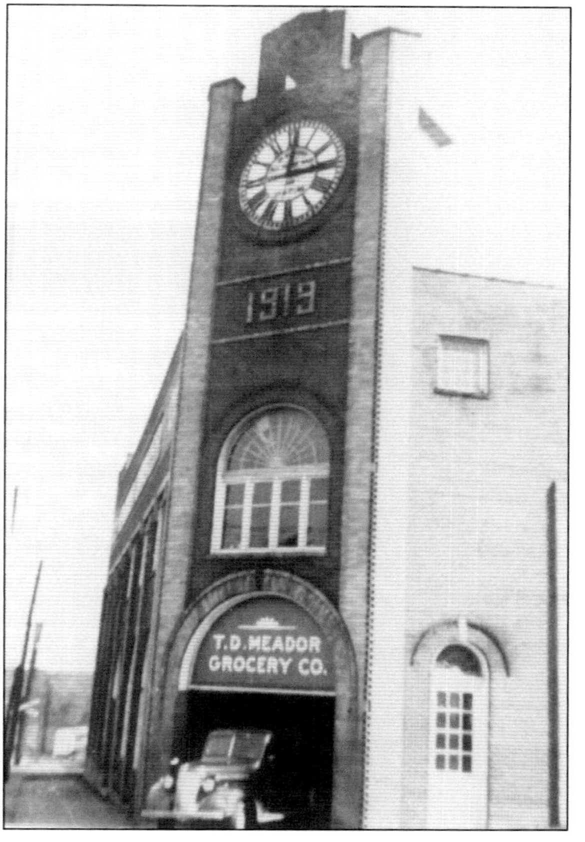

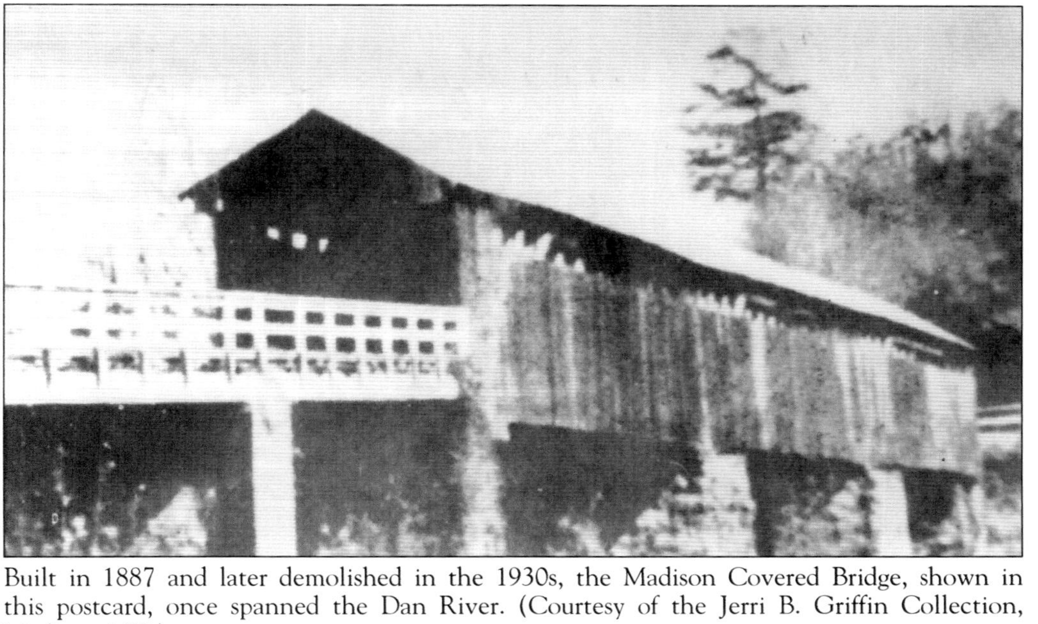

Built in 1887 and later demolished in the 1930s, the Madison Covered Bridge, shown in this postcard, once spanned the Dan River. (Courtesy of the Jerri B. Griffin Collection, Madison, NC.)

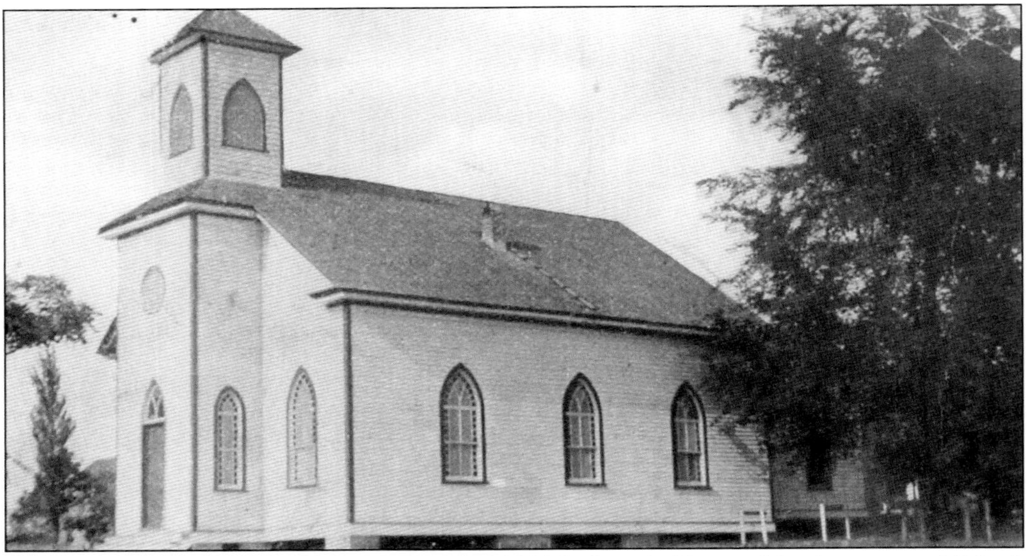

The Madison Baptist Church was organized in 1841, before the Town of Avalon was established. In 1850, this simple, plank structure with its ornate Gothic windows was erected. Later it was remodeled. This tinted postcard dates to the early 1900s. (Courtesy of the Jerri B. Griffin Collection, Madison, NC.)

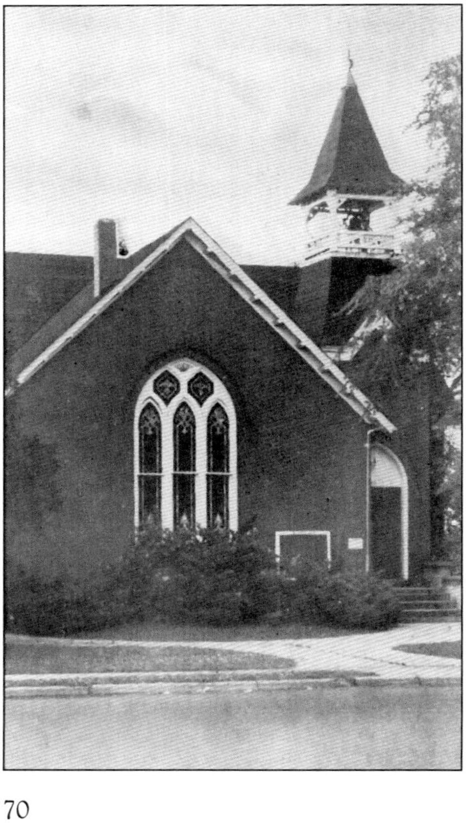

The black-and-white postcard (1940s) depicts the Madison United Methodist Church on Academy Street. This brick sanctuary, topped by fine woodwork on the steeple, was built in 1909, replacing the original structure erected 1845. The building is still in use today. (Courtesy of the Jerri B. Griffin Collection, Madison, NC.)

Organized in 1848, the Madison Presbyterian Church structure, shown in this 1940s black-and-white postcard, is still in use. Though remodeled, the beautiful sanctuary can be viewed on Decatur Street. (Courtesy of the Jerri B. Griffin Collection, Madison, NC.)

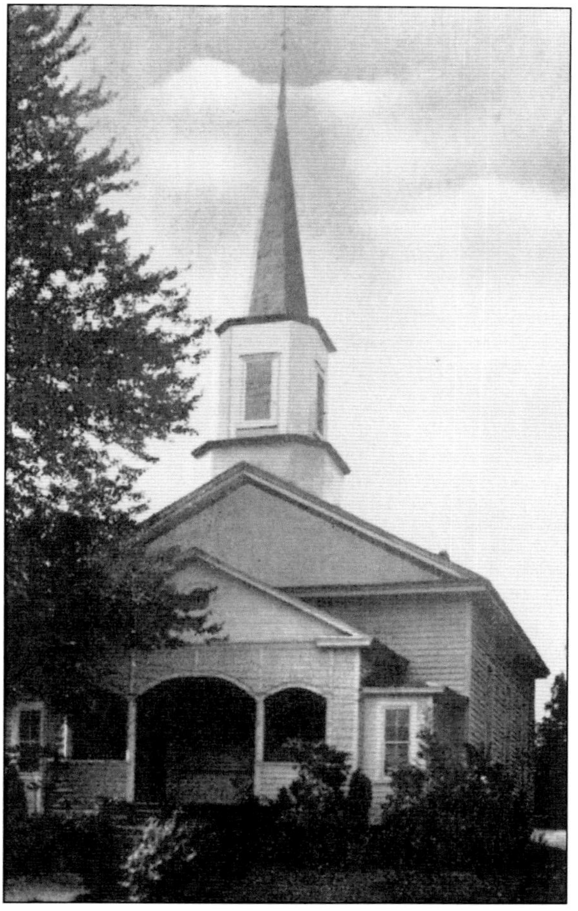

A postcard from the 1920s features the Madison Graded School, and the Grammar Graded School (far right). These facilities on Decatur Street are currently for sale. (Courtesy of the Jerri B. Griffin Collection, Madison, NC.)

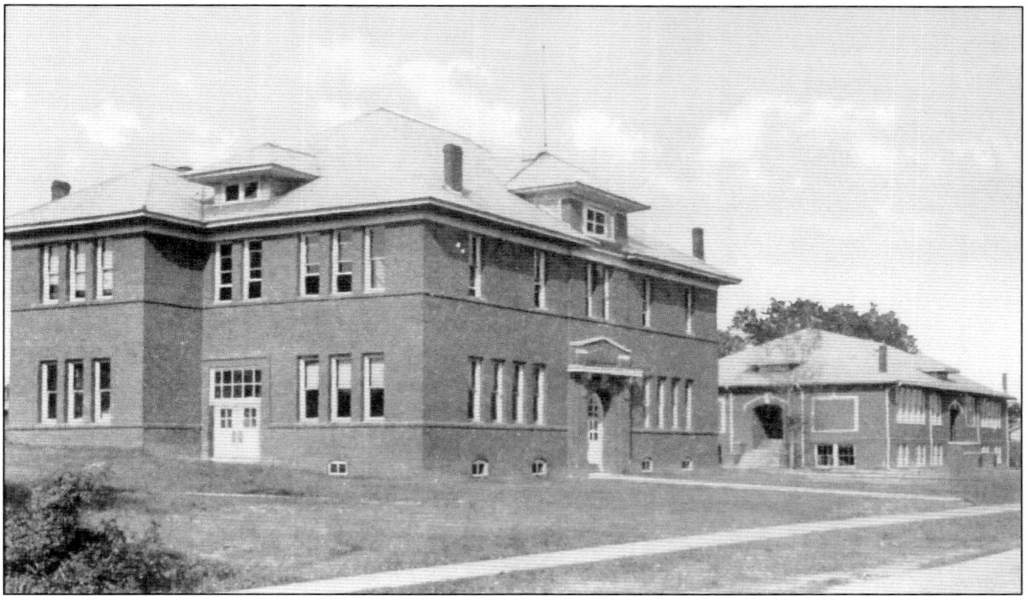

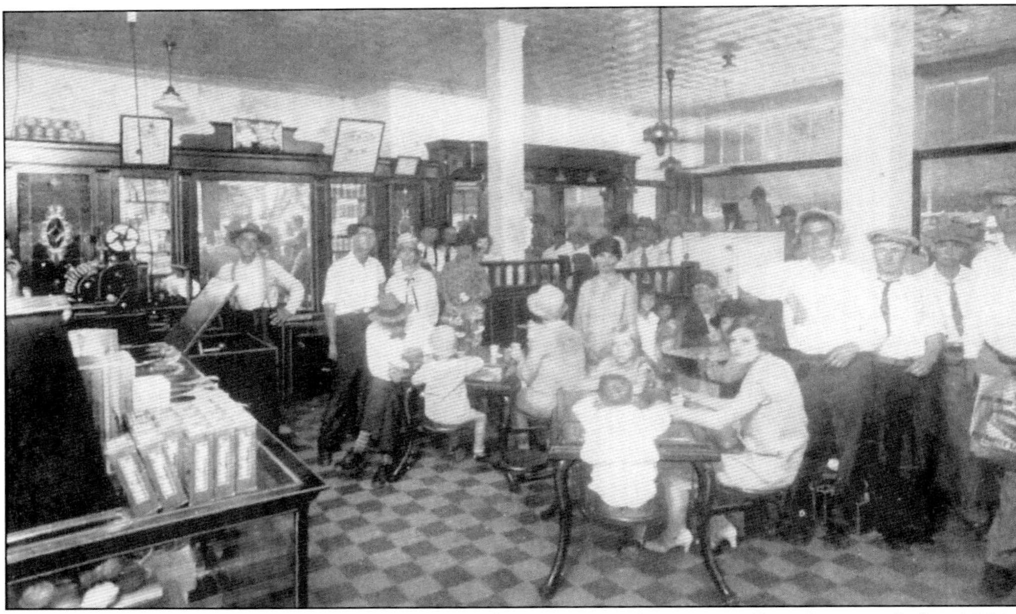

This postcard is an interior view of the Piedmont Drug Company. Dated around the 1930s, the image shows friendly townspeople enjoying the soda shop. (Courtesy of the Jerri B. Griffin Collection, Madison, NC.)

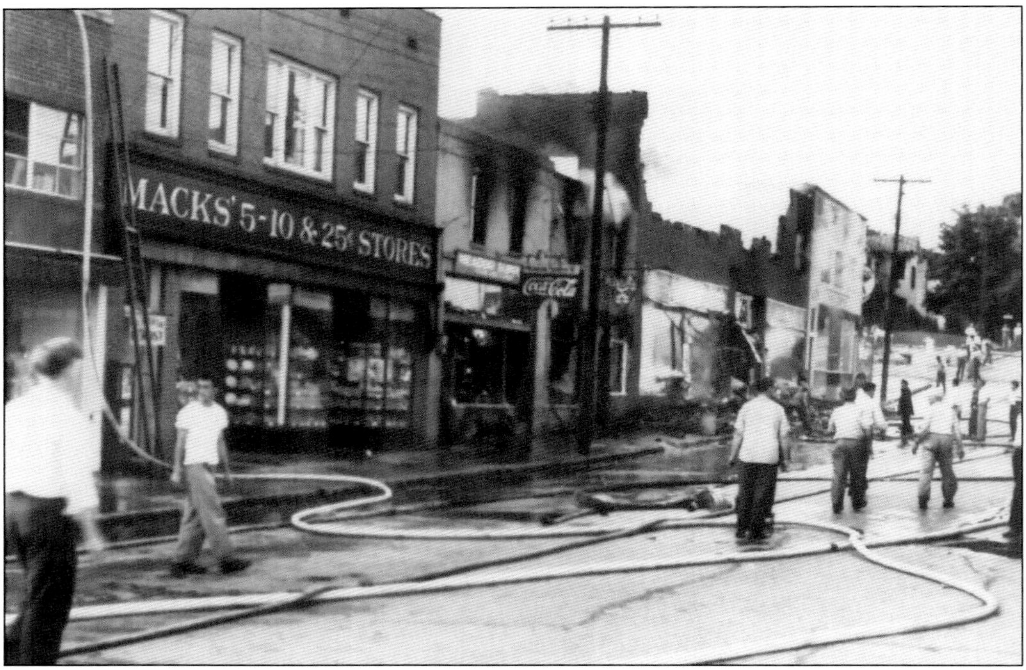

Unlike Avalon's spectacular fires, no postcards were created from the Madison town fires. Still, the village retains its attractiveness and historical structures for visitors and residents to see. (Courtesy of the Jerri B. Griffin Collection, Madison, NC.)

Five

REIDSVILLE

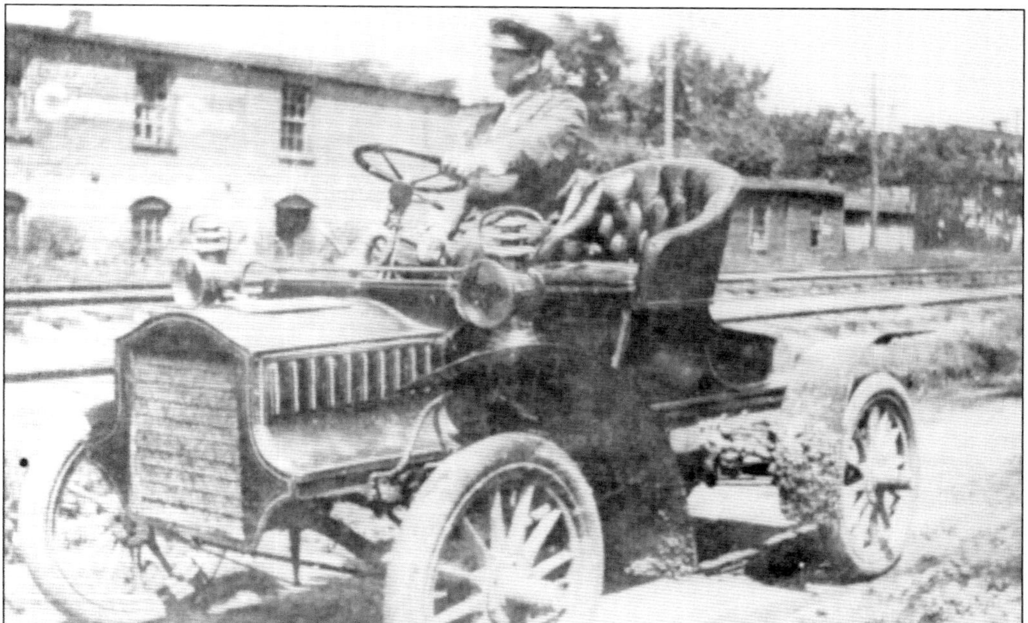

In the early 1900s, Reidsville flourished on tobacco sales and tourism by train-travel. Gradually, the automobile would change the town forever. (Courtesy of the Jimmy Waynick Collection, Reidsville, NC.)

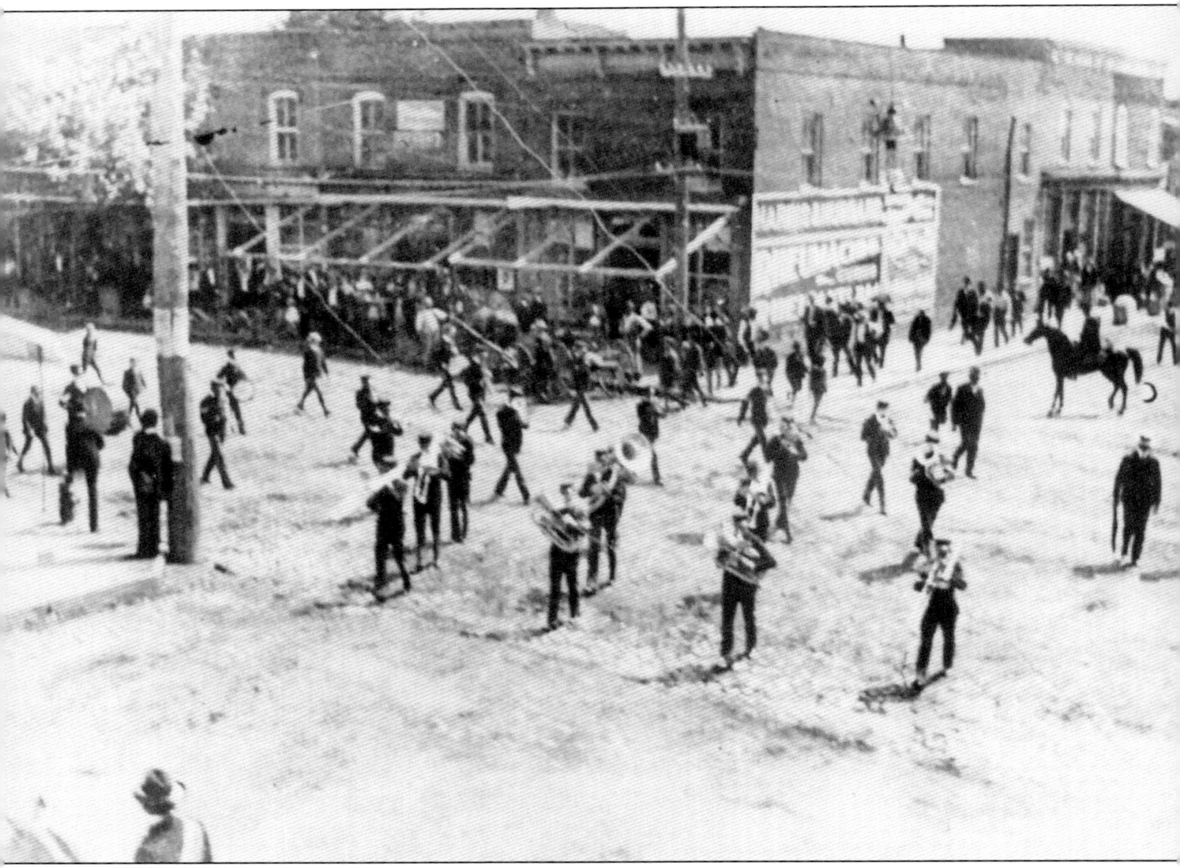

This is a bird's-eye view of the corner of Scales and Gilmer Streets in Reidsville. It shows a 1902 parade honoring Governor Charles B. Aycock. Note that the streets are stone. These stones were incorporated into the landscape of 102 North Main by Billie Jacobs Wright. (Courtesy of the Jimmy Waynick Collection, Reidsville.)

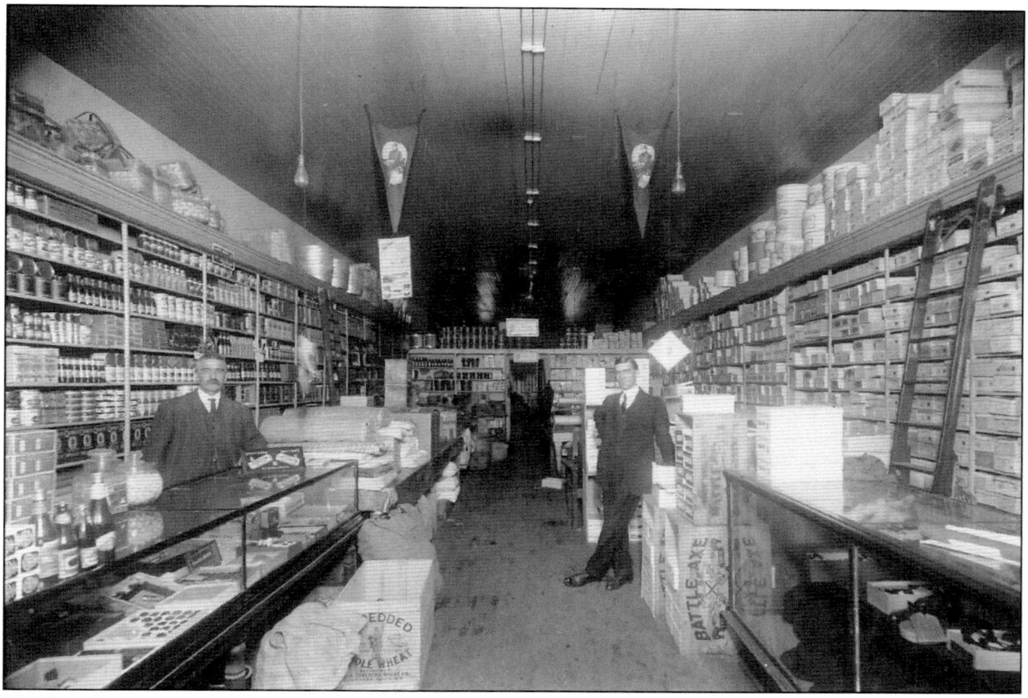

Hubbard's Store, one of Reidsville's early merchandise outlets, specialized in quality and service. (Courtesy of the Jimmy Waynick Collection, Reidsville.)

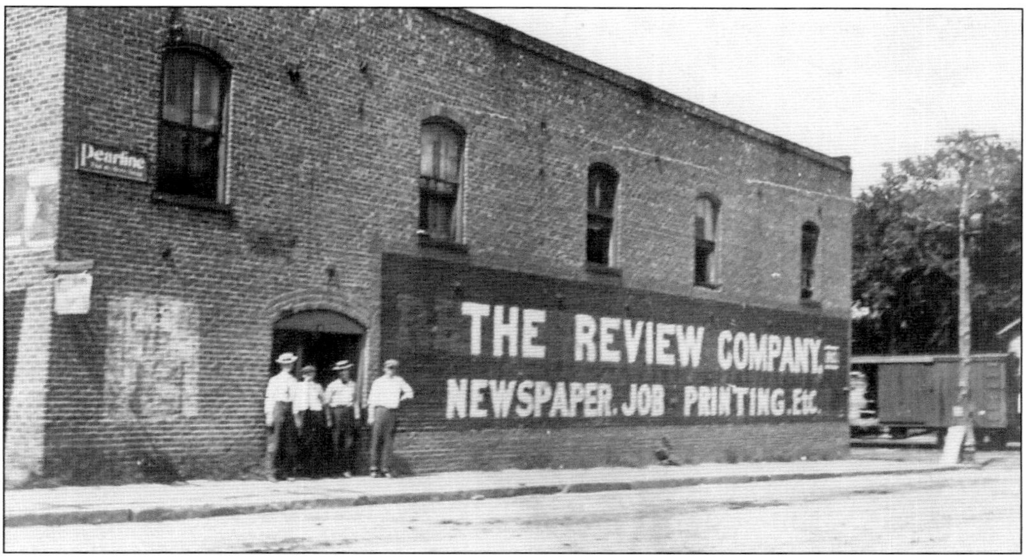

On the corner of Morehead and North West Market Streets, four employees pose in front of the offices of *The Reidsville Review* in this 1916 black-and-white postcard. (Courtesy of the Jimmy Waynick Collection, Reidsville.)

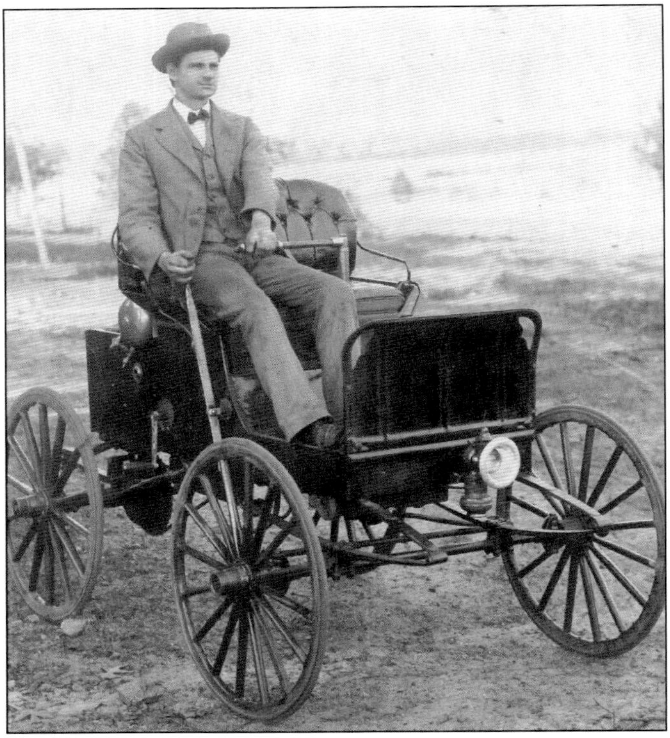

Fletcher Waynick is most recognizable to historians in this portrait. Fletcher, a blacksmith, liked inventions. He put together all the parts of this car—from the commode tank (in the rear) to the kerosene lantern on the front of the carriage. This photograph was taken in 1902, and since Fletcher appears in some postcards, this helps collectors to date their images even when no postmark is clear. (Courtesy of the Jimmy Waynick Collection, Reidsville.)

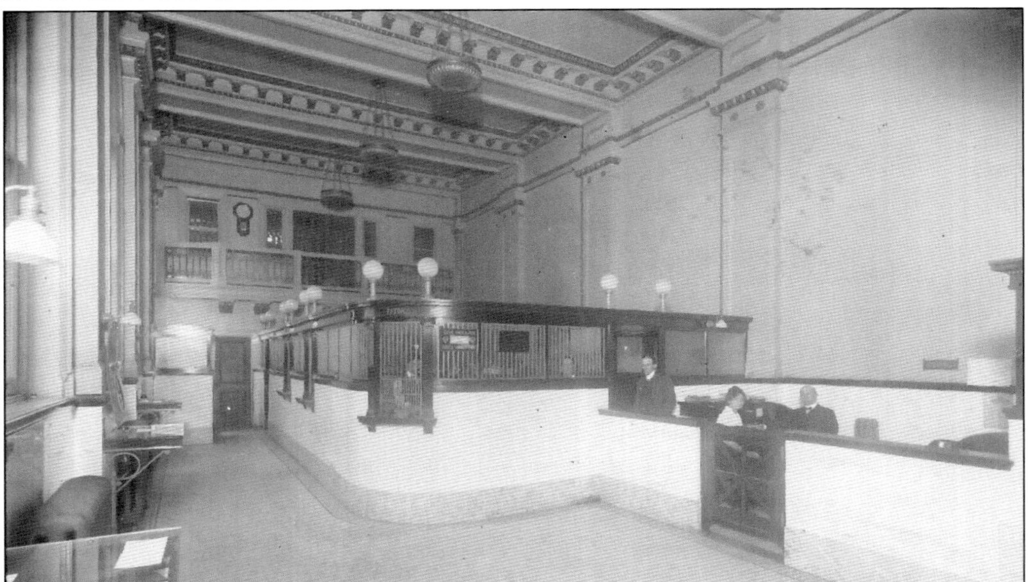

At the southwest corner of Scales and Gilmer Streets a regal, two-story structure once stood; built in 1913, the Citizen's Bank was the subject of several 1920s commercial postcards. Here is an interior shot believed to be used for promotional purposes. Unfortunately, all the cards and advertising in the world did not prevent the bank's failure during the Depression. The building was gutted by fire in 1978 and now is the site of the downtown park. (Courtesy of the Jimmy Waynick Collection, Reidsville, NC.)

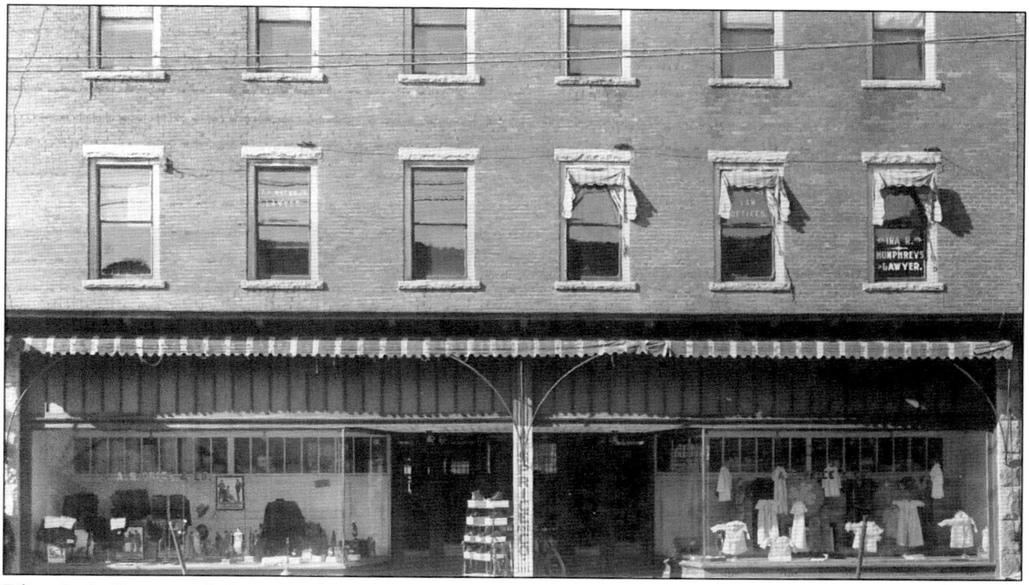

The A.S. Price and Company store is shown above. Located on South Scales Street, the store became Belk-Stevens and is a prominent fixture in the images of the town. The upper level housed Ira R. Humphrey's law offices and the Wrenn law offices. (Courtesy of the Jimmy Waynick Collection, Reidsville.)

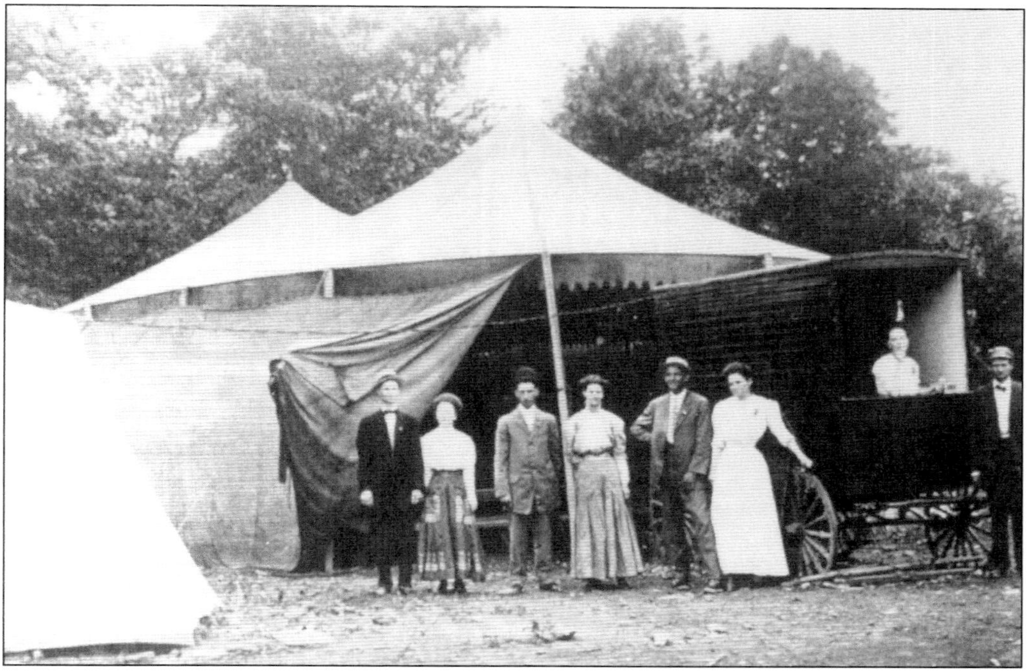

Fletcher Waynick, noted for creating the one motorized jalopy ever built in Rockingham County, enjoyed posing for postcard pictures in his spare time. In this early 1900s black-and-white postcard, Fletcher (far left) stands before a tent constructed as a portable movie house. Fletcher traveled around the county showing movies whenever possible. (Courtesy of the Jimmy Waynick Collection, Reidsville.)

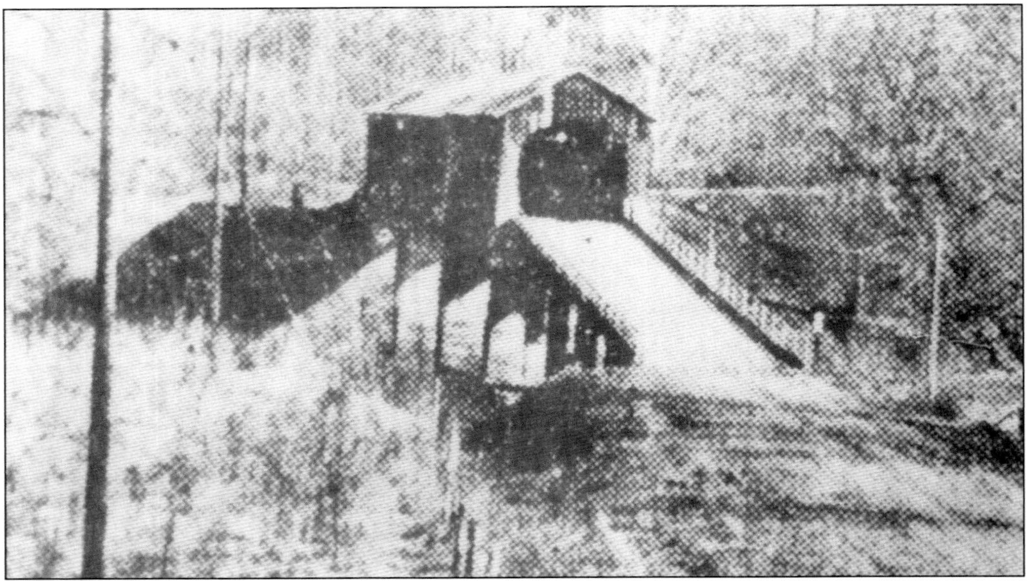

Covered bridges were popular subjects for local and commercial postcard photographers. Settle's Bridge, pictured above, was built in 1870 over the Dan River at the old Dead Timbers Ford near Wentworth. In 1951 it was demolished as the last covered bridge in Rockingham County. All that remains are the postcards that bear its image. (Courtesy of the Jerri B. Griffin Collection, Madison, NC.)

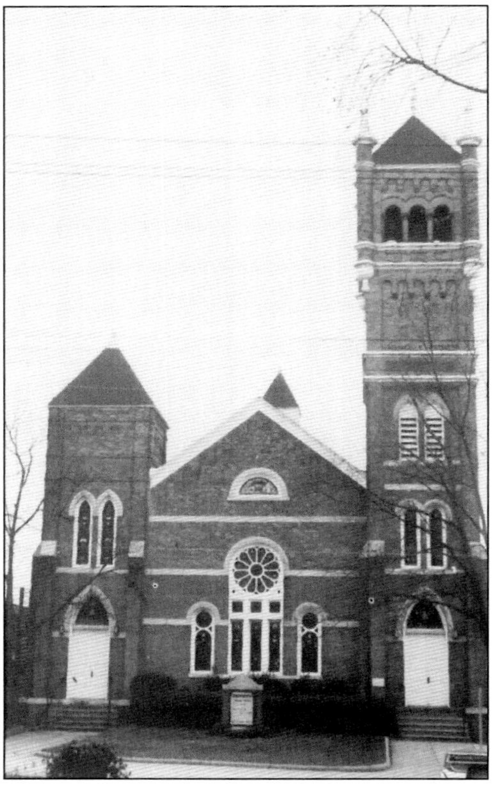

This 1950s black-and-white postcard features the majestic Main Street Methodist Church. It was built around 1892 as a replacement to a facility located on South Scales Street. The congregation was formed in 1874. (Courtesy of the Jerri B. Griffin Collection, Madison, NC.)

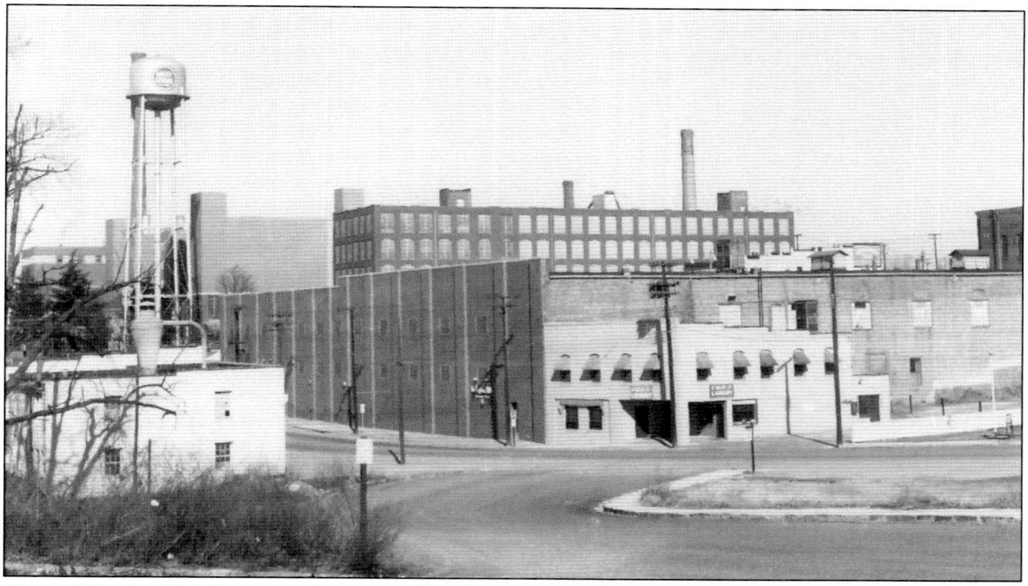

One of Reidsville's larger industries is the American Tobacco Company. It is featured in many postcards from 1917 to the present. The facility is still used today. (Courtesy of the Jimmy Waynick Collection, Reidsville, NC.)

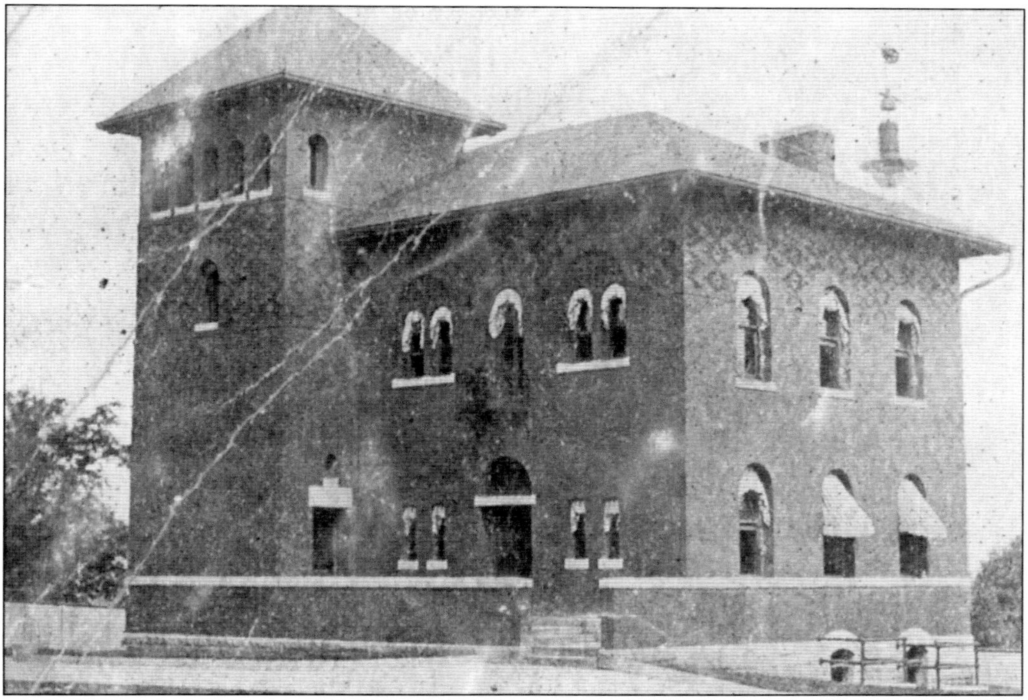

In 1893/94 this structure was erected on the corner of Scales and Morehead Streets. It functioned as the post office until 1953 when it became the city's library. This postcard marked 1911 actually shows the facility as it appeared prior to modifications and the addition of the Confederate Monument (which would have been in the foreground at the far right.) (Courtesy of the Jeff Bullins Collection, Mayodan.)

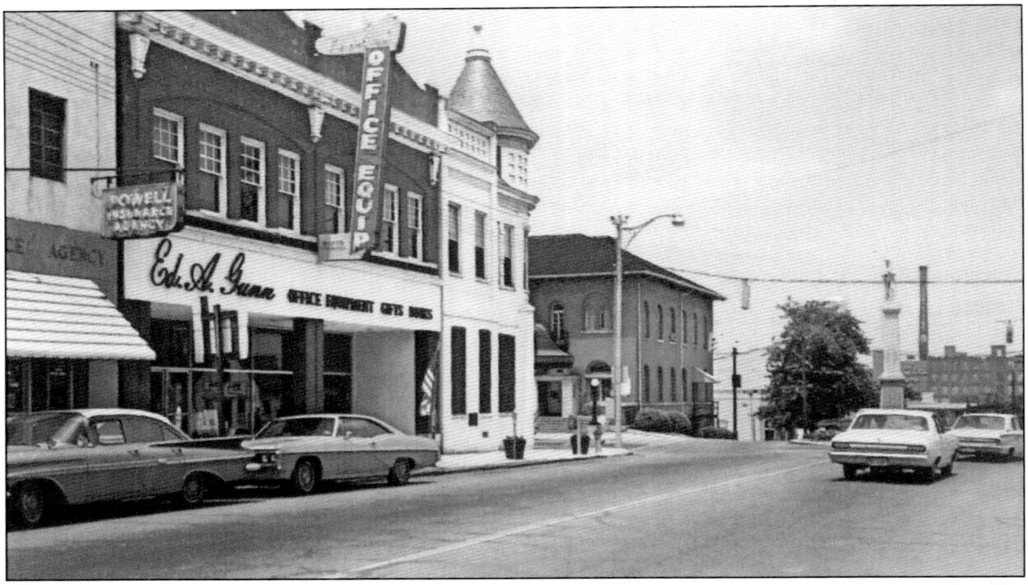

Dated 1969, this postcard depicts Scales Street, the business district of historic Reidsville. This scene looks north to the American Tobacco Plant (background, right). At the left, near the Confederate Monument in the mid-ground, is the city's library building (originally the post office location). (Copyrighted image used with permission of Aerial Photography Services, Inc. 2511 S. Tryon St., Charlotte, NC. Postcard courtesy of the Jerri B. Griffin Collection, Madison, NC.)

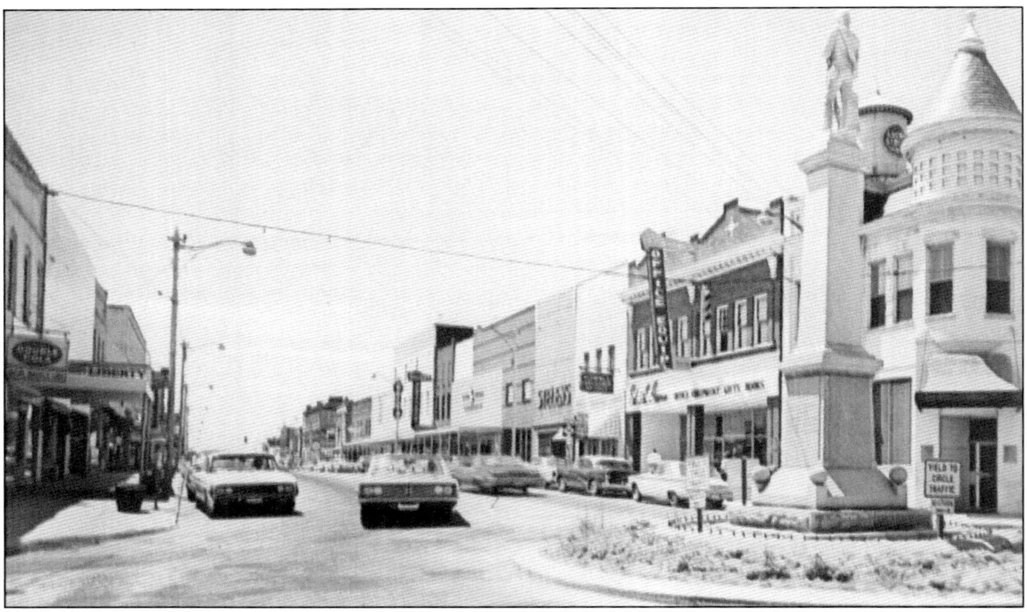

Scales Street is one of the historical gems of the area and is filled with antique stores. Here in this postcard, the Confederate Monument, erected in 1910, faces south (naturally). At the right of the monument is the impressive Victorian structure that housed the former Bank of Reidsville, chartered in 1882. The building still stands today. (Courtesy of the Jerri B. Griffin Collection, Madison, NC.)

Six

Leaksville

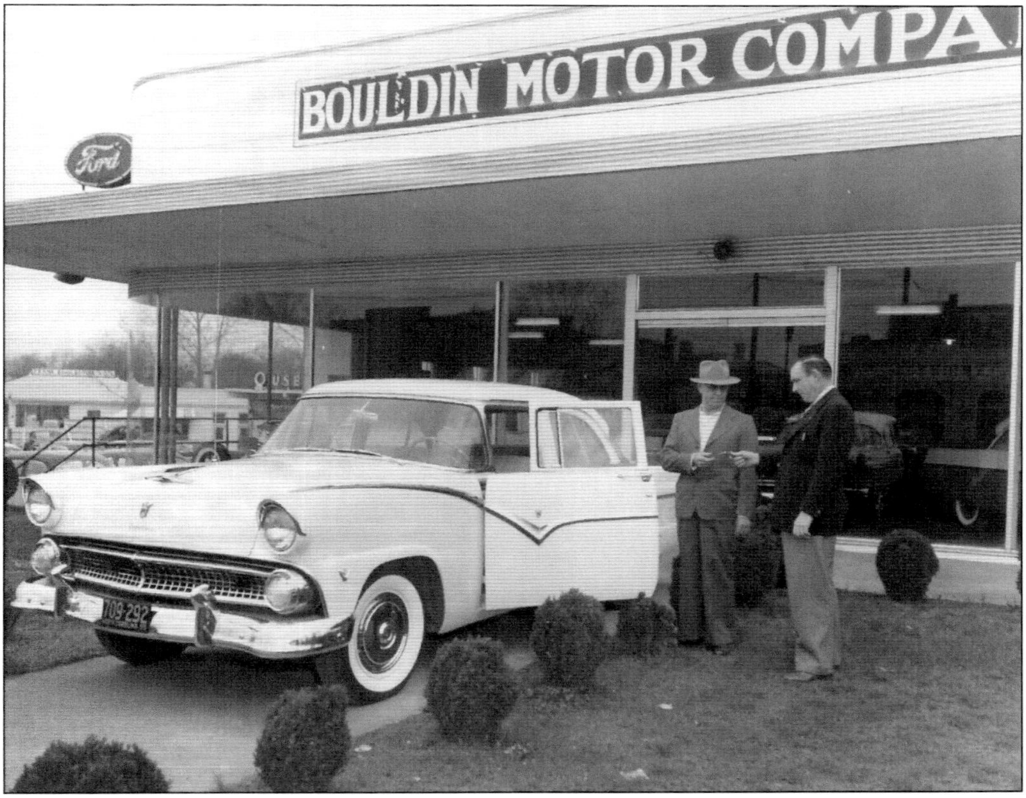

As passenger train rides declined in the late 1940s, the automobile became an important element of Rockingham County's development. It brought the villages along the Mayo, the Dan, and the Smith Rivers closer together until the communities of Leaksville, Spray, and Draper deliberated on consolidation beginning in the late 1950s. Above is one of the more distinctive structures of the "big car" era, Scotties Car Lot in Leaksville. It was located on the corner of Washington and Boone Streets. Here George Scott's dad is seen with the keys to the latest in technology and horsepower. (Courtesy of the Roscoe Hankins Collection, Eden, NC.)

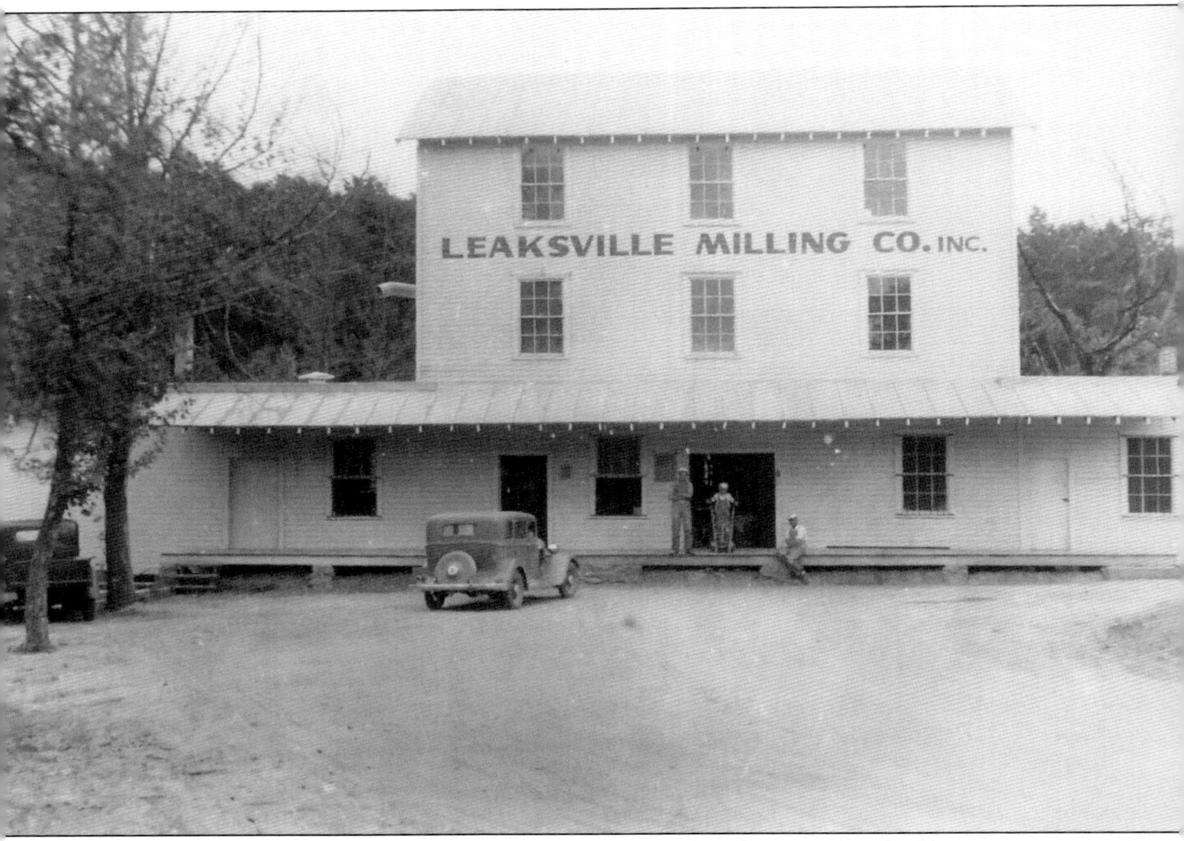

By 1900, the year Avalon Mills began operating, Leaksville Township had been incorporated more than eighty years. Above is the new Leaksville Milling building that replaced King's Mill, a facility that burned in 1938. The site, on the north side of Matrimony Creek just off State Road 1535 near the junction with Clark Street, has a history dating to 1757. The King's Mill was instrumental in the industrial formation of what is now Eden, North Carolina. (Courtesy of the Roscoe Hankins Collection, Eden, NC. Courtesy of the Harold Francis Collection, Eden, NC.)

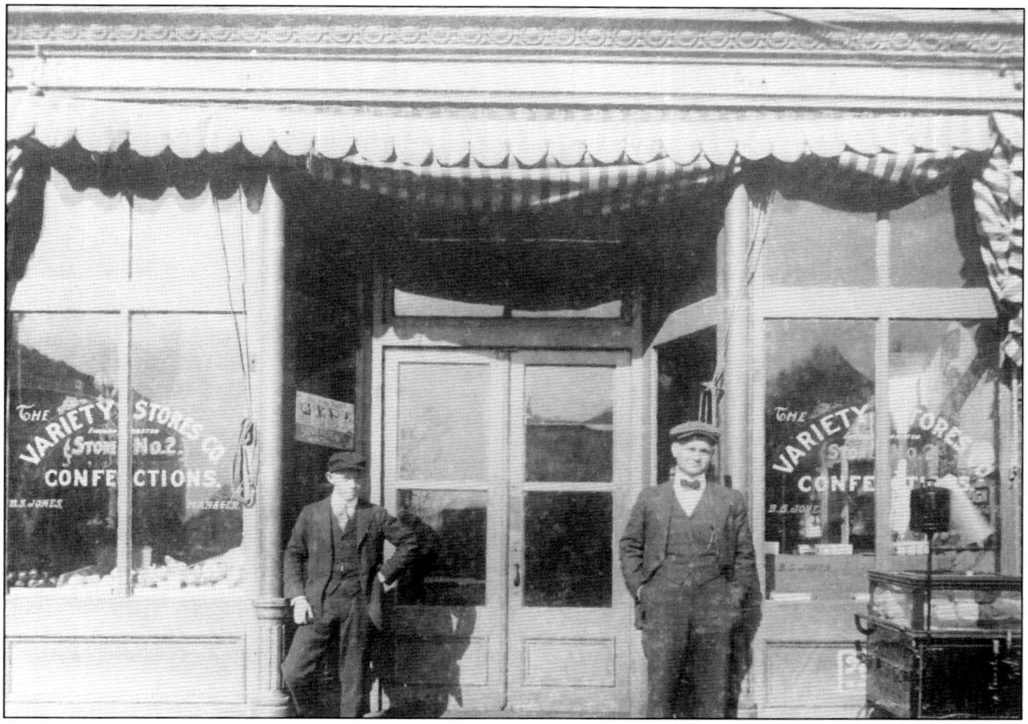

T. Lee Millner (left) and Ben S. Jones (manager) strike a pose before The Variety Stores Company, Store No. 2. Spray resident Thomas Winston Price, also called Picture Price, may have taken the picture. Many photos and postcards of the early 1900s were attributed to Jesse G. Seay and a gentleman called Mr. Wannamaker. Few of Wannamaker's negatives exist since his wife had a bad habit of cleaning the emulsion off the glass negatives and recycling the plates for glass tabletops. (Information provided Harold Francis, Francis Photography, Eden, NC. Image courtesy of the Roscoe Hankins Collection, Eden, NC.)

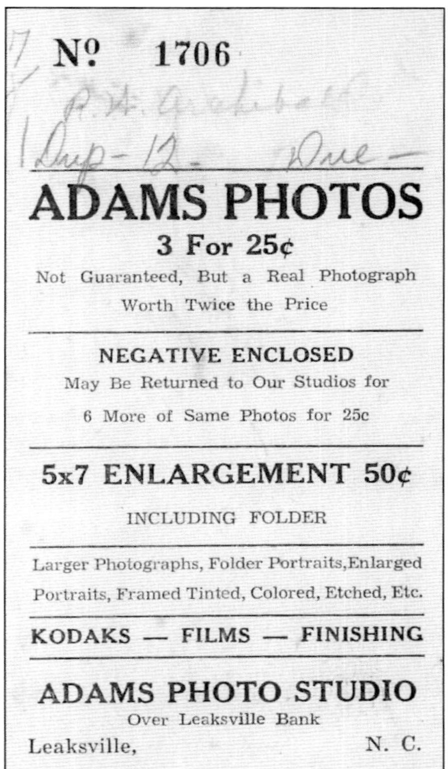

At the right is a negative sleeve from Adams Studio from around 1925. Now called Francis Photography, the studios are located on Washington Street in Leaksville, which was renamed Eden in 1969. (Courtesy of the Bertha Vestal Aheron Collection, Eden, NC.)

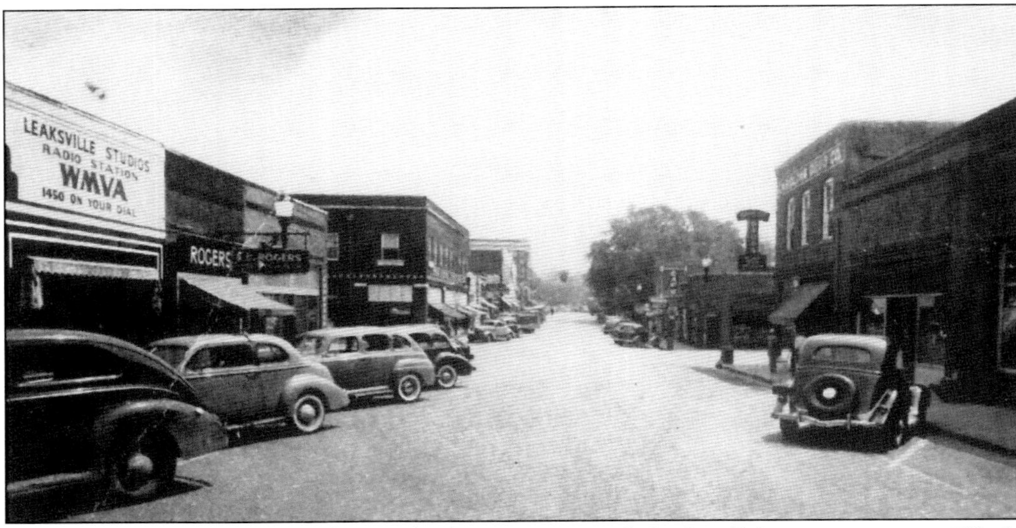

This black-and-white postcard from the late 1940s reveals Leaksville's prosperous post-World War II economy. The photographer is facing east. On the right, in the background, is Robert's Cafe (or G.J. Grill). In the foreground on the right is the Carolina Drug Company (702 Washington Street). Both buildings still stand. On the left in the foreground is WMVA radio. The Pace Building and the Realty Building are in the far background near the centerpoint of the image. (Courtesy of the Roscoe Hankins Collection, Eden, NC.)

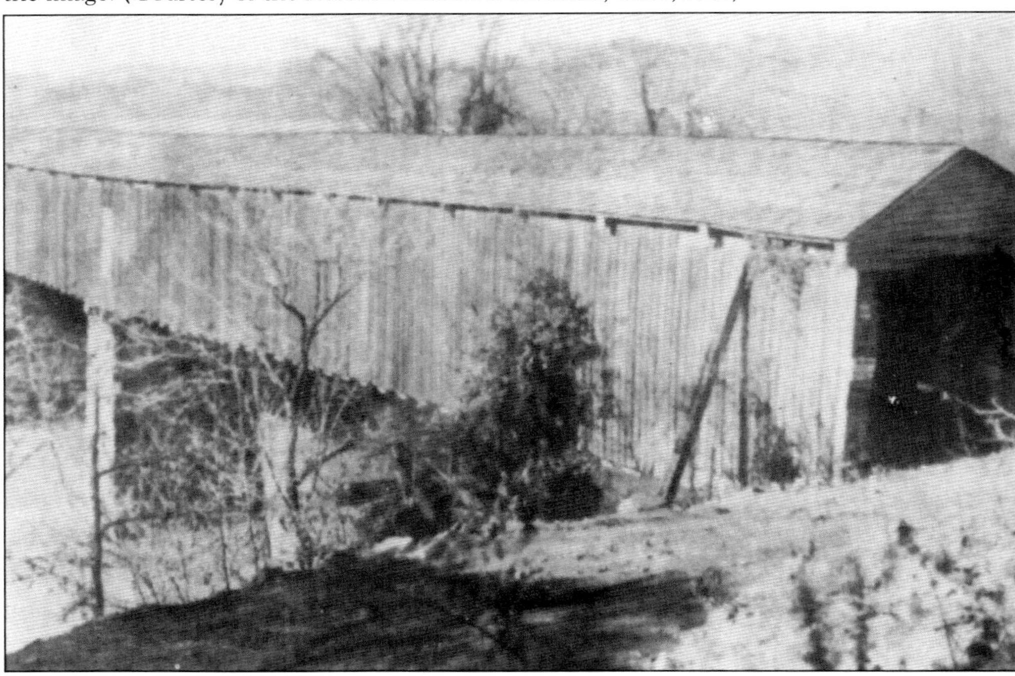
This black-and-white postcard of the Leaksville Covered Bridge depicts a massive structure with piers of rough-cut rubble stones. The bridge spanned the Dan River until it collapsed in the mid-1940s. The remains, one pier, is located in the vicinity of the west side of Bridge Street, northwest of the junction with Highland Drive. (Courtesy of the Jerri B. Griffin Collection, Madison, NC.)

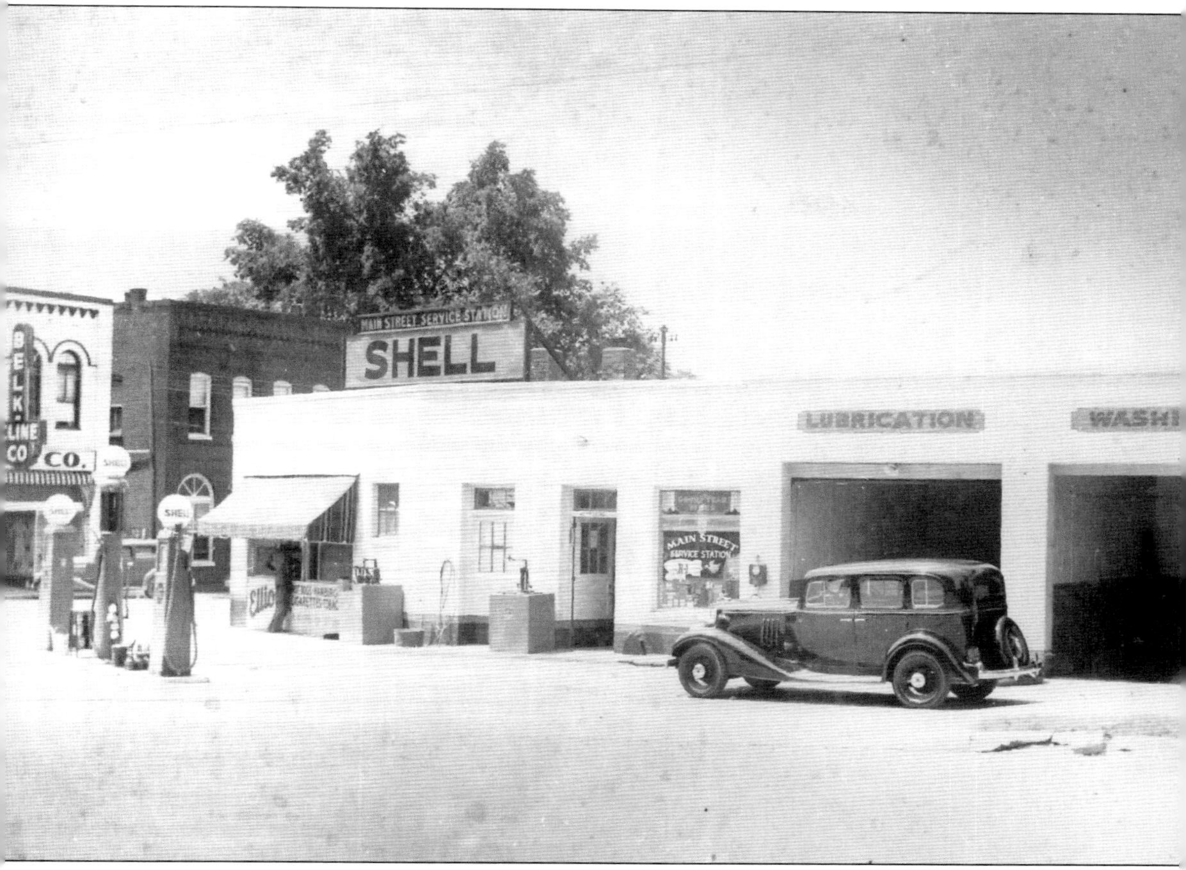

Elliott's Hot Dogs and Hamburgers was a grill located in the modern Main Street Shell Service Station, near present-day Washington Street. It was a favorite for many Leaksville residents. This photograph was taken around the 1930s. (Courtesy of the Roscoe Hankins Collection, Eden, NC. Courtesy of Harold Francis Collection, Eden, NC.)

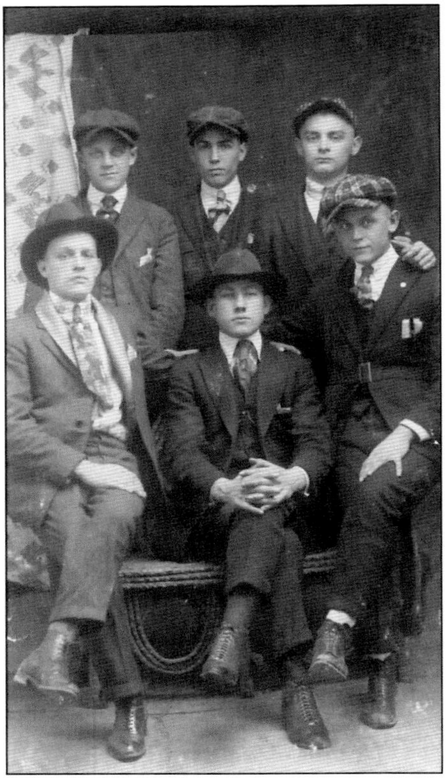

The postcard here is from the 1920s. It features some boys from Leaksville. Individuals pictured are from left to right, as follows: (front row) Willie Chambers, Mr. Moore, and Lymon Cheek; (back row) Dick Grogan, Everet Buschell, and Rucker Martin. Dan Aheron of Spray may have taken the photograph, as Dan used quilts—a typical backdrop for gentleman photographers who could not afford the expensive hand-painted backdrops. Little did these photographers know that the quilts would later mark their works like a signature. (Courtesy of the Lavender Cheek and Mary Cheek Collection, Eden, NC.)

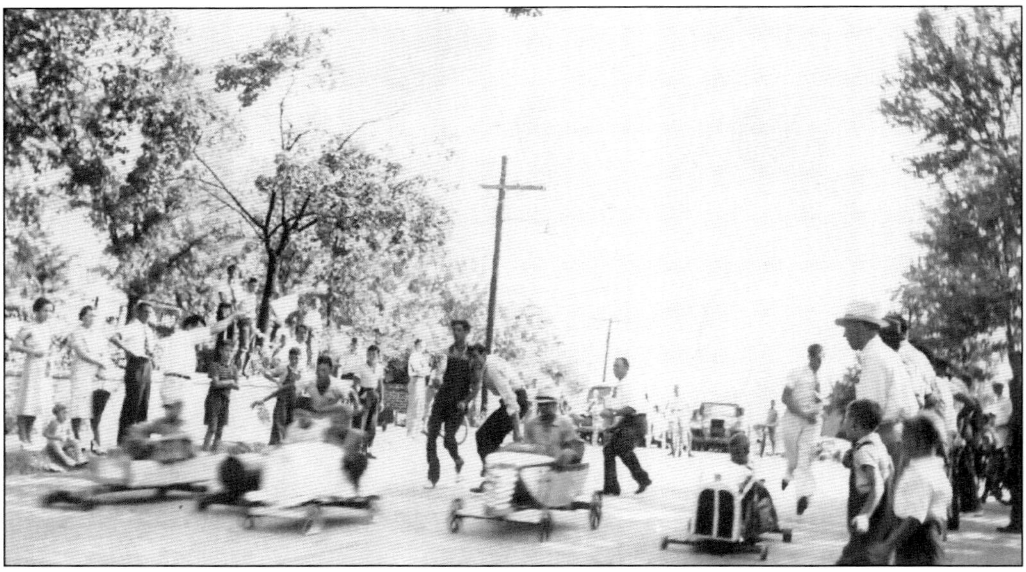

Dan Aheron of Spray photographed Fair Funeral Home's Annual Soap Box Derby. The races were on Boone Road. The Fair Funeral Home still exists on Boone Road. The date of this image is not known, but the races began after 1939. (Courtesy of the Bertha Vestal Aheron Collection, Eden, NC.)

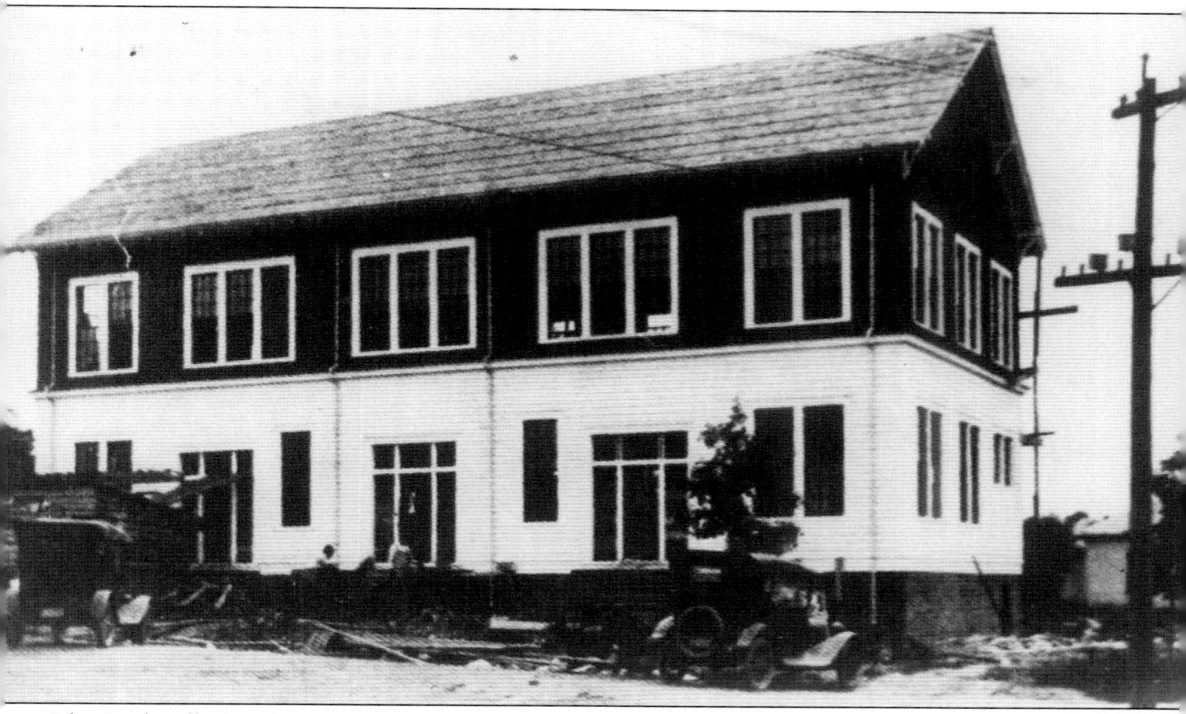

The Leaksville YMCA was constructed in 1921 with the financial support of industries like Marshall Field and Company. Unlike its Spray counterpart, the Leaksville structure was seldom illustrated in local postcards. (Courtesy of the Lavender Cheek and Mary Cheek Collection, Eden, NC.)

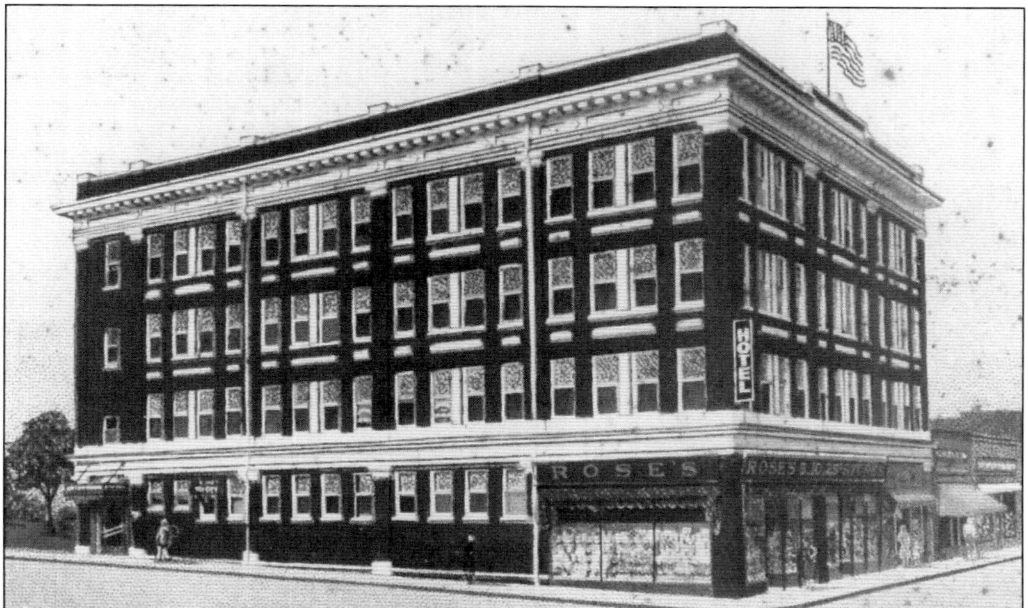

A postcard from the 1920s shows the John B. Ray Building, which still stands today on Washington Street. (Courtesy of the Harold Francis Collection, Eden, NC.)

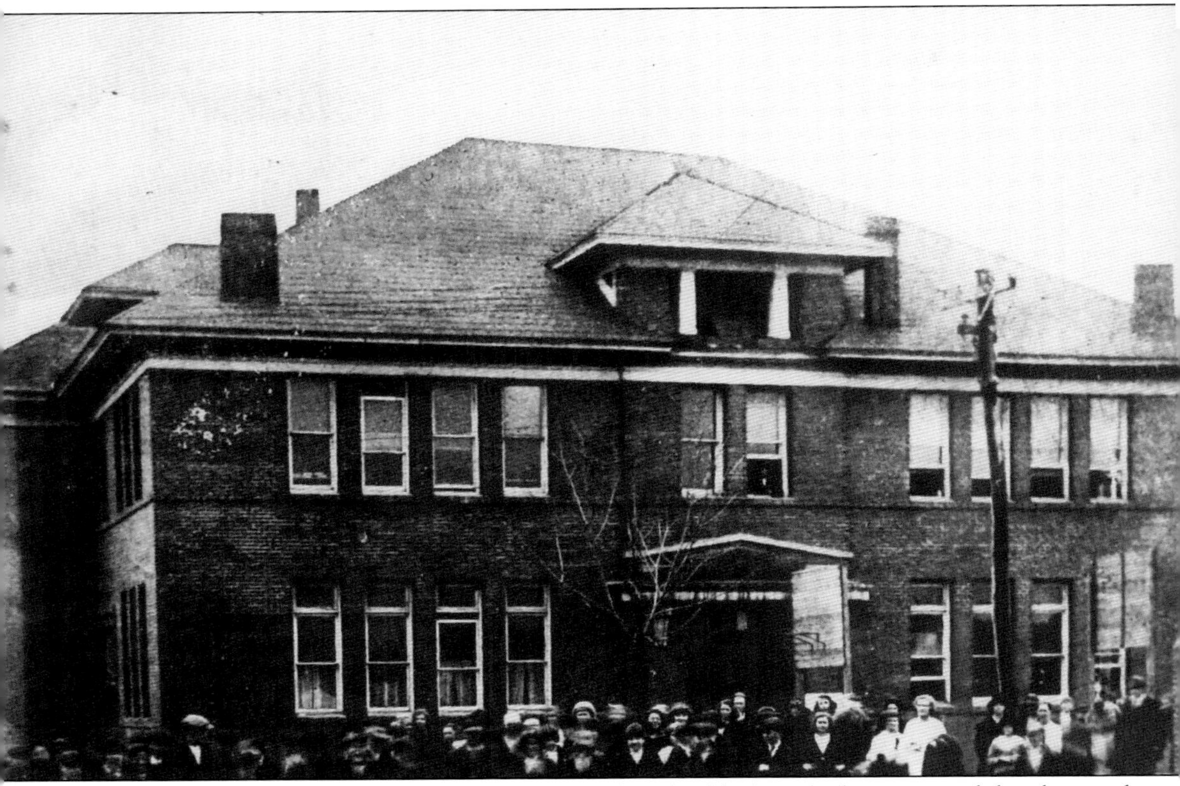

The grand Leaksville Graded School is pictured in this black-and-white postcard dated around the 1920s. Located on Bridge Street, it was built in 1915. Today a recreation facility exists on the site. (Courtesy of the Lavender Cheek and Mary Cheek Collection, Eden, NC.)

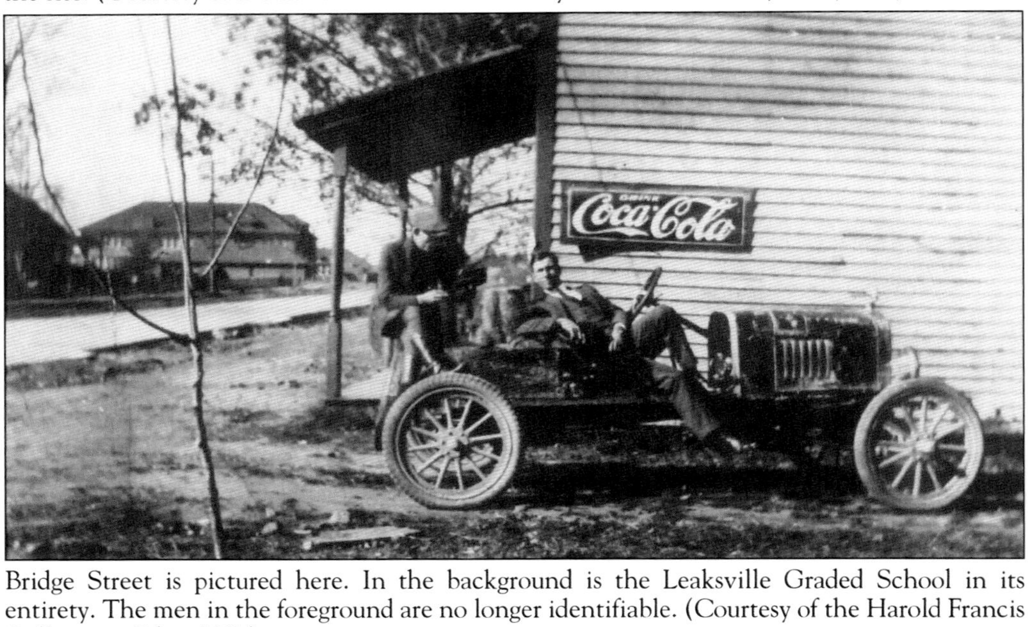

Bridge Street is pictured here. In the background is the Leaksville Graded School in its entirety. The men in the foreground are no longer identifiable. (Courtesy of the Harold Francis Collection, Eden, NC.)

Seven

SPRAY

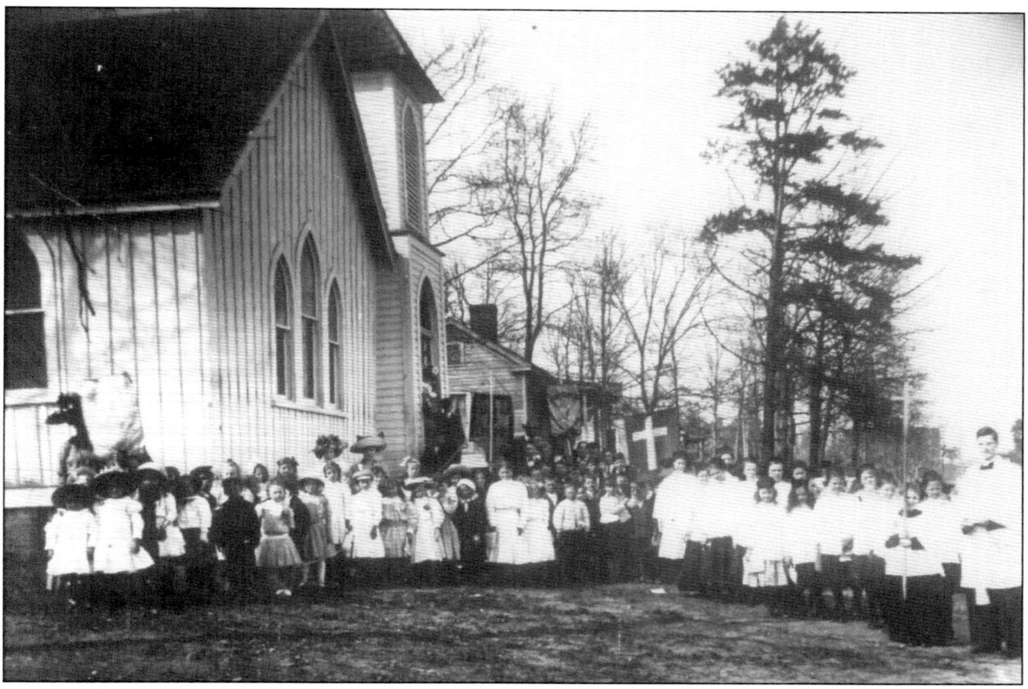

Not far from the Smith River, the Town of Spray was founded. It was called Spray due to the waterfalls at the mills. Pictured here is Rev. Gordan (far right) and the congregation which created the Rock Church on 604 Morgan Road. Most congregations did not use the river for baptism; instead, they used Spray Park's pond. (Courtesy of Harold Francis Collection, Eden, NC.)

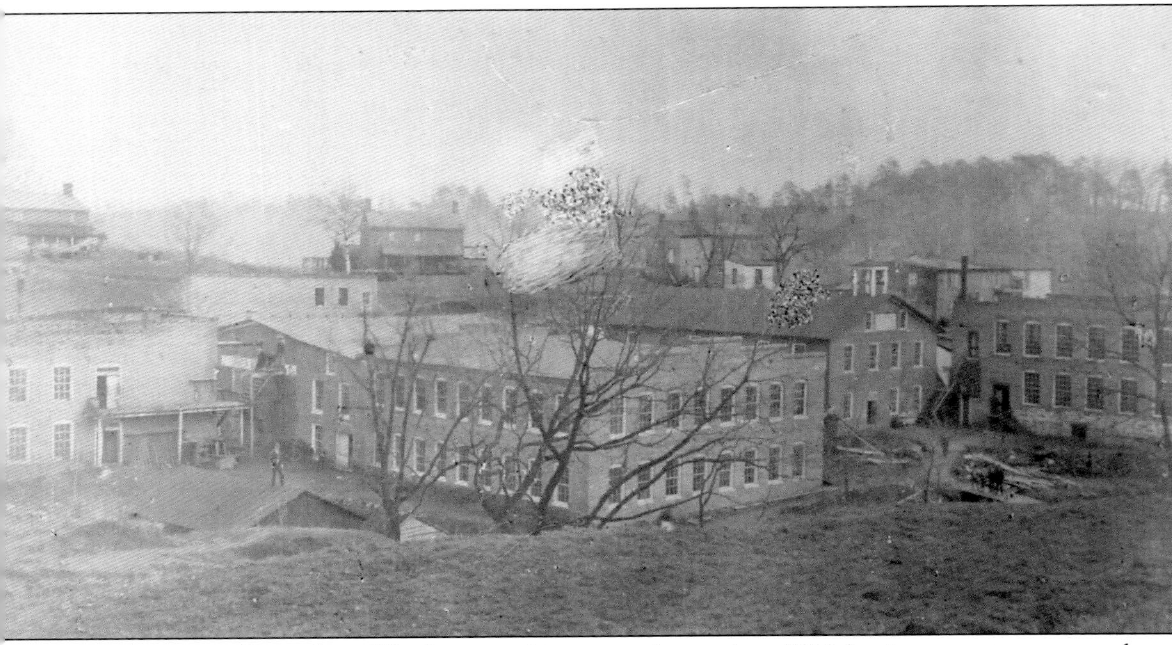

The town of Spray (now Eden) appeared in postcards as early as 1906, but it was not incorporated until 1950. The area, an industrial site along the Smith River, had its first mill as early as 1833. Above is Spray around 1850. The facility in the center is marked by a sign that reads, "J. Turner Moorehead and Company," making this structure a Leaksville Factory Interest. (Courtesy of Lavender Cheek and Mary Cheek Collection, Eden, NC.)

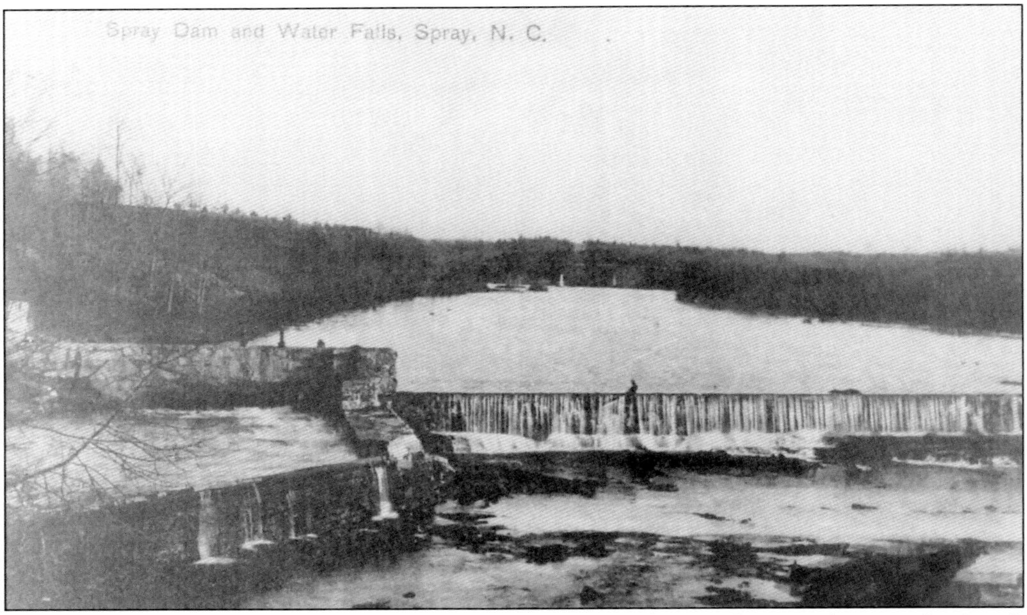

This postcard printed in Germany is postmarked 1908. It depicts the new dam on the Smith River which replaced the wooden one. Eden now surrounds this monumental structure. (Courtesy of the Harold Francis Collection, Eden, NC.)

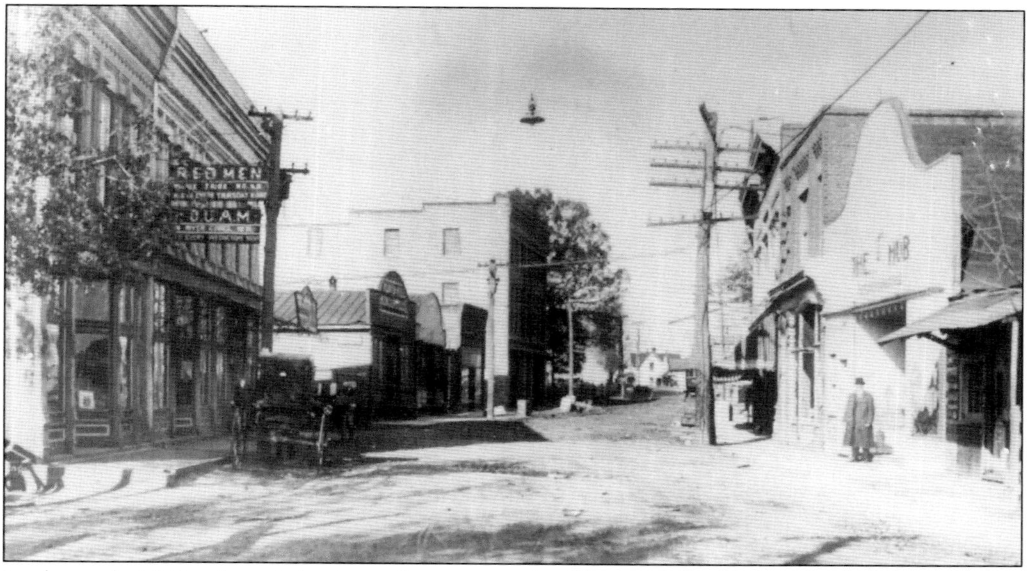

In the early 1900s, Spray's business district was the "Boulevard" which still exists. On the left of the image is the M.L. Heiner's clothing store. Next to it is the Floyd-Hill Mercantile. The house (center) at the end of the street is believed to be the Grogan House. The majority of these buildings no longer exist. (Courtesy of Lavender Cheek and Mary Cheek Collection, Eden, NC. Courtesy of the Harold Francis Collection, Eden, NC.)

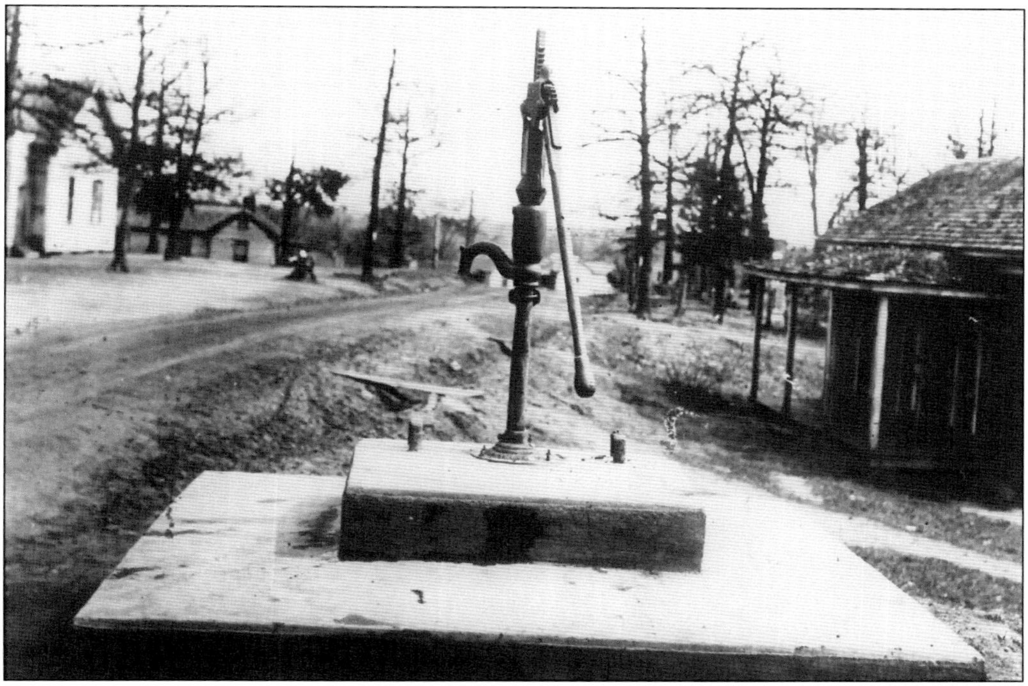

Spray had a public water system in the early 1900s. Neighborhood wells dotted the town. This one was located on Church Street. All the structures in the image survived the pump, even the Wesleyan Church in the background on the left. (Courtesy of Lavender Cheek and Mary Cheek Collection, Eden, NC. Courtesy of the Harold Francis Collection, Eden, NC.)

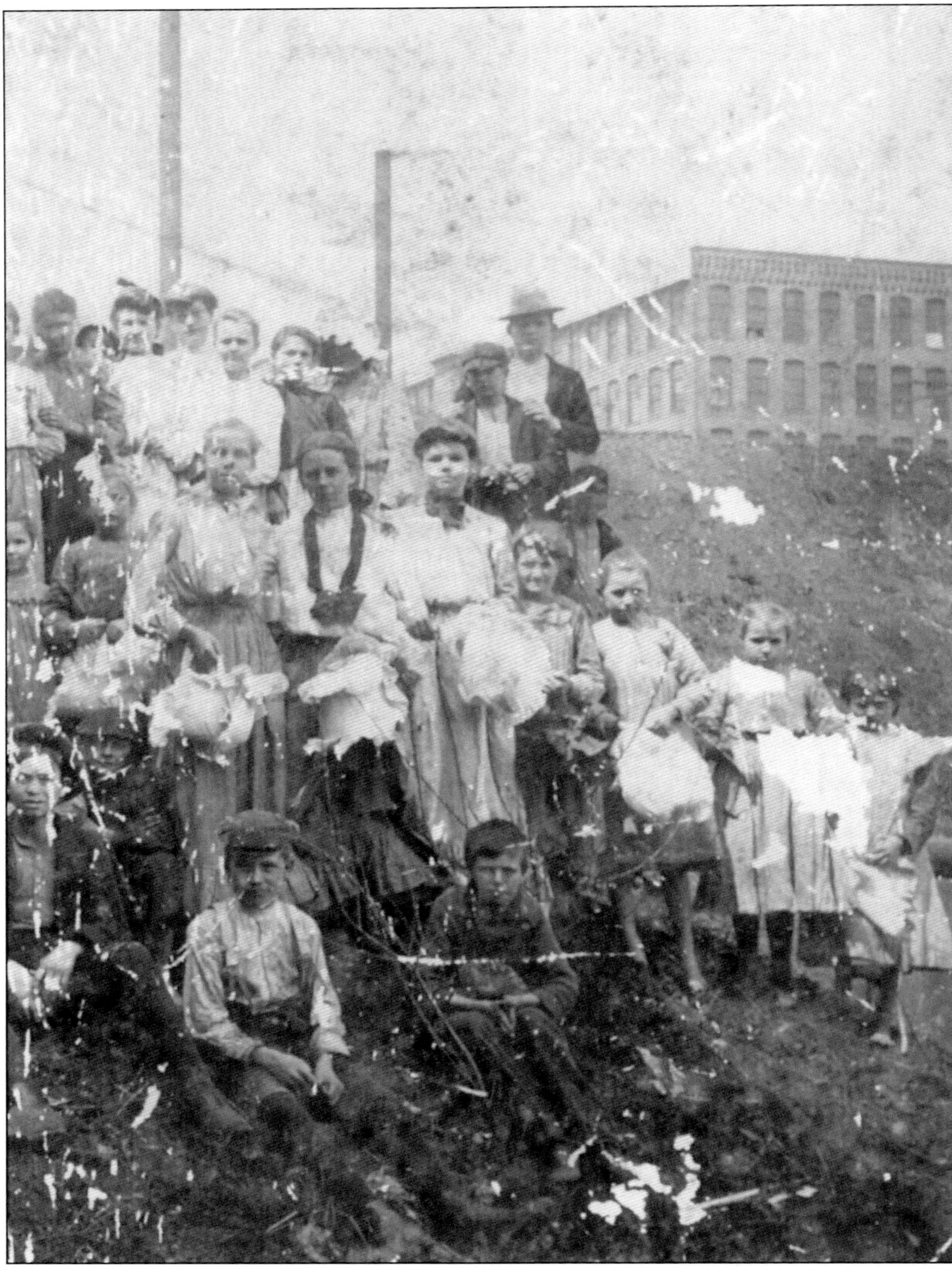

Child labor laws were introduced in North Carolina around 1907. Pictured above is part of an original photograph from Jackson's Studio in Spray in 1904. Behind the children is the Spray Cotton Mill (also called Fieldcrest). (Courtesy of Bertha Vestal Aheron and the Aheron family, Eden, NC.)

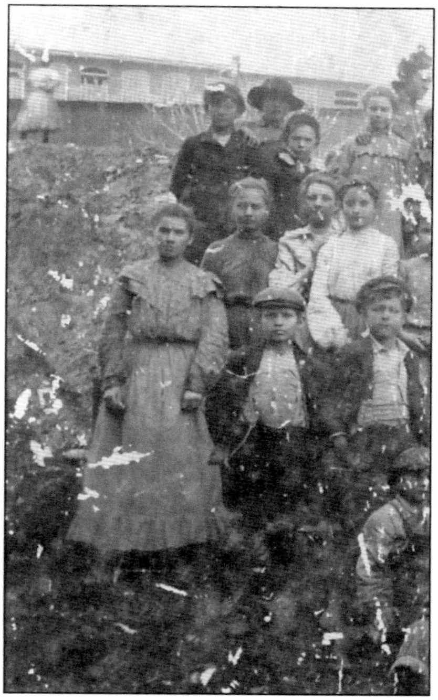

As a boy, Dan Aheron worked at Spray Cotton Mill. He is at the upper left of the image. The mill buildings behind the children still exists near Morgan Street. (Courtesy of Bertha Vestal Aheron and the Aheron family, Eden, NC.)

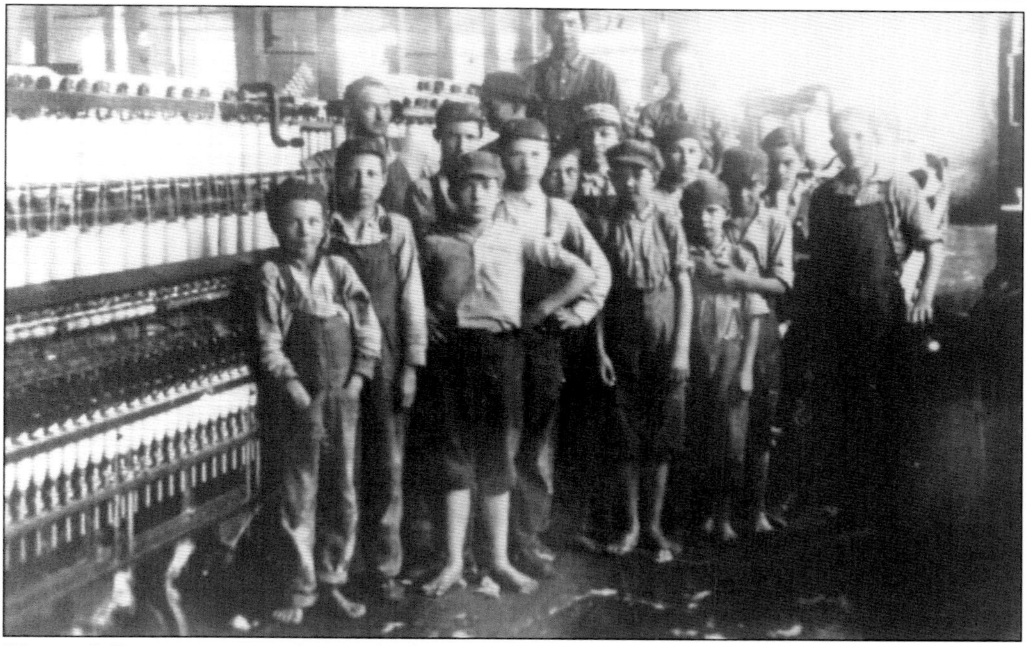

"Picture" Price was a professional photographer. He did many shoots for area businesses. Appearing in this picture are (in no particular order): Ernest Murphy, Cecil Fulcher, Mr. Reece, Mr. Fowler, Rush Mabes, Willie Lee Burchell, Roy Murphy, Eugene Bondurant, Tyler Bondurant, Roger Kirkman, Jim Alcorn, Jesse Via, Lum Rutledge, Clyde Fulcher, Alvis Via, and Elma Axsom. Dan Aheron is standing on a crate at the very top of the group. (Courtesy of the Roscoe Hankins Collection, Eden, NC. Courtesy of Iris Aheron Earps and the Aheron family, Eden, NC.)

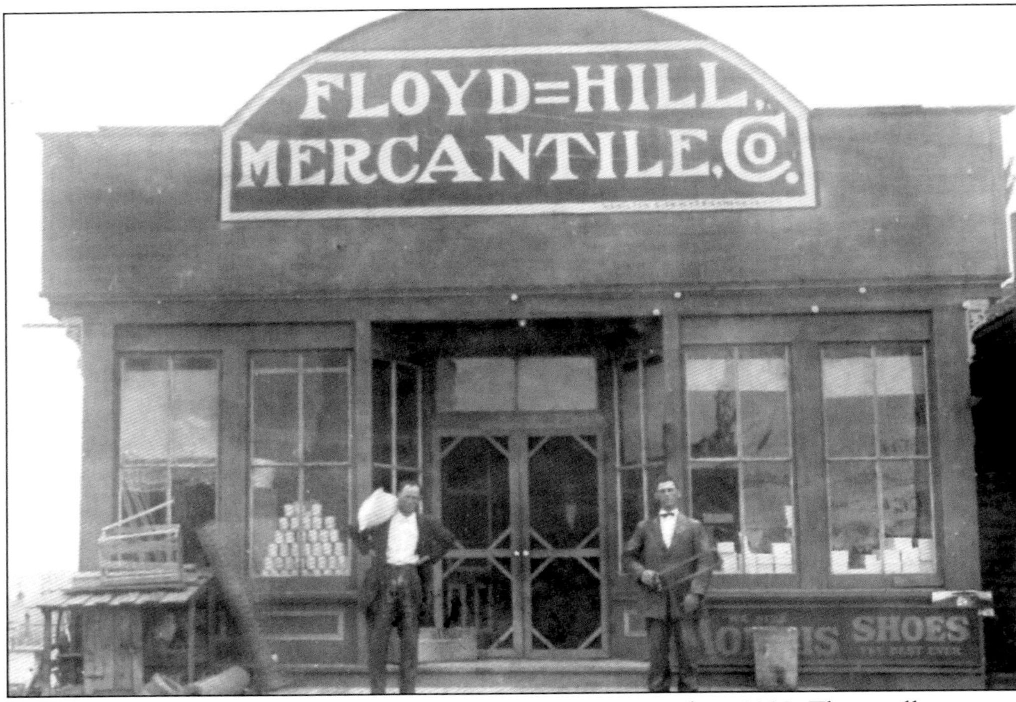

This image is from a Floyd-Hill Mercantile Company postcard, c. 1908. The small store was located on the Boulevard in Spray. Tan Martin and Hover Martin hold a few products that they sale. (Courtesy of the Roscoe Hankins Collection, Eden, NC.)

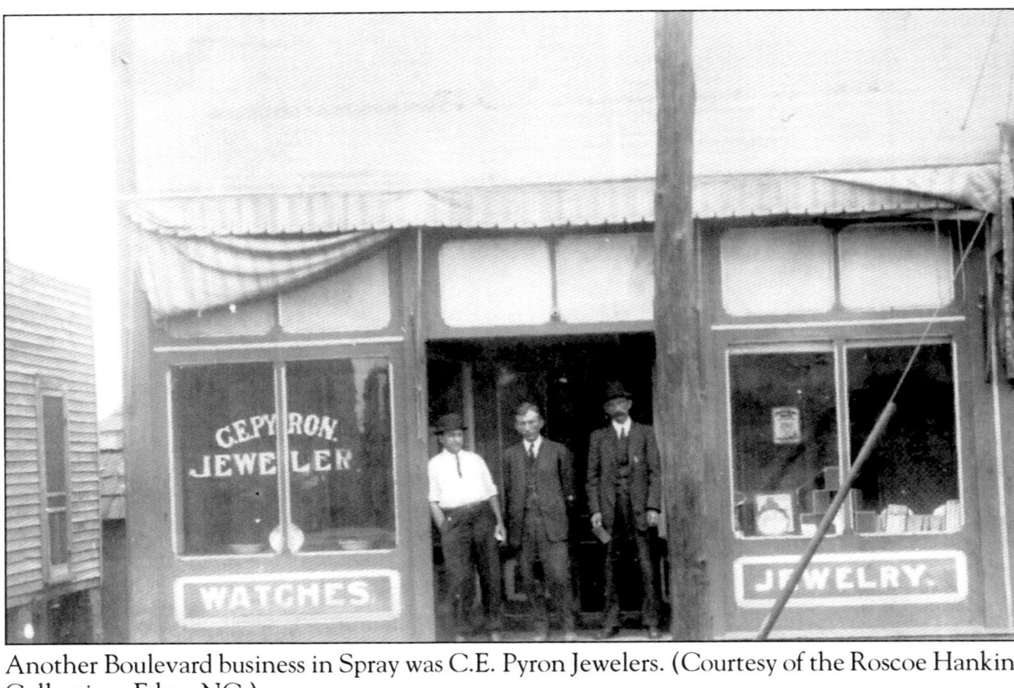

Another Boulevard business in Spray was C.E. Pyron Jewelers. (Courtesy of the Roscoe Hankins Collection, Eden, NC.)

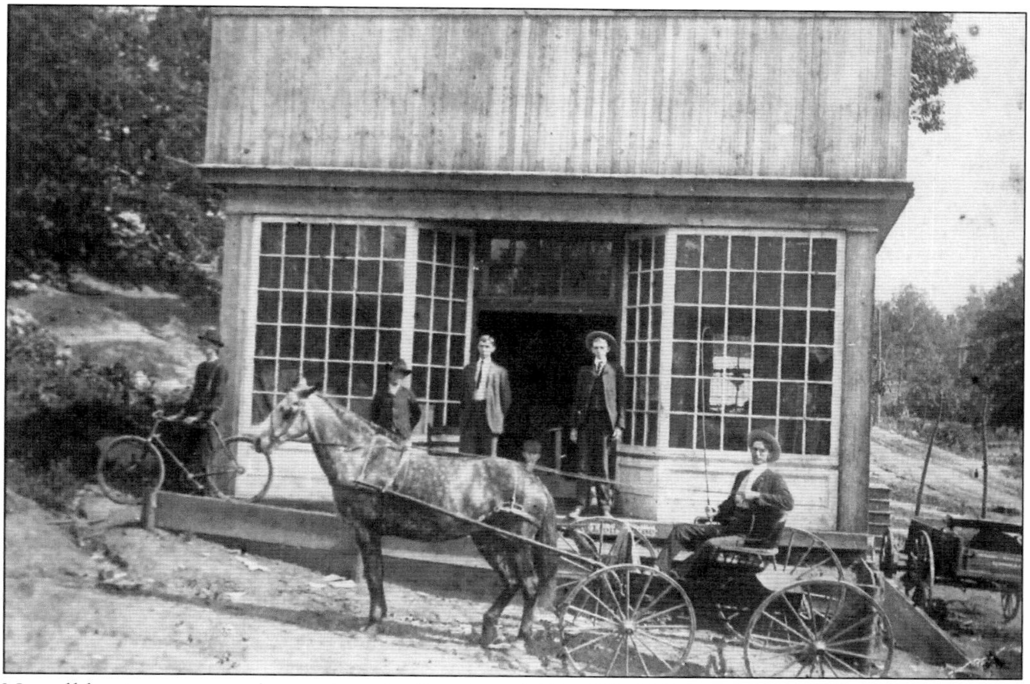

Not all businesses were located on the Boulevard. The "Red" Store, as it is called today, was on Church Street. A spring behind the store made it an attractive gathering place in the 1900s for those who used the pure water for moonshine. Unfortunately, its patrons fought more than they bought things. Blood seemed to flow often at the "Red" Store. (Courtesy of the Roscoe Hankins Collection, Eden, NC.)

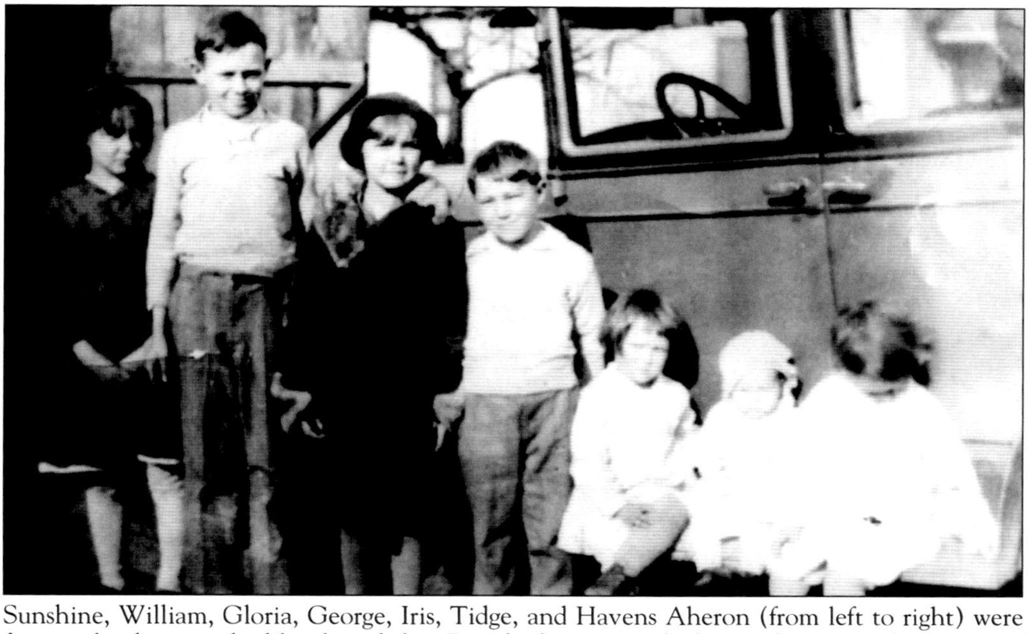

Sunshine, William, Gloria, George, Iris, Tidge, and Havens Aheron (from left to right) were frequently photographed by their father Dan for his postcards during the 1930s. (Courtesy of Bertha Vestal Aheron and the Aheron family.)

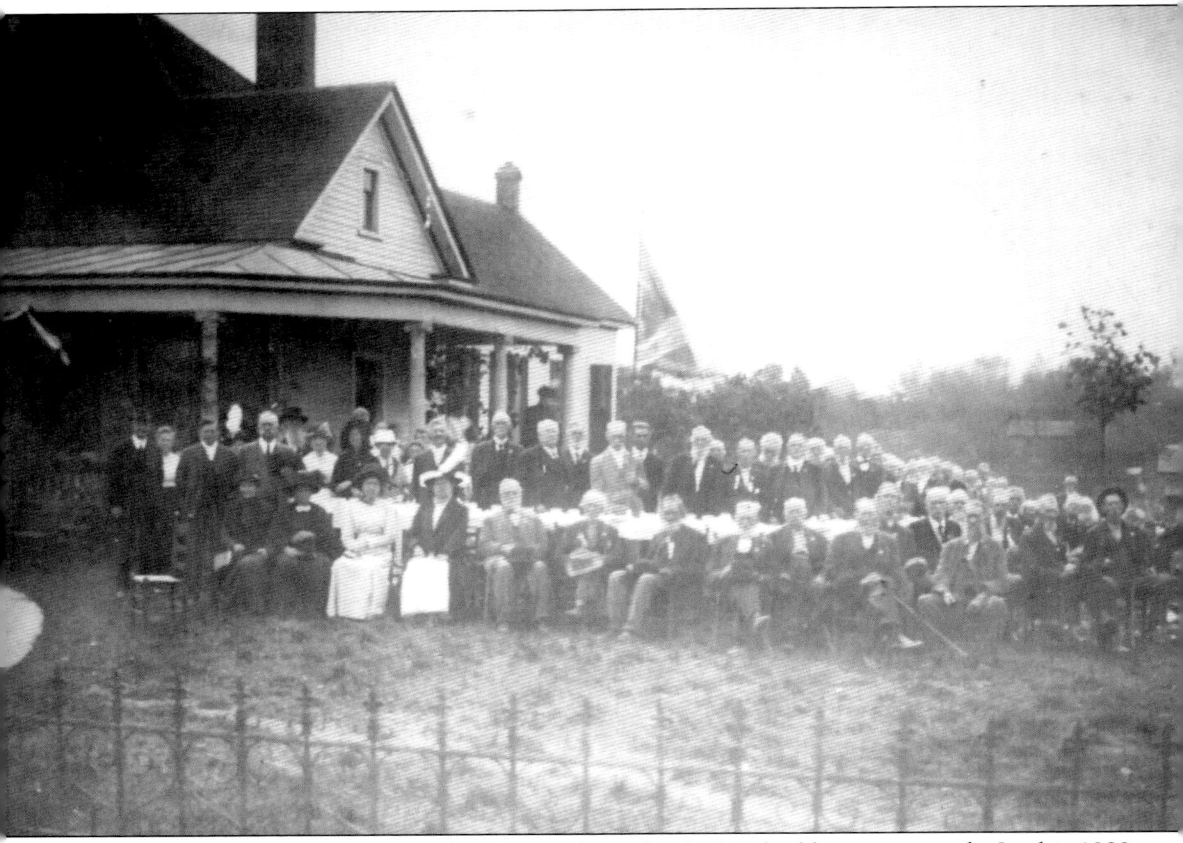

The Heiner House was on Bridge Street where the A & P building now stands. In this 1929 photograph, Confederate soldiers from Rockingham County gather for a meal and fellowship. (Courtesy of Lavender Cheek and Mary Cheek Collection, Eden, NC.)

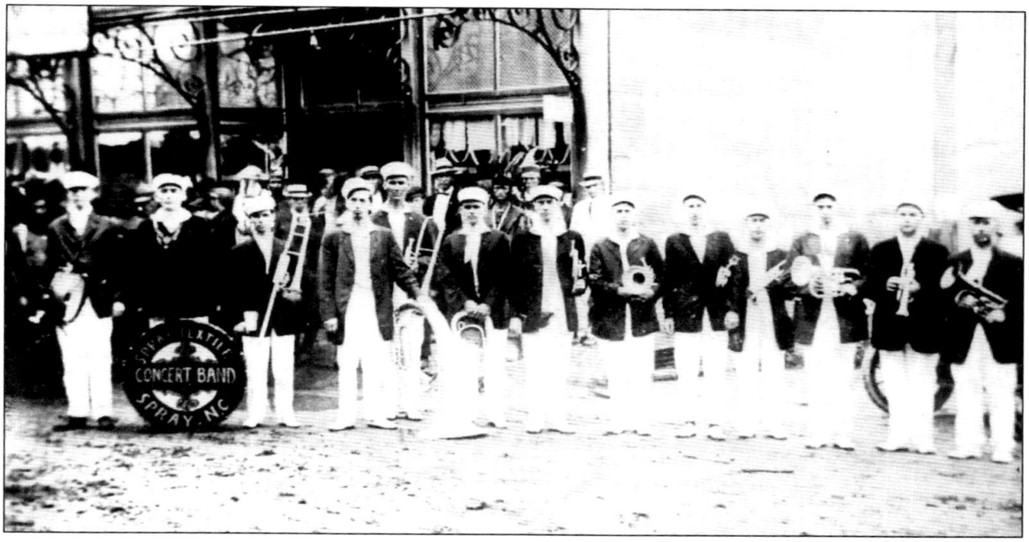

This is a postcard of the Spray Mill Band in front of Heiner's. Members, pictured from left to right, are as follows: unknown, Buck Baughn, B.O. Austin, D.C. Yarbrough, Bob Frazier, John Parker, Reaves Cooper, James Murphy, Maryl Yarbrough, A.D. Parker, Stafford Dillion, Ramie Kendrick and J.M. Coward. The photograph was taken around July 4, 1914. (Courtesy of Bertha Vestal Aheron and the Aheron family, Eden, NC.)

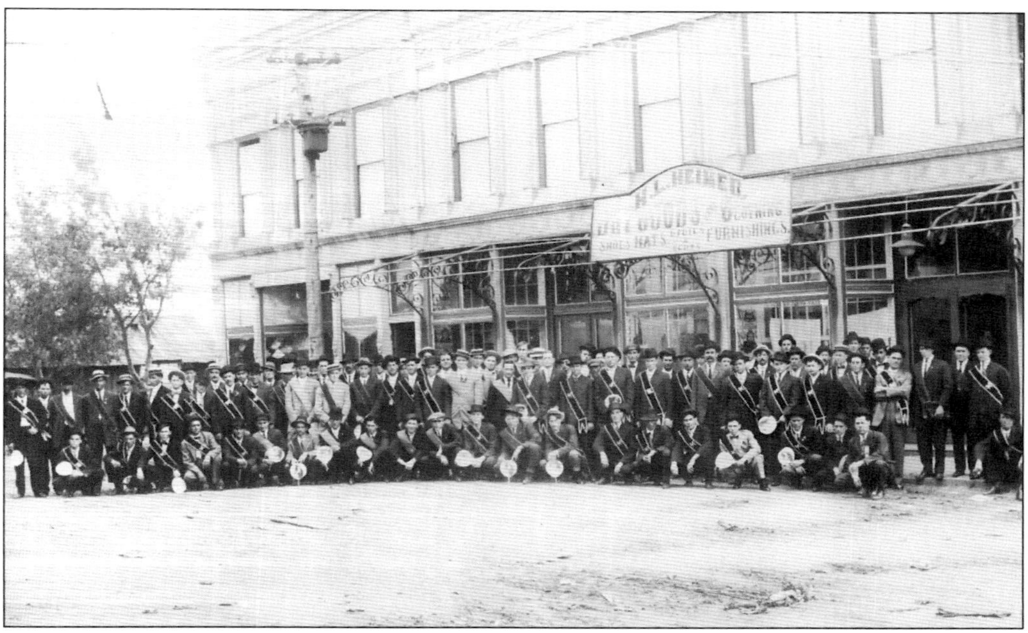

Heiner's Dry Goods is shown here with the "Redmen," a manly man's club. They met in the Heiner's upstairs. Notice the clay that made up the Boulevard in 1916. (Information courtesy of Harold Francis, Francis Photography, Eden, NC. Courtesy of Lavender Cheek and Mary Cheek Collection, Eden, NC.)

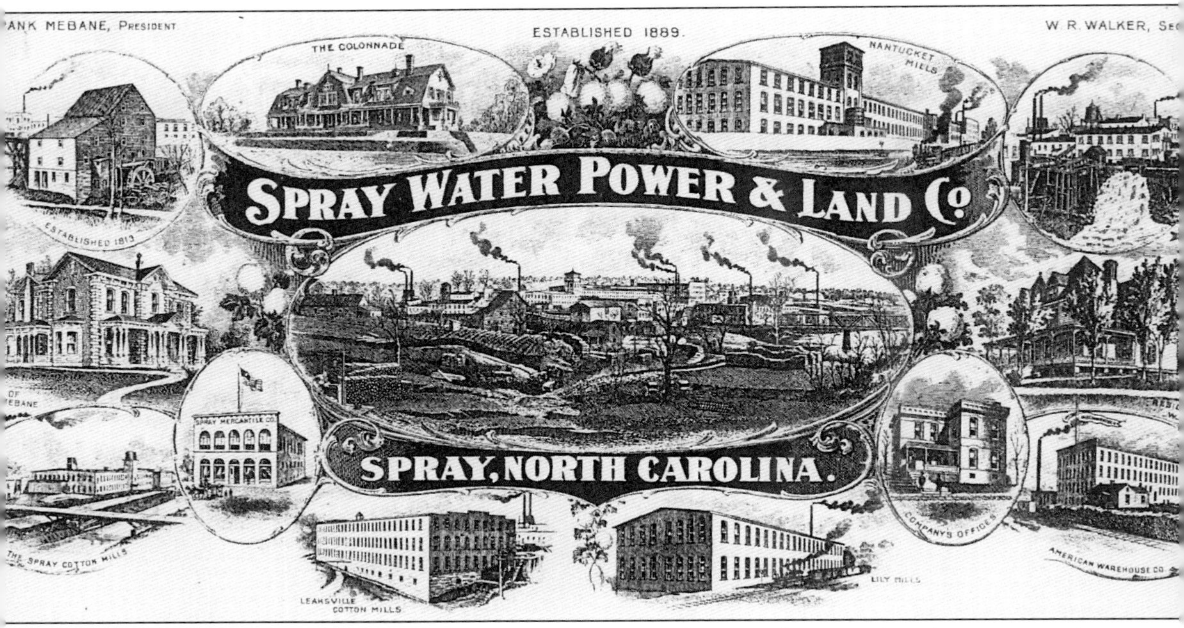

Spray Water Power and Land Company incorporated postcard images into its corporate logo. Beginning on the upper left (clockwise) we can see Barnett's 1813 grist mill, the first structure on the Smith River; The Colonnade Hotel; the 1905 Nantucket Mills; the old mill (its postcard is entitled *The Waterfall*, c. 1906); the Walker House; the American Warehouse; the Company's Offices; Lily Mills; Leaksville Cotton Mills; Spray Mercantile; Spray Cotton Mills; and the B. Frank Mebane residences. The letterhead of Spray Water Power and Land was printed by American Lithographic, New York, around the early 1900s. (Courtesy of Lavender Cheek and Mary Cheek Collection, Eden, NC.)

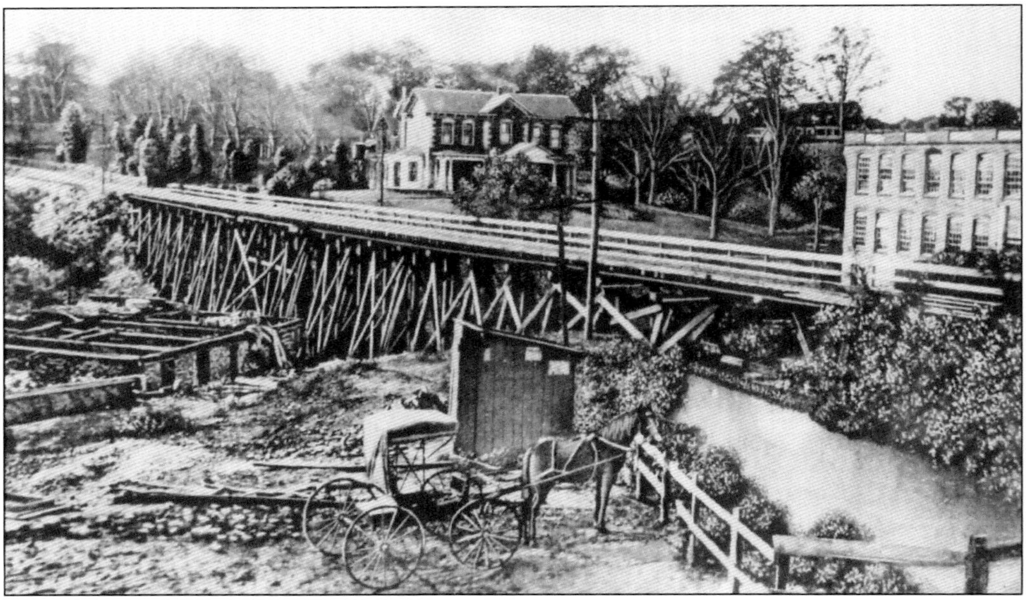

B. Frank Mebane's residence is featured in this 1910 sepia; Mebane created the Town of Draper. (Courtesy of the Harold Francis Collection, Eden, NC.)

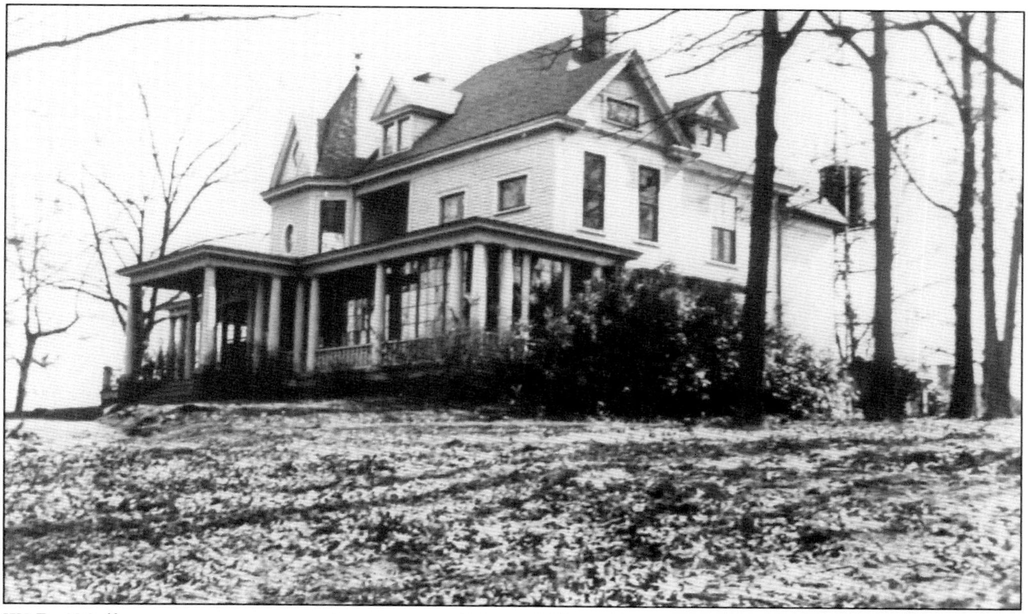

W.R. Walker was secretary and treasurer of Spray Water Power and Land Company. His stately home burned to the ground in the mid-1900s. (Courtesy of Lavender Cheek and Mary Cheek Collection, Eden, NC.)

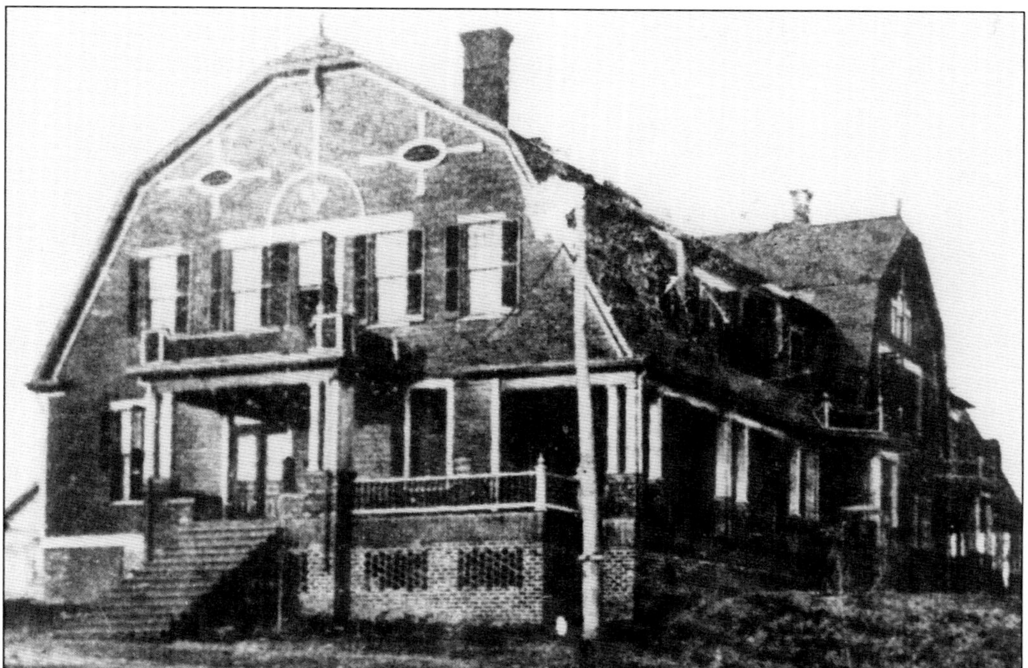

This early postcard depicts the Colonnade Hotel, located between Chestnut Street and Boone Road. The hotel burned in 1957 and no longer exists. (Courtesy of Harold Francis Collection, Eden, NC.)

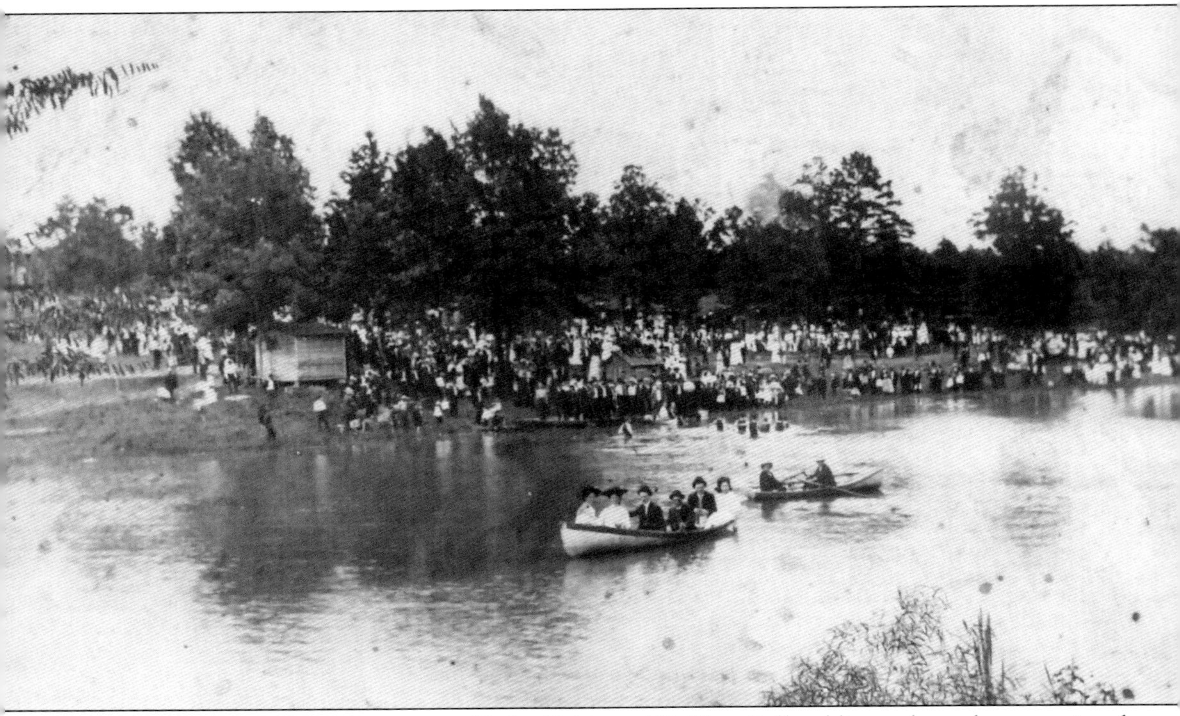

Spray Park (now in the vicinity of Lake Drive and DeHart Ballpark) was the only recreational area in the city at the time this photo was made on July 4, 1908. The park was the site of plenty of baptismal services. "Picture" Price took the picture. (Courtesy of the Roscoe Hankins Collection, Eden, NC.)

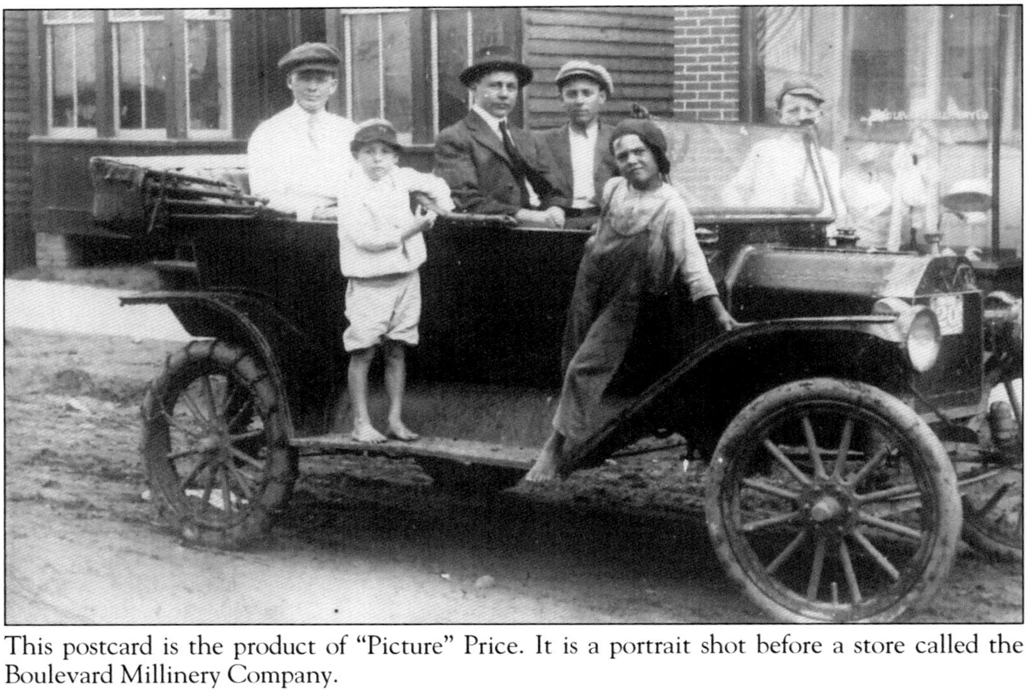

This postcard is the product of "Picture" Price. It is a portrait shot before a store called the Boulevard Millinery Company.

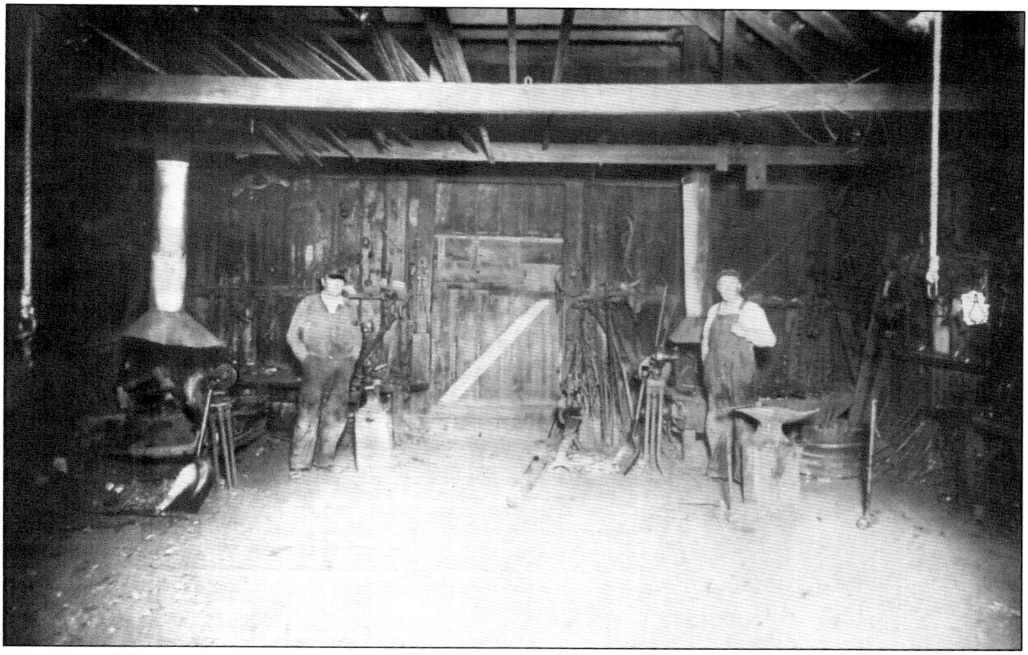

The first fifty years of the twentieth century brought dramatic changes to Spray. Pictured above are two blacksmiths, Tony (left) and Smythe Eggleston (right). (Courtesy of the Roscoe Hankins Collection, Eden, NC.)

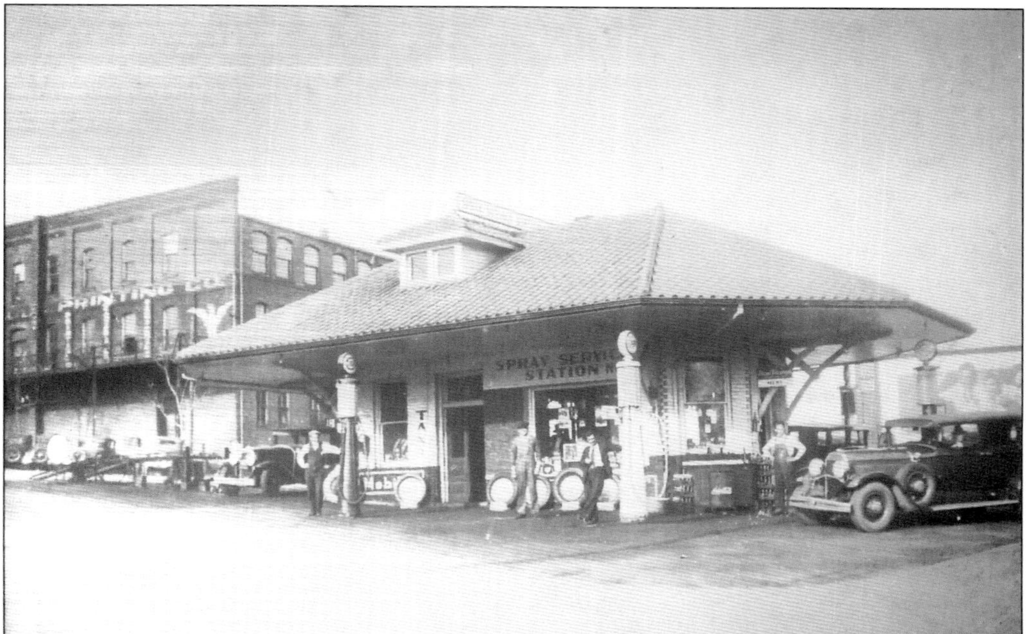

Horsepower replaced horses. As a result, by the 1930s, gas stations popped up all over Spray, Draper, and Leaksville. This one was located near the Mercantile Building; it no longer exists. (Courtesy of the Harold Francis Collection, Eden, NC.)

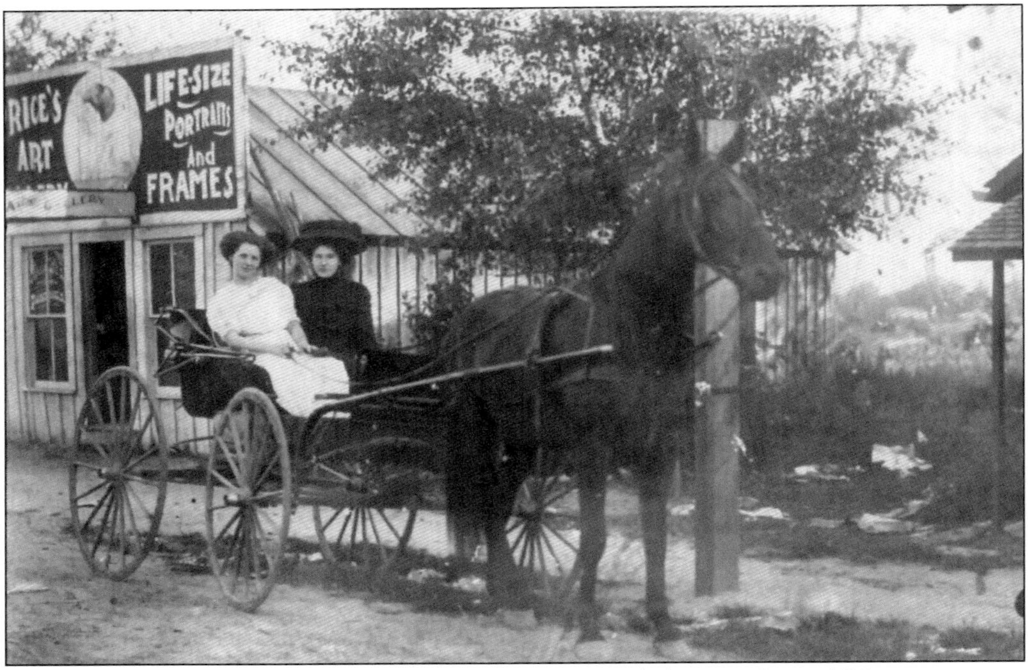

Commercial photographers of Eden unknowingly captured much of history on glass plates (film negatives came later). Above is the studio of "Picture" Price, one of the more well-known photographers from East Rockingham County. Behind the ladies and their buggy is his studio, which was located on the Boulevard in Spray in the early 1900s. (Courtesy of Roscoe Hankins Collection, Eden, NC.)

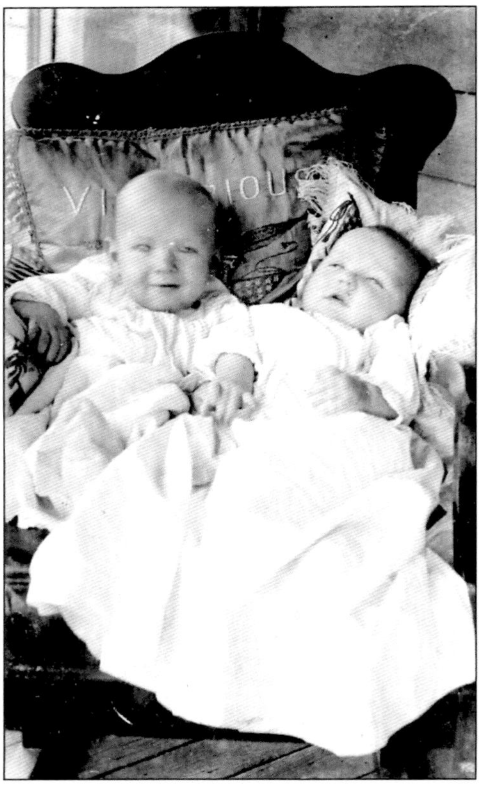

William "Bill" Aheron (left) and cousin Clarence "Fats" Vestal (right), an Eden policeman, are propped on top of the Victory pillow in this family postcard from the 1920s. The Victory pillow was a gift to Dan Aheron for being a soldier who returned from World War I. Dan took this picture of his firstborn son, who is now retired and residing in Texas with his wife, Dottie. (Courtesy of Iris Aheron Earps and the Aheron family, Eden, NC.)

Dan Aheron was a gentleman photographer who made the bulk of his living in the Spray Cotton Mills. This formal portrait postcard (on the right) was taken by Dan's friend, "Picture" Price, prior to World War I. When Dan returned from the war, he had a camera from Europe with him. On the weekends, he began taking informal portraits for postcards which supplemented his low wages at the mill. Below is an image of the Nantucket Mill (on the corner of Morgan and Church) taken as the veterans returned from the war by train in 1918. People everywhere are waving their American flags. (Courtesy of Bertha Vestal Aheron and the Aheron family. Courtesy of The Roscoe Hankins Collection, Eden, NC.)

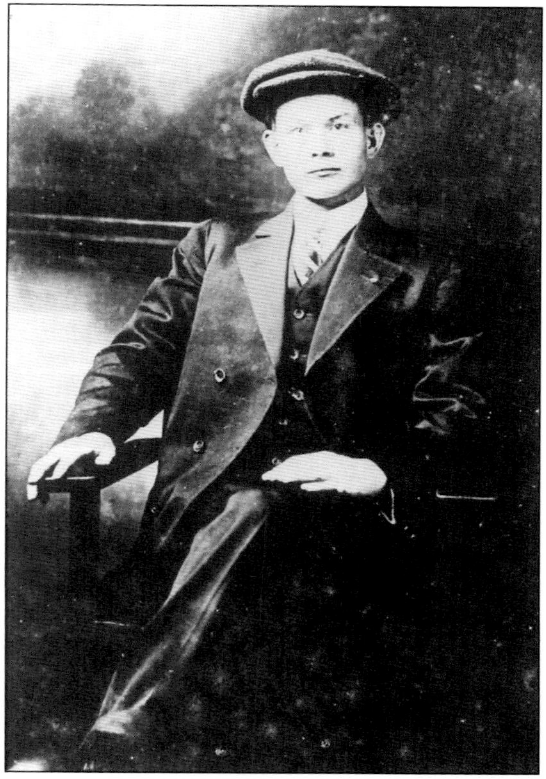

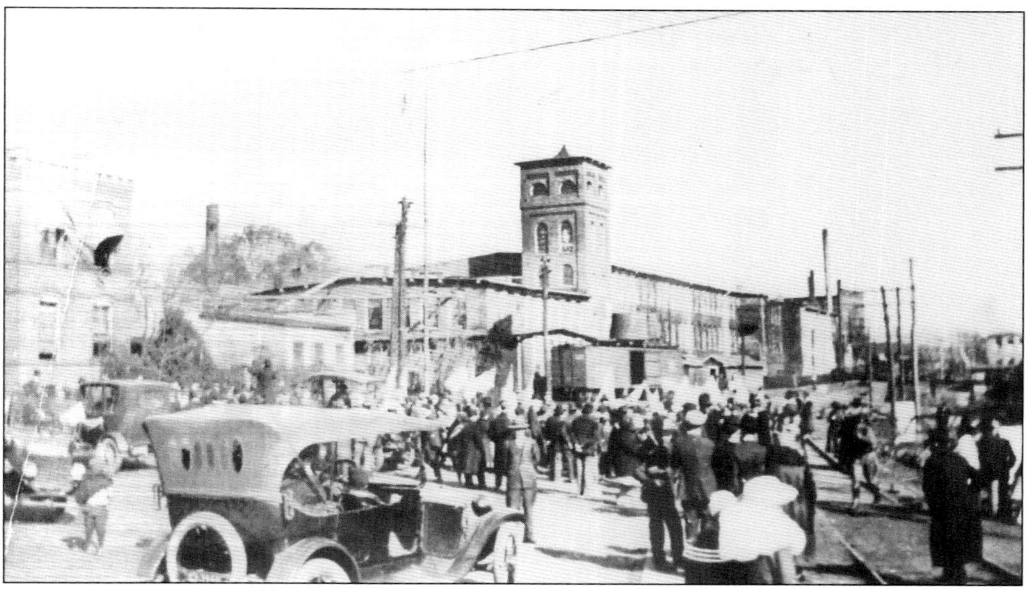

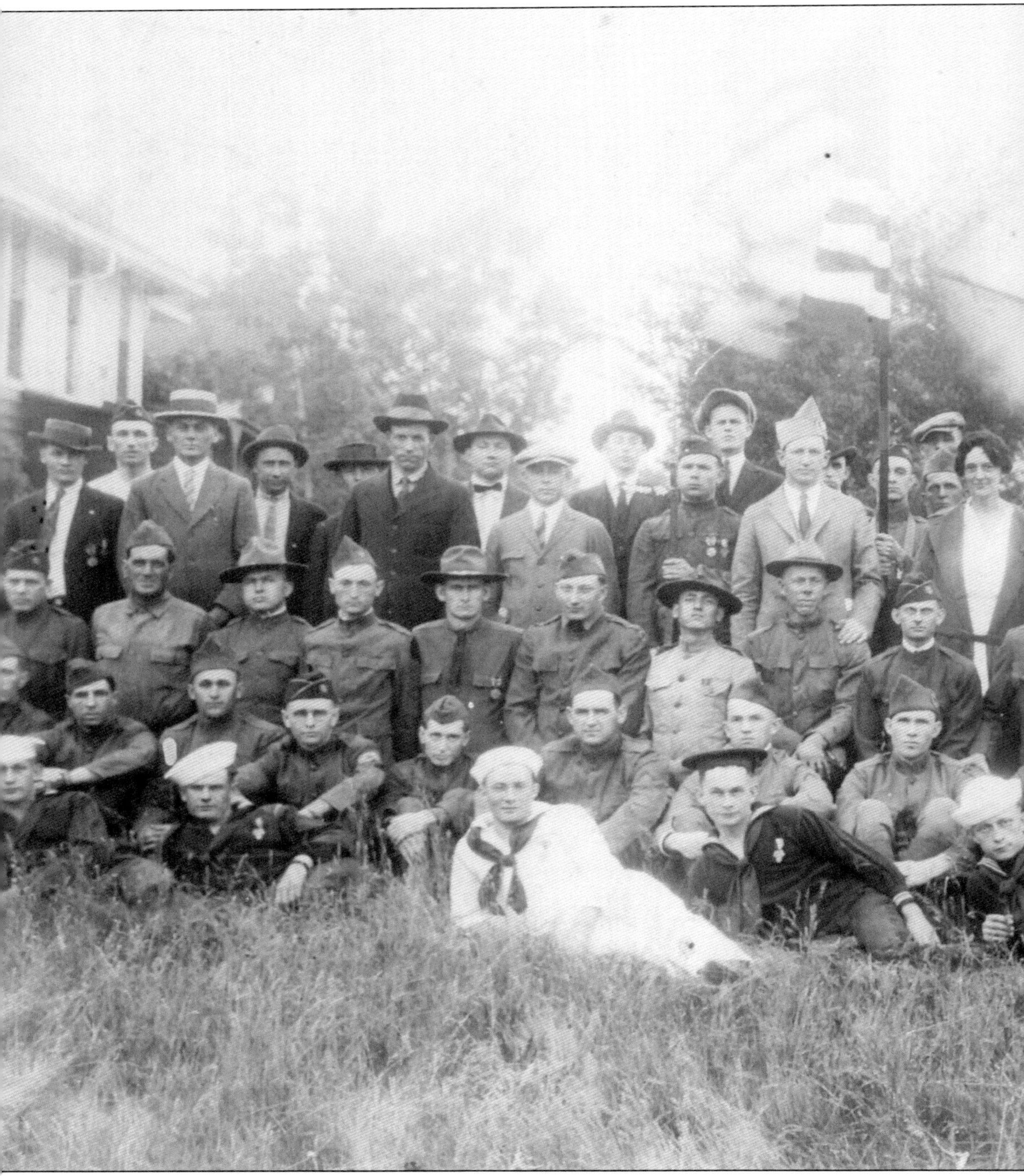

Here is a portrait of World War I veterans from the tri-city area—the common name given to Leaksville, Spray, and Draper prior to towns' consolidation into the City of Eden in 1967. Some of the men are identified, but the list is out of order. Among them are Melvin Tucker Sr., Bill Hopper, Allen Hancock, Mr. Morgan, Mr. Matthews, G.D. Scott, Judson Hall, George Bateman, Luther H. Hodges, Tom C. Stanley, Ernest I. Hankins, Will Vernon,

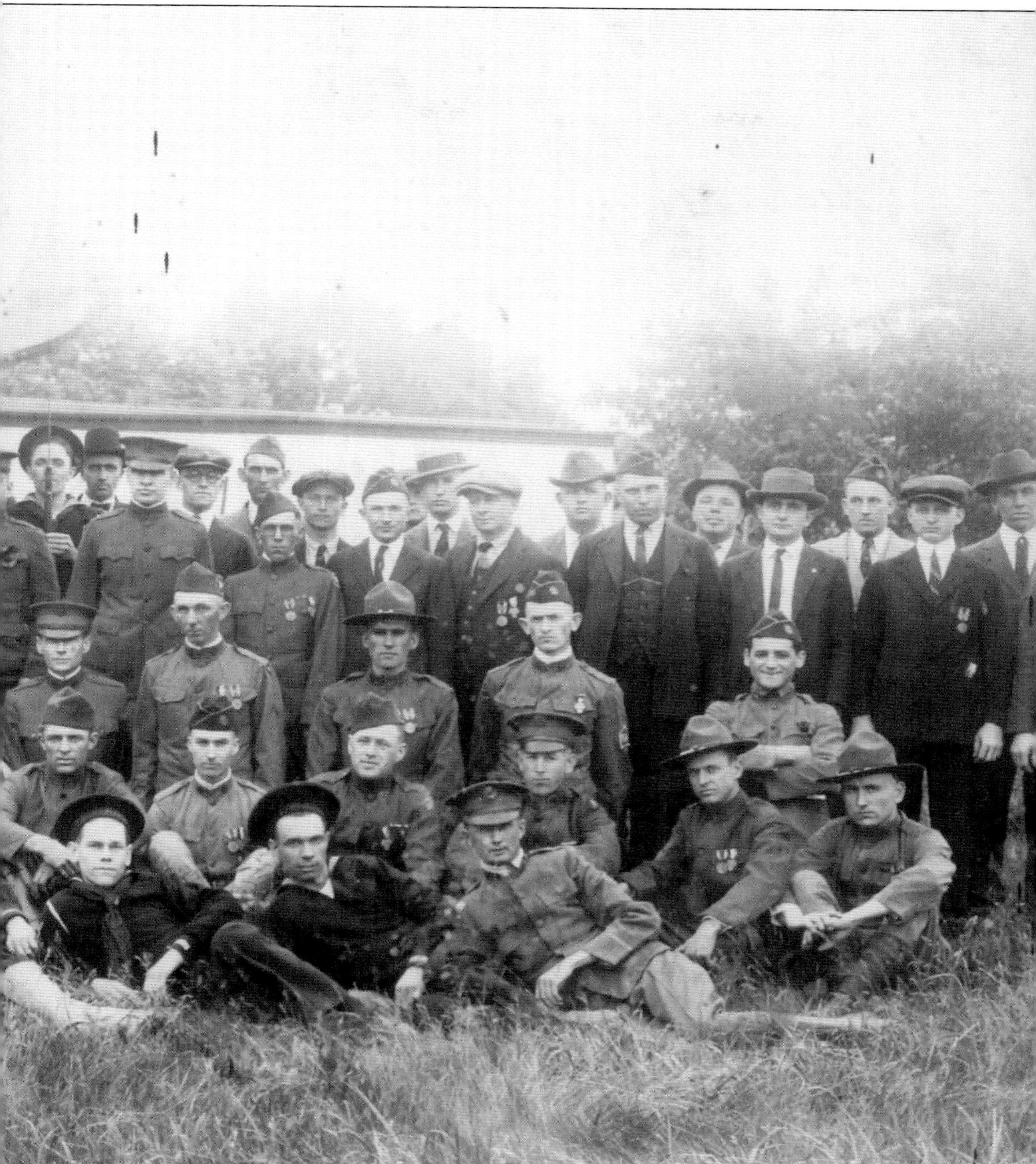

Dan Lashly, Bremy Vernon, Cornelious Purdy, Mr. Brown, Curt Moore, and Fred Hundley. Dan Aheron is the second individual from the left in the first row, wearing Navy blues. (Courtesy of Bertha Vestal Aheron and the Aheron family. Courtesy of the Roscoe Hankins Collection, Eden, NC.)

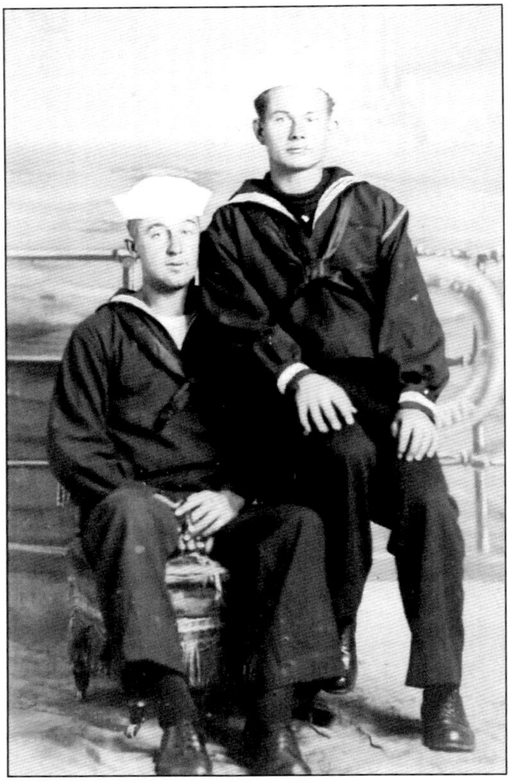

This postcard features World War I sailors Charles Clark (left) and his friend, Dan Aheron. They served on the USS *Mississippi*. Bertha Aheron used this postcard by Price to announce her husband's safe return from overseas. (Courtesy of Bertha Vestal Aheron and the Aheron family, Eden, NC.)

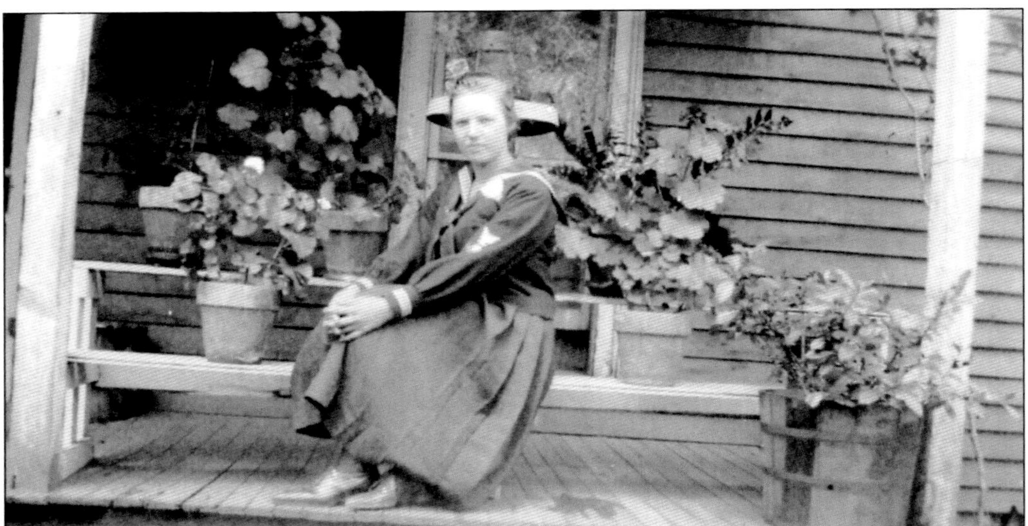

Dan Aheron frequently photographed his assistant and wife, Bertha Vestal Aheron, at their home on Clifton Street. According to Bertha, Dan did shoots on weekends and she processed the film on weekdays when the children napped. Most of their cards featured people, not businesses. (Courtesy of Bertha Vestal Aheron and the Aheron family, Eden, NC.)

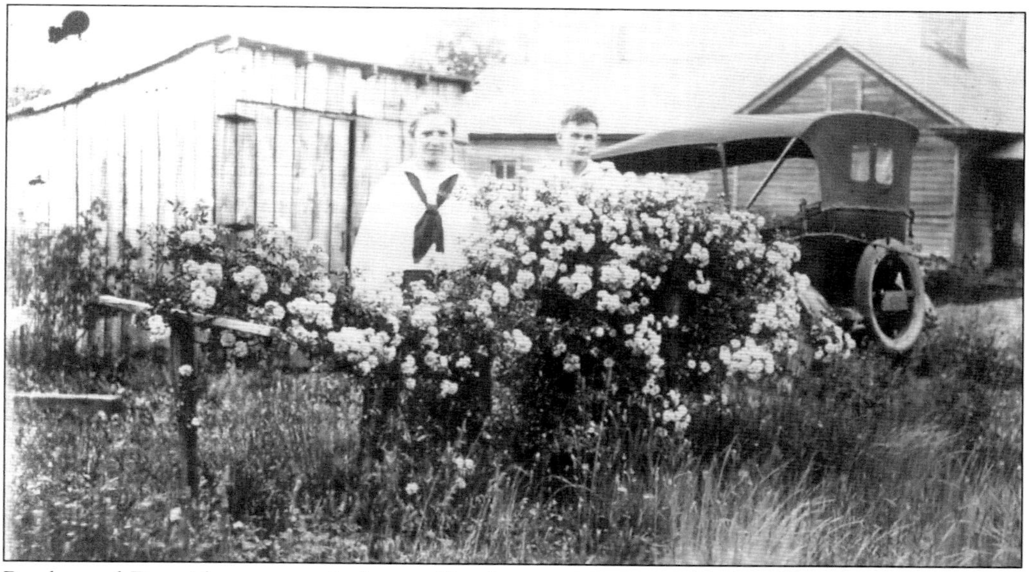

Bertha and Dan Aheron pose in front of his first touring car and behind her favorite tea roses. The house behind them and the shed still exist on Clifton Street on Aheron property. A family member took the postcard picture using Dan's camera. The impromptu moment was captured a couple of days after Dan's return from the war. (Courtesy of Iris Aheron Earps and the Aheron family, Eden, NC.)

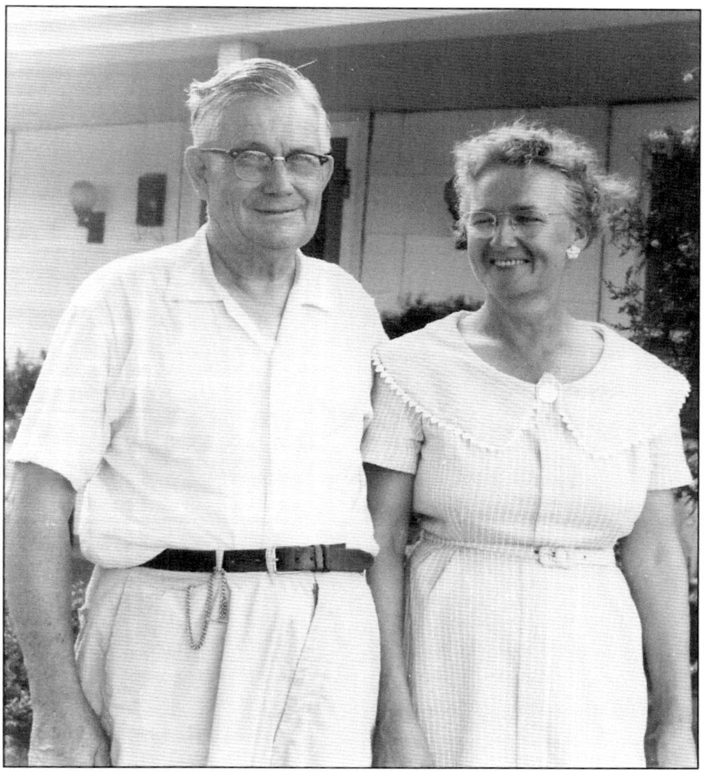

This is a photograph of Dan and Bertha Aheron at their Clifton Street house in 1959. Dan had retired from Spray Cotton Mill (Fieldcrest Mills). (Courtesy of Iris Aheron Earps and the Aheron family, Eden, NC.)

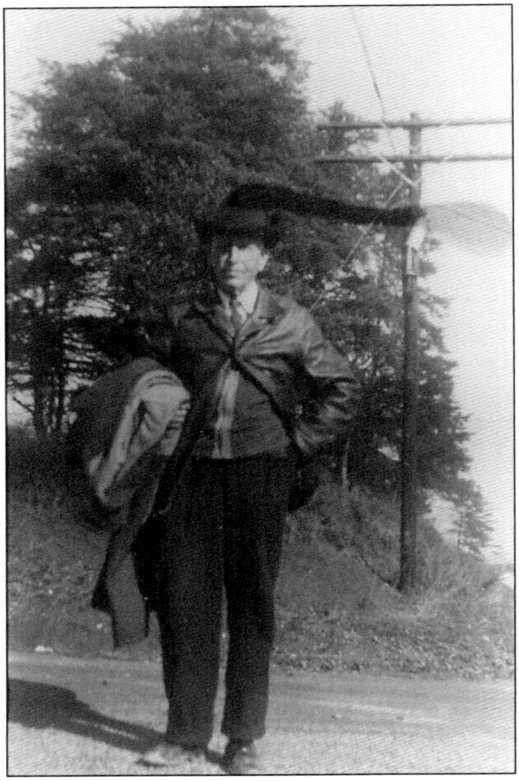

Joseph Henry Aheron, Dan's father and a Spray carpenter, greets his son upon his return from overseas. (Courtesy of Iris Aheron Earps and the Aheron family, Eden, NC.)

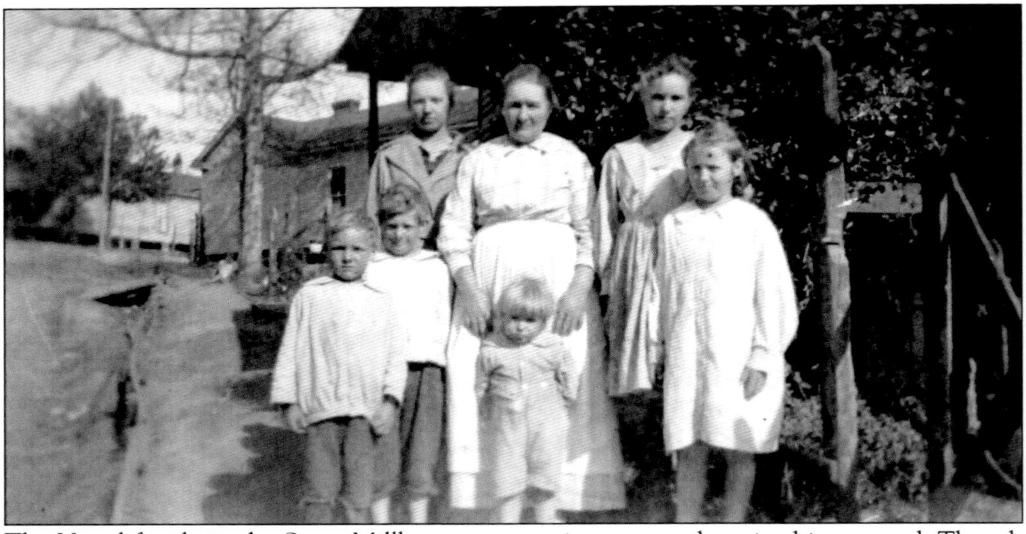

The Vestal family in the Spray Millhouse community are seen here in this postcard. Though refurbished, many of the original structures in this picture still exist along Church, Oak, and Clifton Streets. (Postcard by Dan Aheron. Courtesy of Iris Aheron Earps and the Aheron family, Eden, NC.)

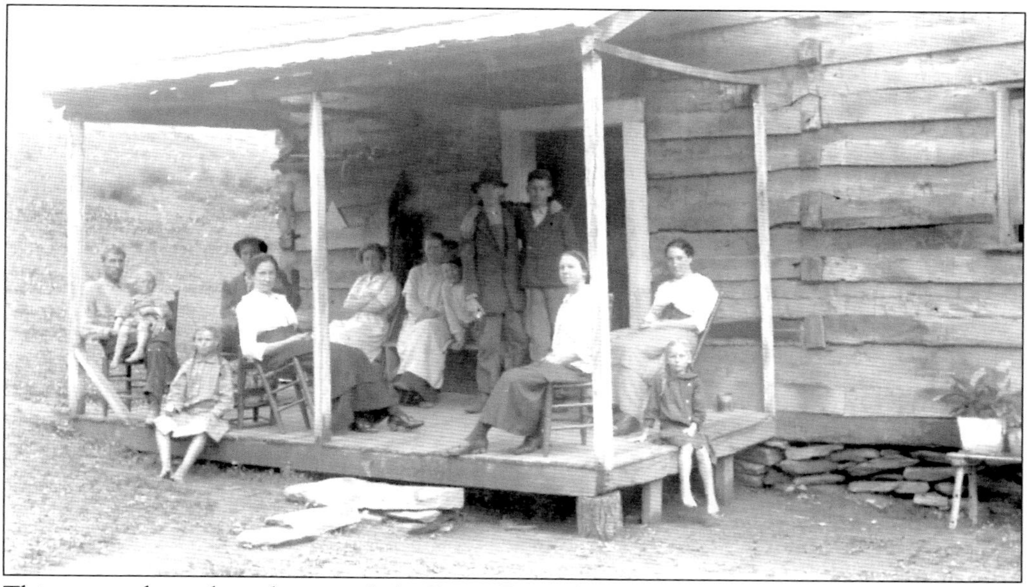

This postcard may have been made by Price. Dan Aheron (left) embraces a friend and fellow millworker. The card was made prior to World War I. Some of the people are believed to be Dan's maternal cousins in Spray. (Courtesy of Bertha Vestal Aheron and the Aheron family, Eden, NC.)

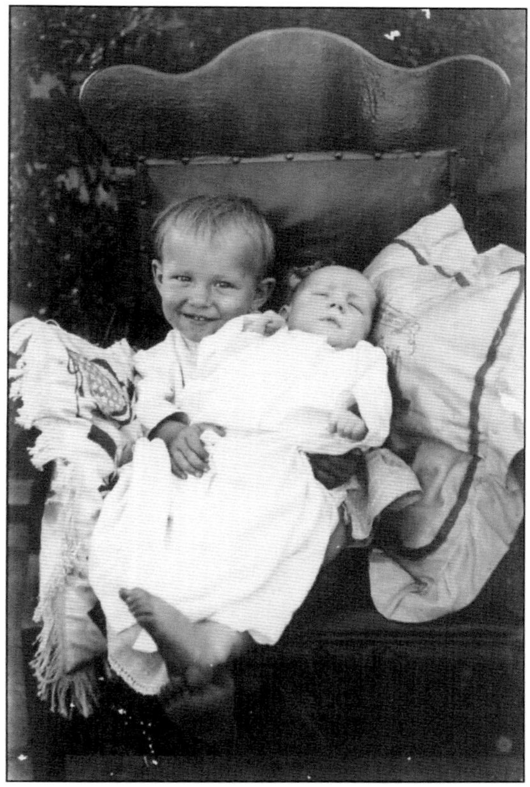

William Aheron holds his sister Sunshine so his Dad can make another 1920s postcard/birth announcement. Dan and Bertha had five girls and three boys during their many years together. (Courtesy of Bertha Vestal Aheron and the Aheron family, Eden, NC.)

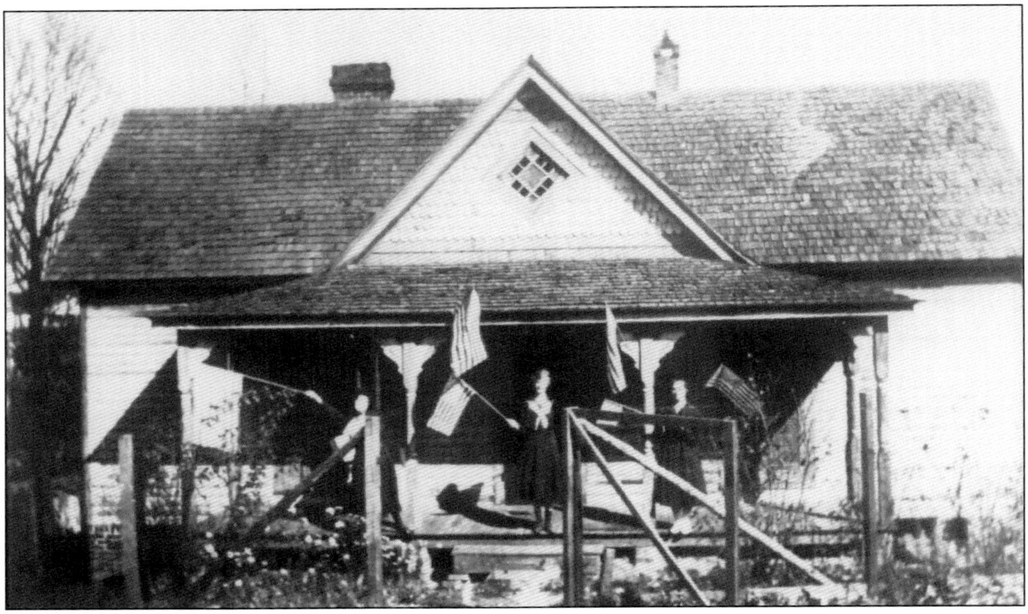

The home of John H. Vestal was on Grammond Street in Spray. Bertha Vestal is on the right. Flags are waving as the soldiers return home by way of the Dick & Willie train in 1918. (Courtesy of the Roscoe Hankins Collection, Eden, NC.)

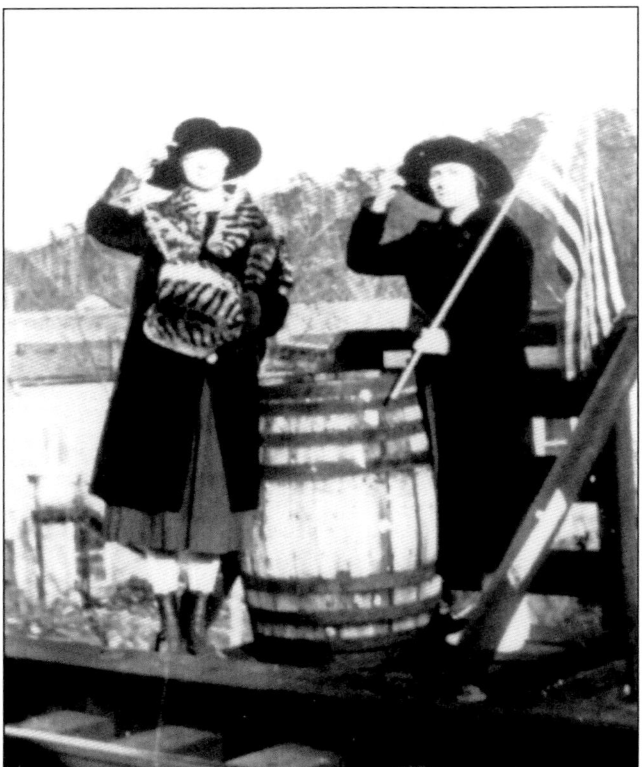

Mithie (left) and Rosa Vestal (right) stand on the Spray trestle to get a better view of the celebration. Note the white eagle painted on the Spray Mercantile Building at the left of this 1918 image. (Courtesy of The Roscoe Hankins Collection, Eden, NC.)

This postcard of a 1920s Spray couple was typical of Dan Aheron's subject matter. (Courtesy of Bertha Vestal Aheron and the Aheron family, Eden, NC.)

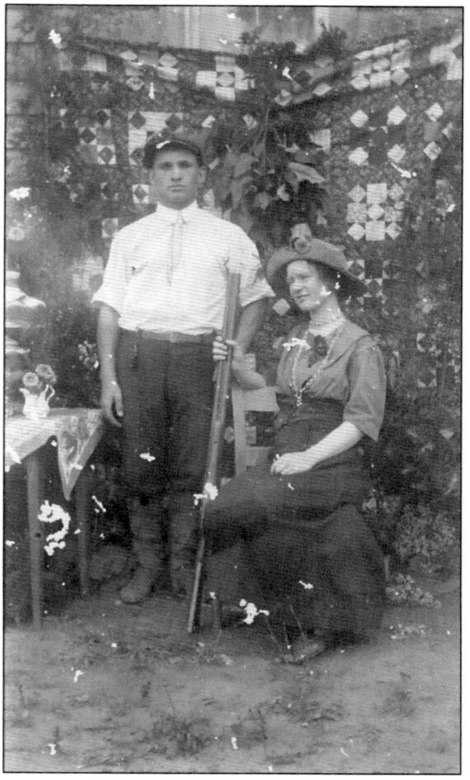

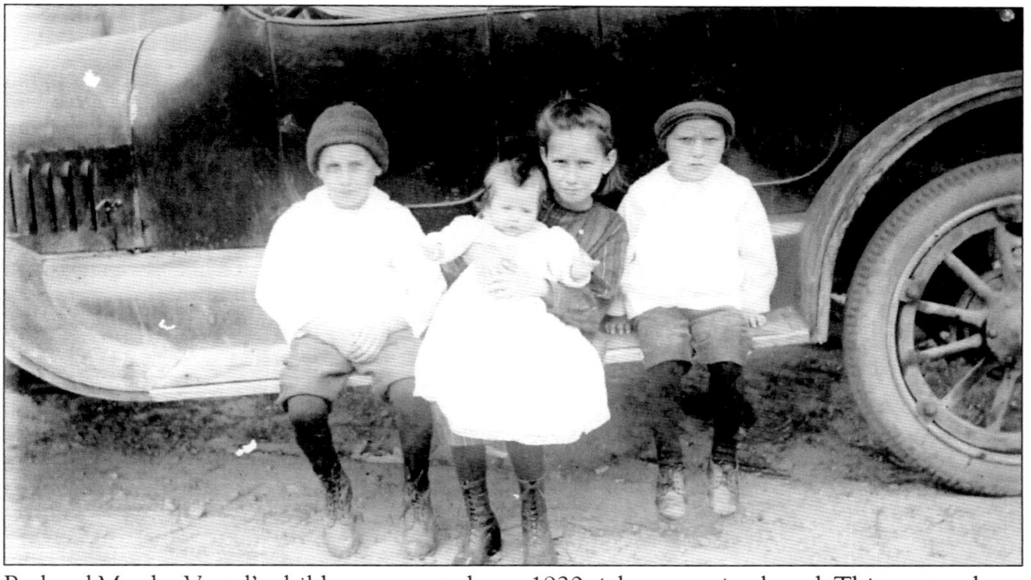

Bud and Martha Vestal's children are seated on a 1920s jalopy running board. This postcard was created by Bertha Aheron. (Courtesy of Iris Aheron Earps and the Aheron family, Eden, NC.)

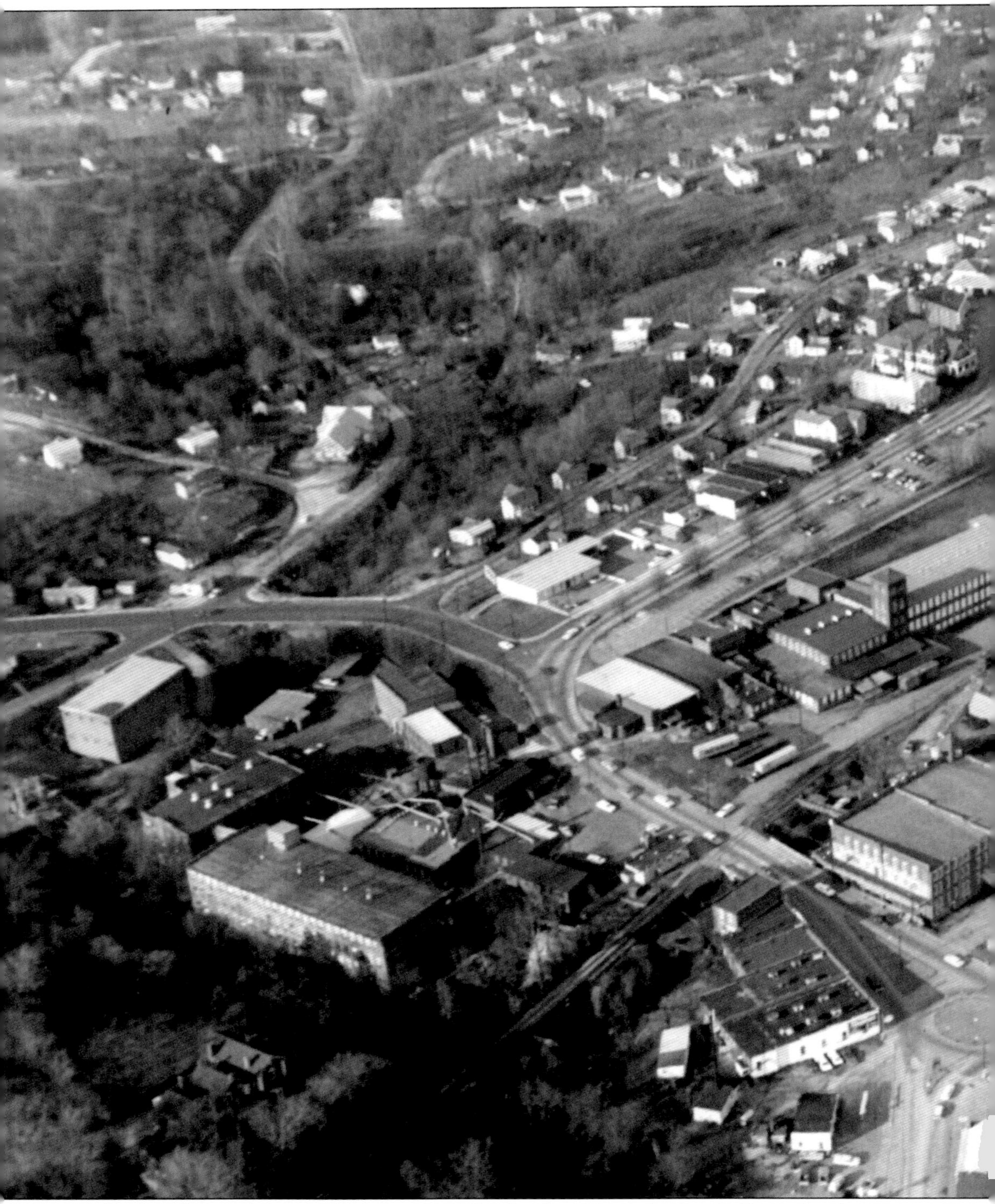

This aerial view features Spray around 1959. At the right is the Smith River. In the center of the image is Nantucket Mills (also called Fieldcrest). In an effort to provide better city services for their residents, Leaksville, Spray, and Draper consolidated on September 13, 1967. By a

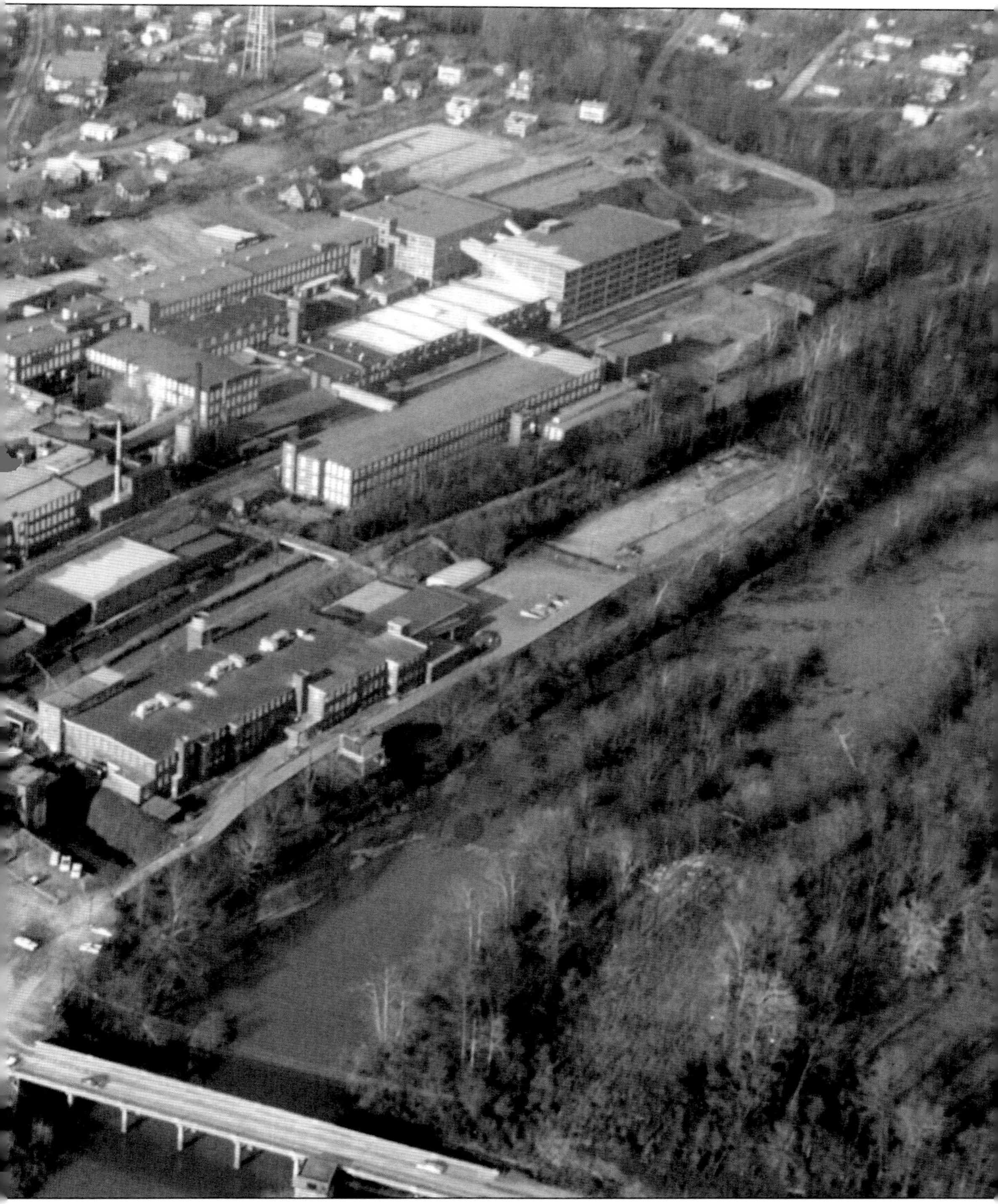

unanimous vote, the new city was named Eden. (Courtesy of the Lavender Cheek and Mary Cheek Collection, Eden, NC.)

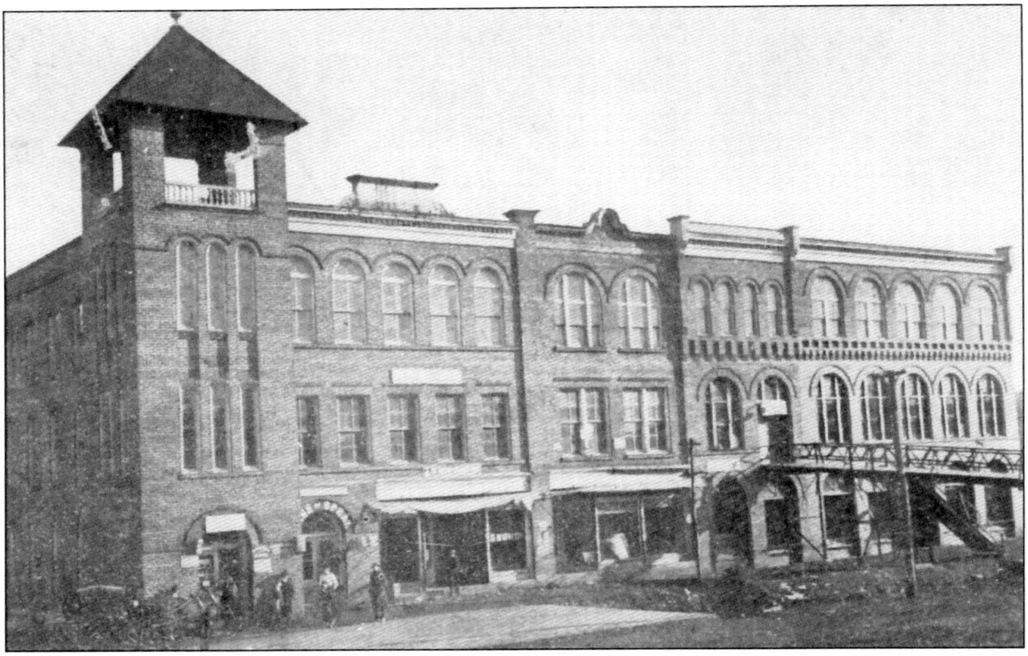

The Spray Mercantile building dates from the 1890s. The original two-story unit now stands on the northeast corner of Spray Power Canal and Church Street. This postcard features one of the nation's first shopping malls. (Courtesy of Harold Francis Collection, Eden, NC.)

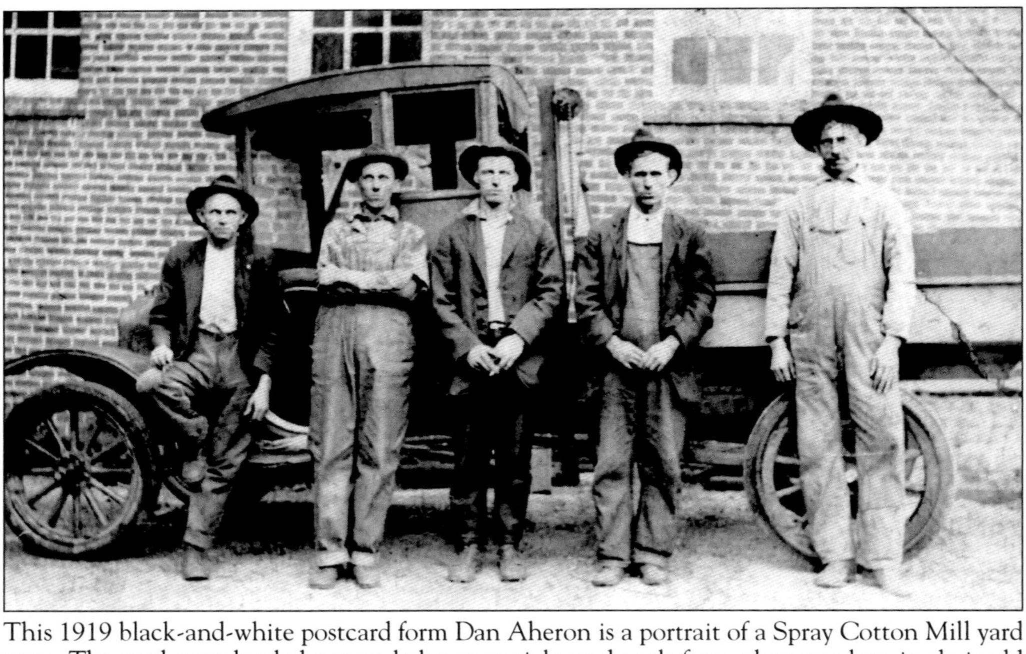

This 1919 black-and-white postcard form Dan Aheron is a portrait of a Spray Cotton Mill yard crew. The yard crew hauled cotton bales, materials, and tools from place to place in their old truck. Sometimes, they had to get mules to haul the truck and its load. (Courtesy of Bertha Vestal Aheron and the Aheron family, Eden, NC.)

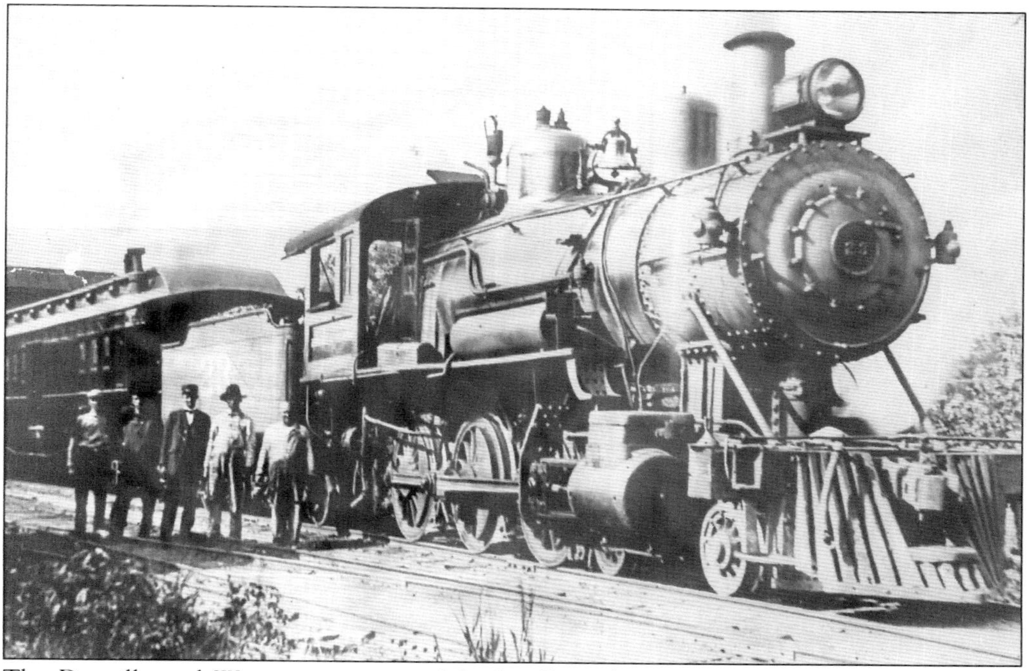

The Danville and Western train served Leaksville and Spray. (Photograph courtesy of the Harold Francis Collection, Eden, NC).

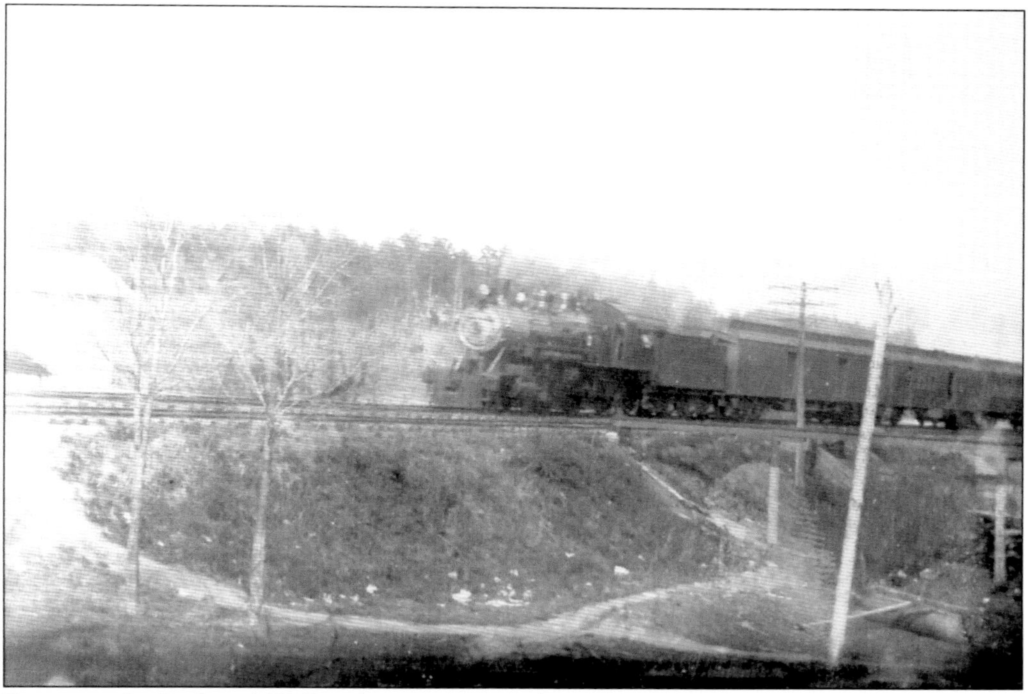

Known as the Dick and Willie, the train approaches Spray in this 1920s postcard shot by Dan Aheron. (Courtesy of the Bertha Vestal Aheron Collection, Eden, NC.)

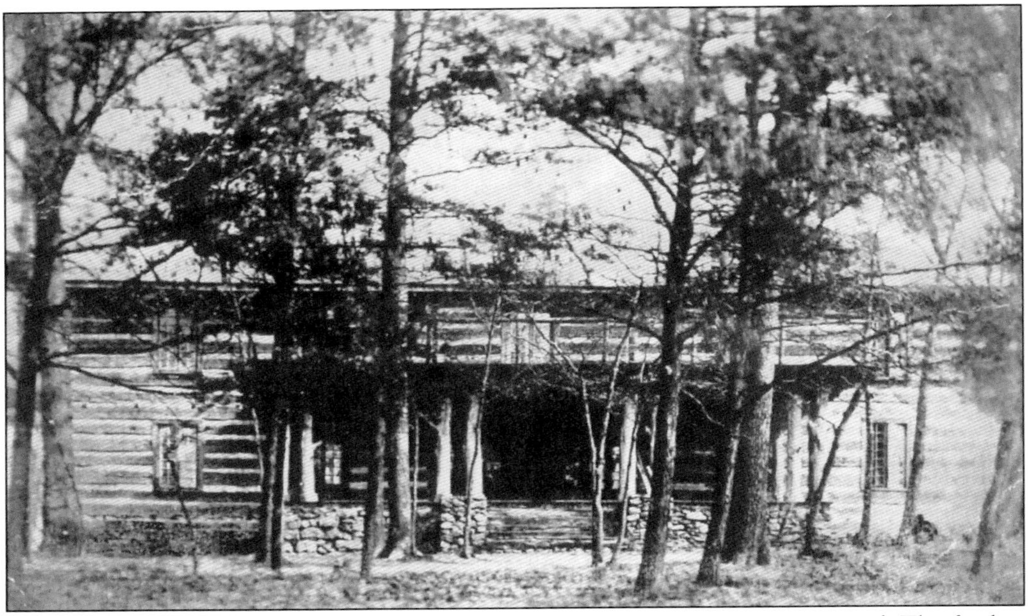

The Club House in Spray was a log structure as shown this 1923 sky-tint postcard. The facility no longer exists. (Courtesy of Lavender Cheek and Mary Cheek Collection, Eden, NC.)

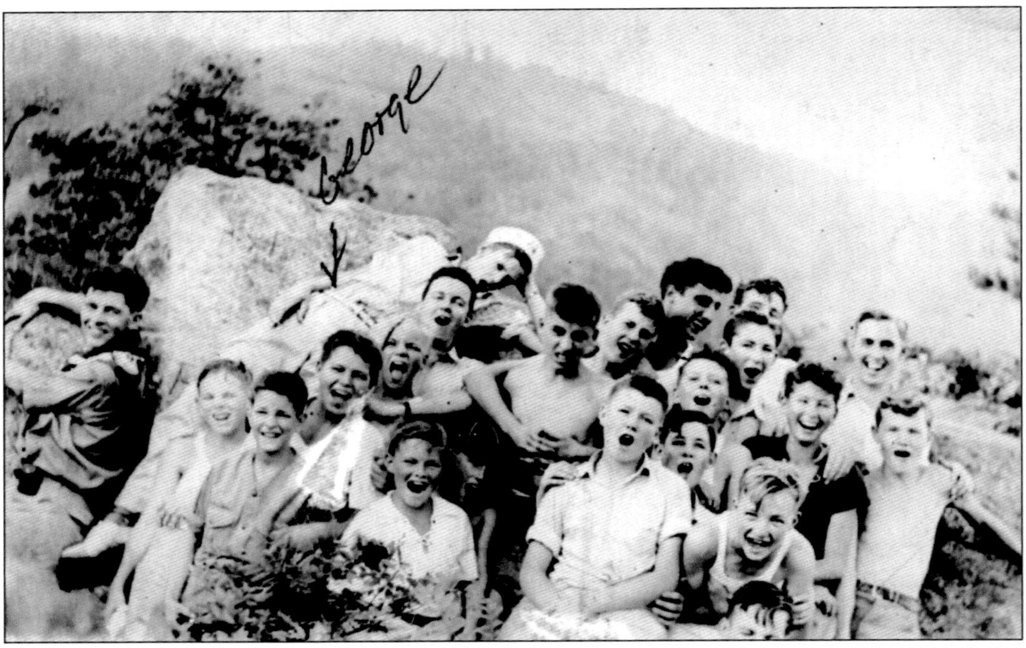

Tommy Jones (far left) and the Spray Baptist Boy Scout Troop Number 33 are at the Pinnacles of Dan near the Blue Ridge Parkway. This postcard dates from the mid-1930s. Dan or Bill Aheron took the picture so that parents could be assured their children were safe and having a good time. (Courtesy of George Aheron and the Aheron family, Eden, NC.)

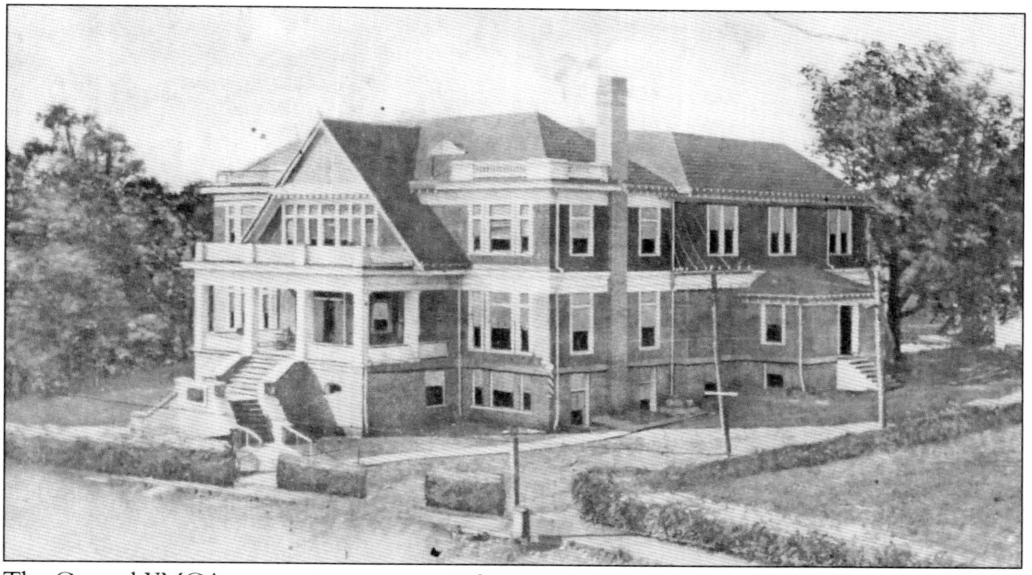

The Central YMCA was an intricate part of community life in Spray. This sepia image is from 1910 when the facility had been completed. It was located across the street from Spray Cotton Mills, but it has since been demolished. It was built by Marshall Field. (Courtesy of the Jeff Bullins Collection, Mayodan, NC.)

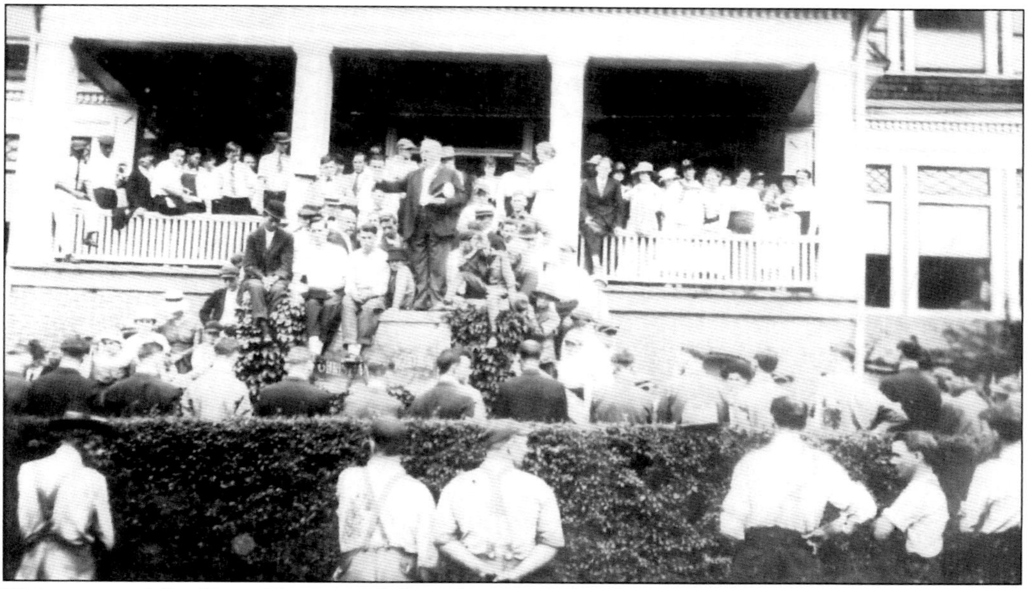

This postcard by Dan Aheron exhibits details of the front portico at the Central YMCA. Perched on the steps is Preacher Otta. (Courtesy of Bertha Aheron and the Aheron family, Eden, NC.)

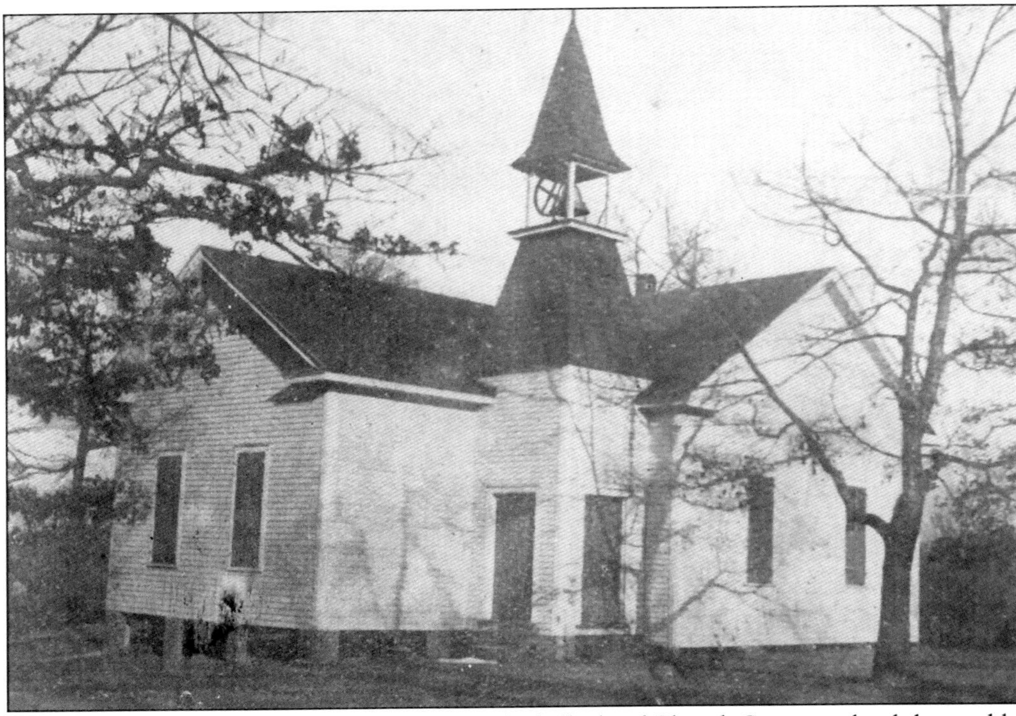

First Christian Church was built in 1892 on the hillside of Church Street on land donated by J. Turner Morehead. Several postcards of the planked architecture exist. This card dates to around 1914. (Courtesy of the Roscoe Hankins Collection, Eden, NC.)

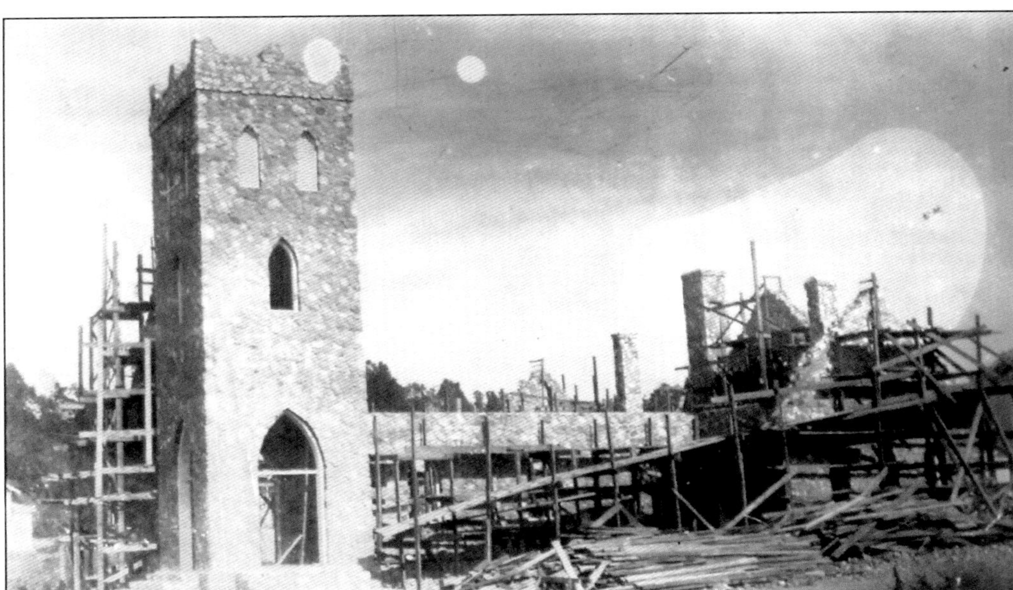

A postcard created by Dan Aheron exhibits St. Luke's Episcopal (the Rock Church) under construction. The sanctuary was built from 1924 to 1926. It is still at 604 Morgan Road. (Courtesy of Bertha Vestal Aheron and the Aheron family, Eden, NC.)

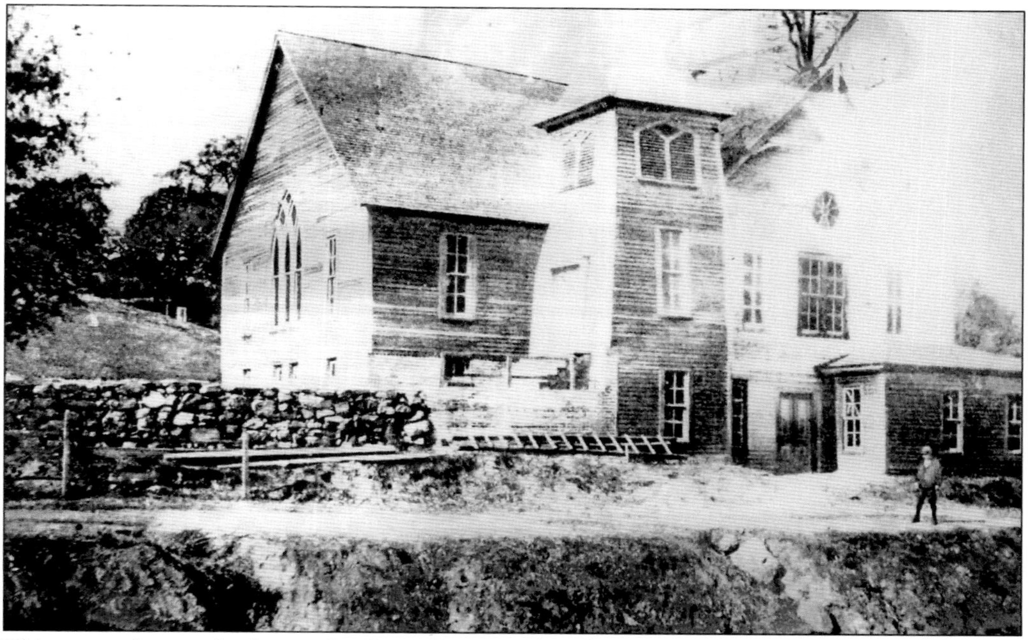

This new religious facility is the Spray Baptist Church. It was built at the junction of Spring Street and Park Road in 1903 as a Spray mission. This postcard is marked 1908. (Courtesy of the Roscoe Hankins Collection, Eden, NC.)

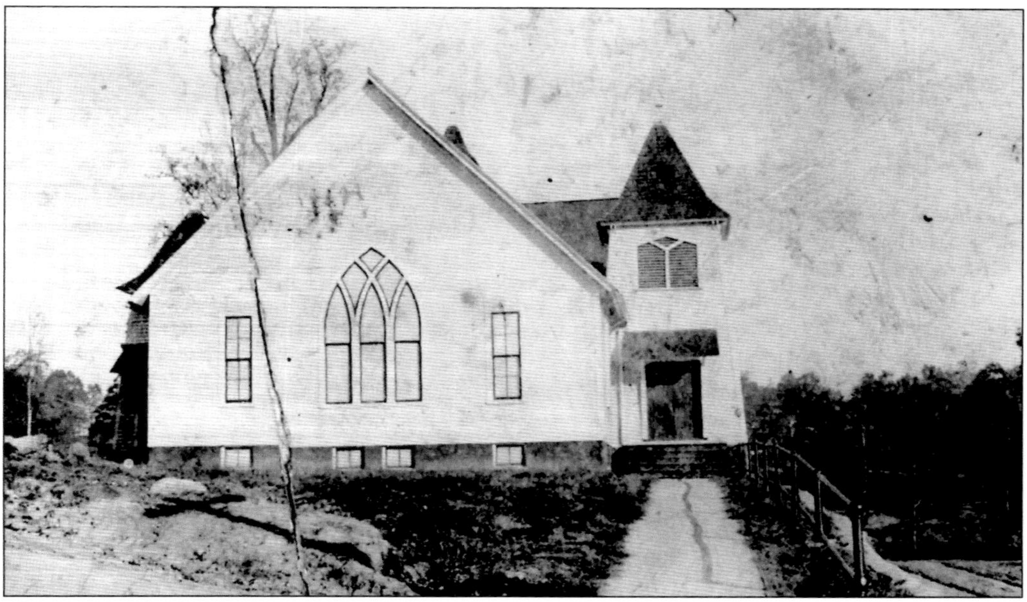

This postcard of Spray Baptist was photographed by Dan Aheron for his daughter Sunshine. This image was produced in the late 1920s after the planks had been freshly white-washed. (Courtesy of the Bertha Vestal Aheron Collection, Eden, NC.)

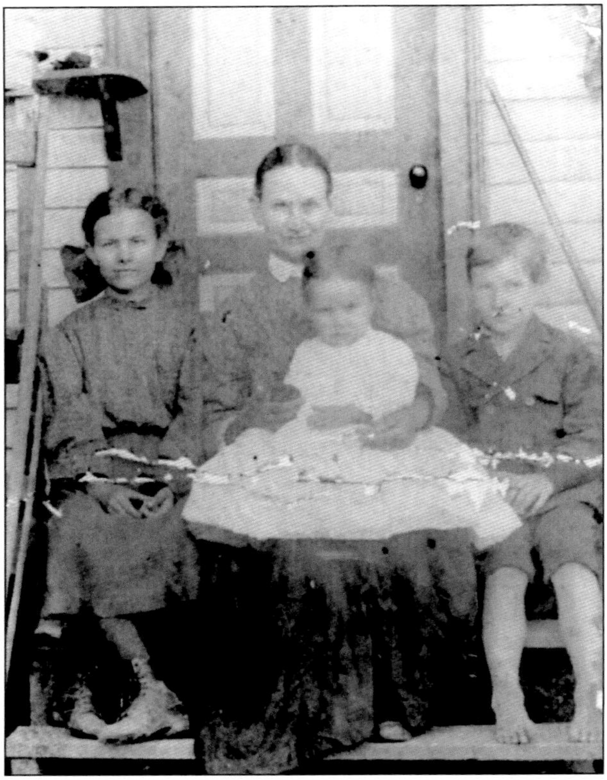

This is a photograph of the Joseph Henry Aheron family seated on the steps of their Spray home. From left to right are: Etta Aheron Black, Betty Alice Harvey Aheron (Dan's mother), little Joe Aheron, and Frank Aheron (far right). This picture was probably taken by son Dan Aheron in the early 1920s. (Courtesy of Iris Aheron Earps and the Aheron family Collection, Eden, NC.)

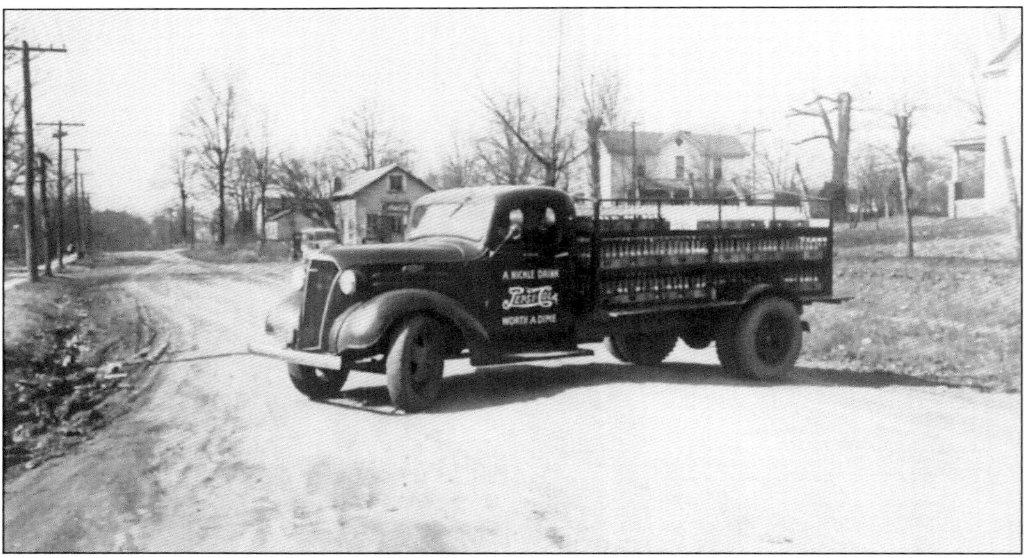

Dan Aheron photographed the Pepsi Cola truck as it delivered bottles to Clifton Street, Spray, in the 1940s. Behind the truck's cab is the competitor's store. The "Cola War" was on and the Cold War of the 1960s would soon follow. In 1967, however, the peaceful towns of Leaksville, Spray, and Draper merged to become the largest city in Rockingham County, the City of Eden. (Courtesy of Bertha Vestal Aheron and the Aheron family Collection, Eden, NC.)

Eight

DRAPER

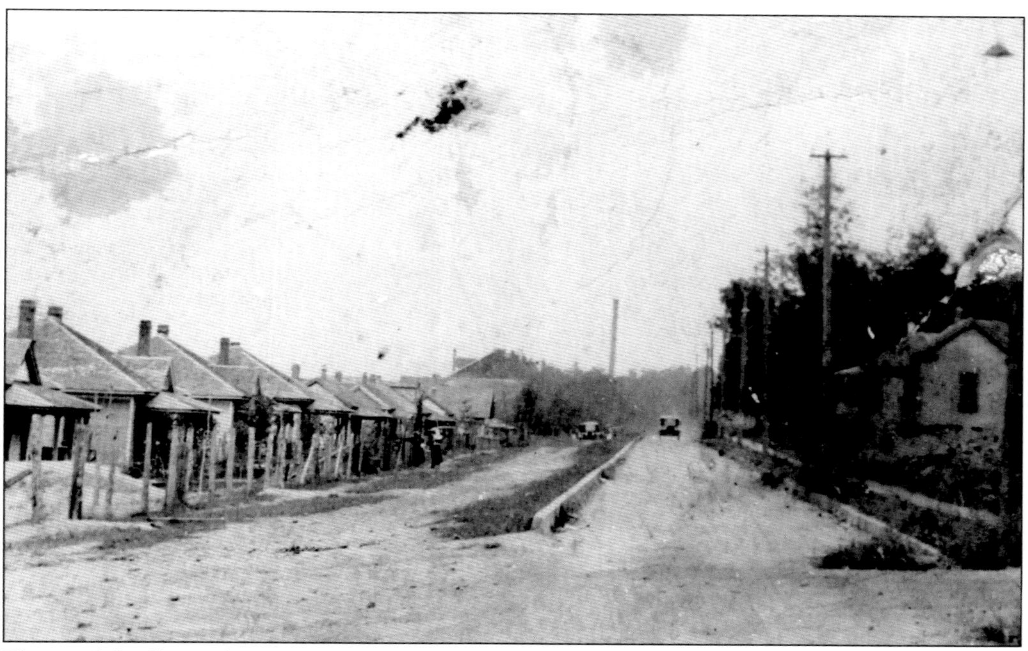

The model village of Draper, once a railroad flagstop called Sharp, is located east of the Smith River along Highway 770. Also known as the Meadows, Draper was built around 1905 by B. Frank Mebane. It was incorporated in 1949 and consolidated into the City of Eden in 1967. This is a 1920s postcard of Fieldcrest Road. (Courtesy of the Harold Francis Collection, Eden, NC.)

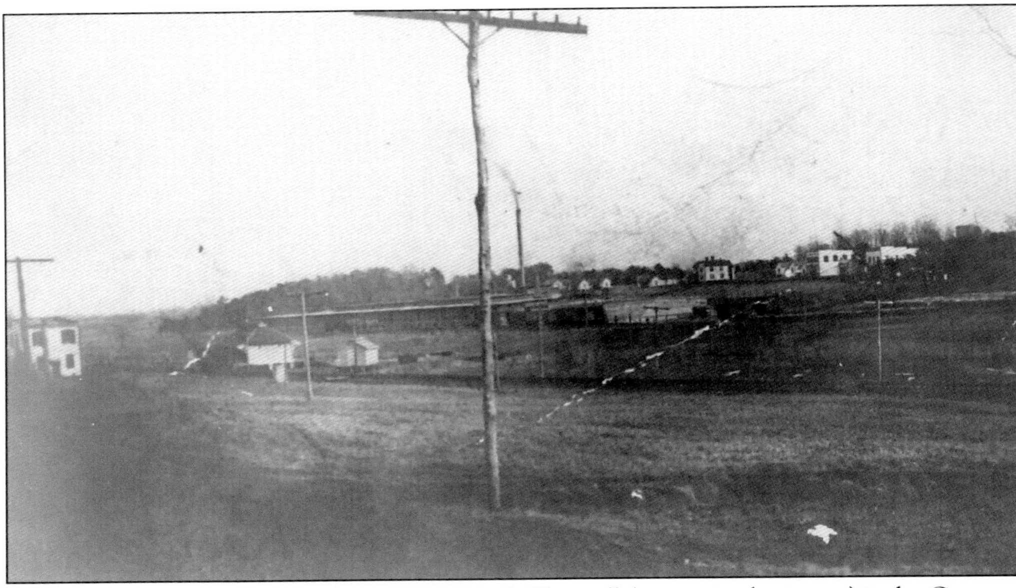

This is believed to be a copy of a 1906 postcard. The mill (center in the image) is the German-American. At the right, note the white box buildings. This is the business district called the Front, which no longer exists. (Courtesy of the Roscoe Hankins Collection, Eden, NC.)

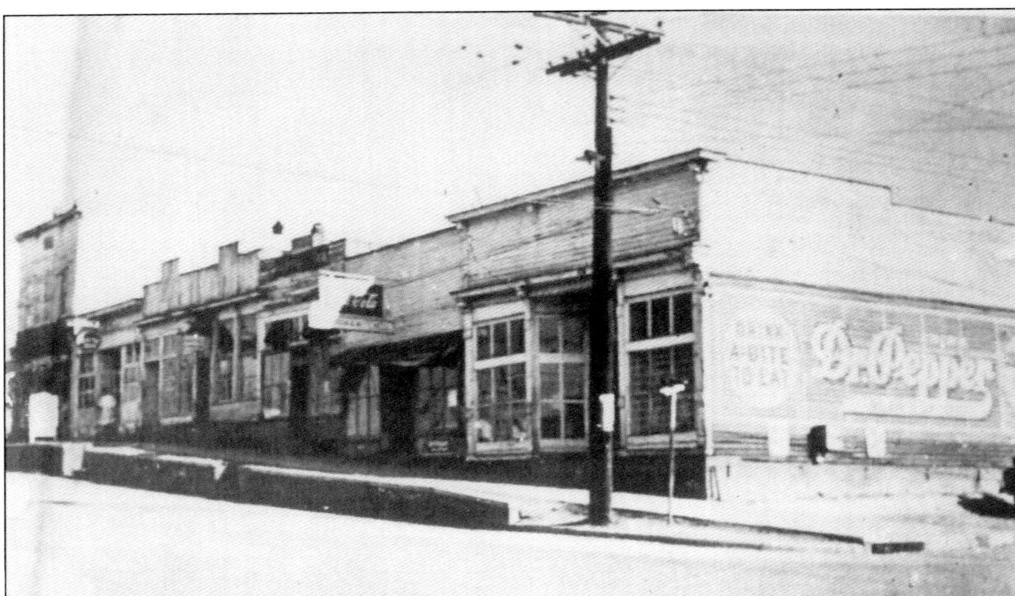

Here is a close-up of the Front in Draper, 1938. This picture was snapped by commercial photographers Claude Gillie and Harold Francis. Harold Francis, a man born in Draper, states that the Front was on Mill Avenue. Pictured here, from left to right, are: Barker's Grocery (over which was Woodmen's Hall), P.J. Holland's Cafe, Walker DeHart's dime store, Sanitary Barber Shop, Morrison & Hall Grocery, R.S. Sledge's drug store, and Clarke Grocery and Dry Goods. (Courtesy of the Harold Francis Collections, Eden, NC.)

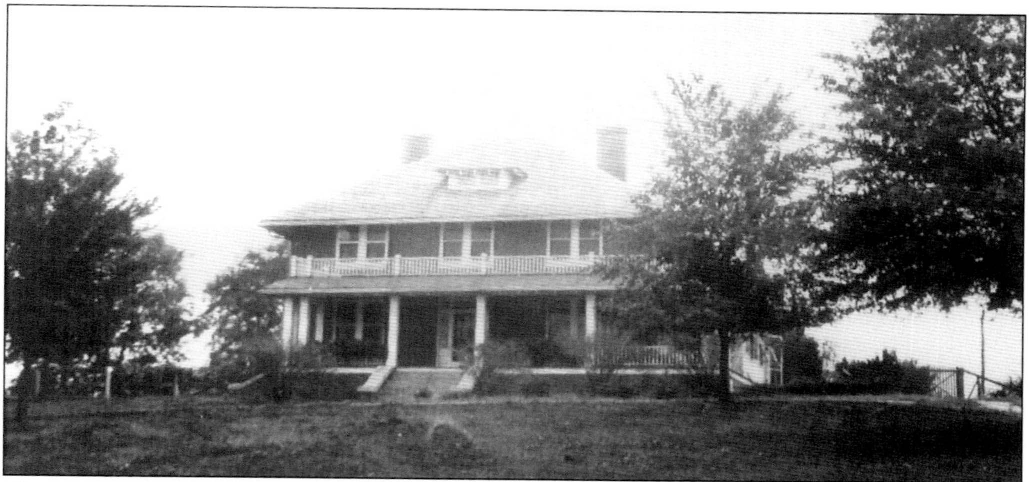

This is a postcard of the superintendent's house on 141 North Main, *c.* 1916. The property was originally in the heart of Draper and belonged to the German-American Mill. In 1926 the house was home for mill superintendent G.C. Truslow. Truslow, employed under the Southern Group of Marshall Field Mills, developed and patented several machines for producing quality textiles. The superintendent's house is now a private residence. (Courtesy of the Harold Francis Collections, Eden, NC.)

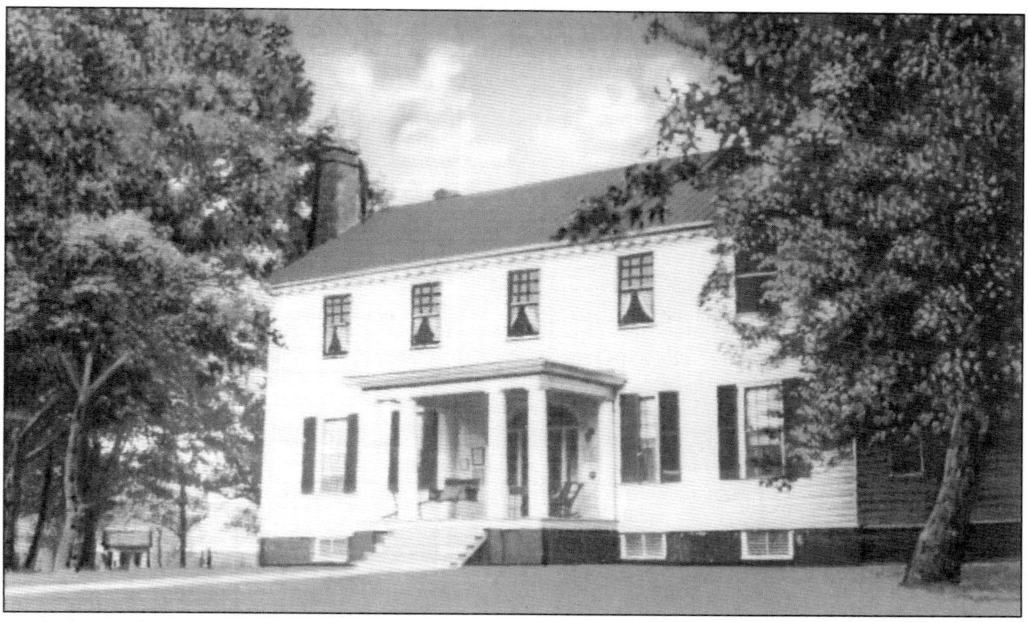

Built by Robert Brodnax on his Cascade Plantation about 1823, this beautiful structure depicted on a full-color postcard still stands on Willow Oak Drive. It was renamed in 1916 by R.I. Smith Sr. and still remains in the Smith family. (Courtesy of the R.I. Smith Jr. Collection, Eden, NC.)

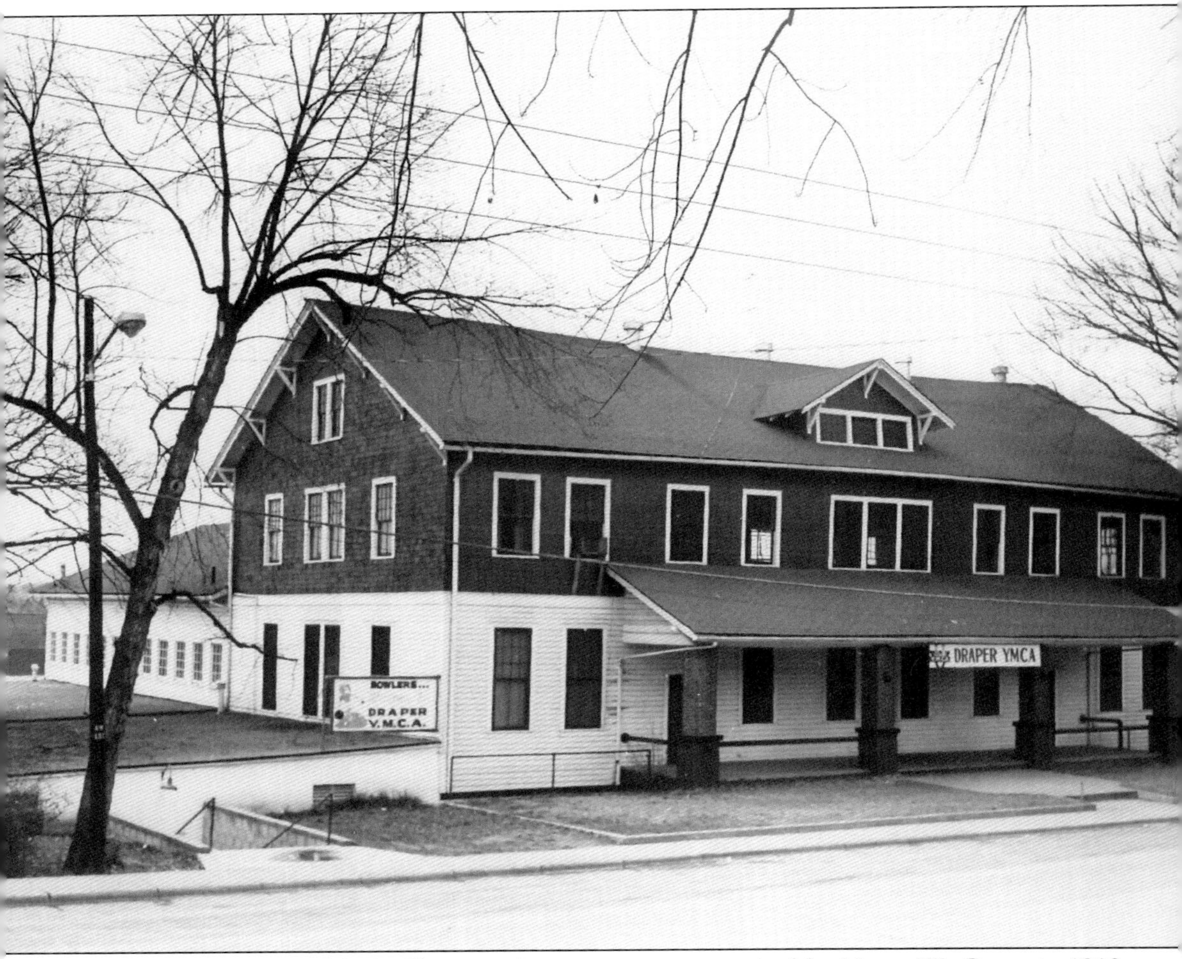

The Draper Young Men's Christian Association was organized by Henry W. Owen in 1918. This community center was dedicated in 1919 and it was the subject of several postcards. As time progressed, the facility expanded until it resembled the image above. Most postcards do not reveal the alterations to the the left of the large porch. (Courtesy of the Lavender Cheek and Mary Cheek Collections, Eden, NC.)

Nine

Rockingham County

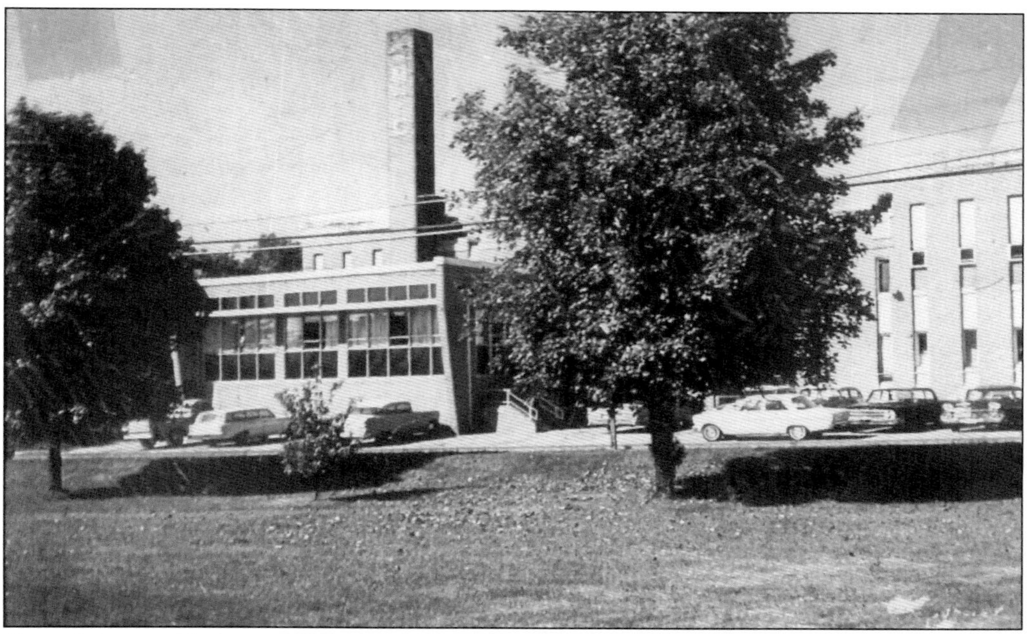

One of the world's largest Nylon throwing plants was the Madison Throwing Company. The facilities are now operated by Unifi on Ayersville Road. This postcard is from the early 1960s. The throwing company, like so many industries in Rockingham County, grew from the power generated by the rivers—the Mayo, the Dan, and the Smith. (Courtesy of the Jerri B. Griffin Collection, Madison, NC.)

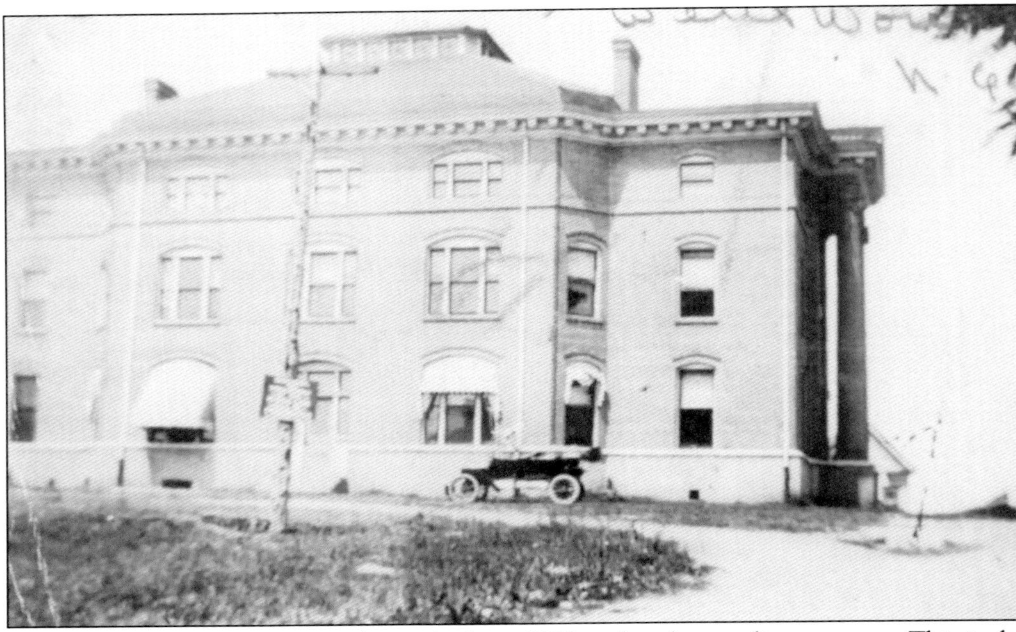

The Rockingham County Courthouse built in 1907 replaced an earlier structure. This is the courthouse in 1912. It is located in Wentworth, which, at this writing, is in the process of incorporation. (Courtesy of the Jimmy Waynick Collection, Reidsville, NC.)

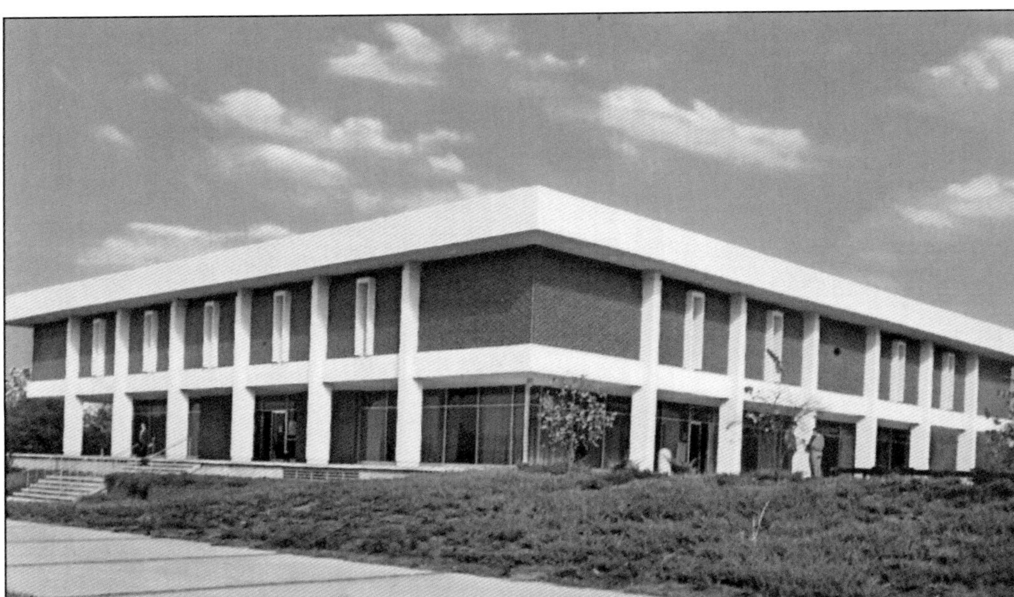

In 1966 Rockingham Community College was established at the county seat, Wentworth. Located near NC 65, the college offers a variety of studies. This 1969 postcard features the administration building, one of the four original structures on the campus. (Courtesy of the Jerri B. Griffin Collection, Madison, NC.)

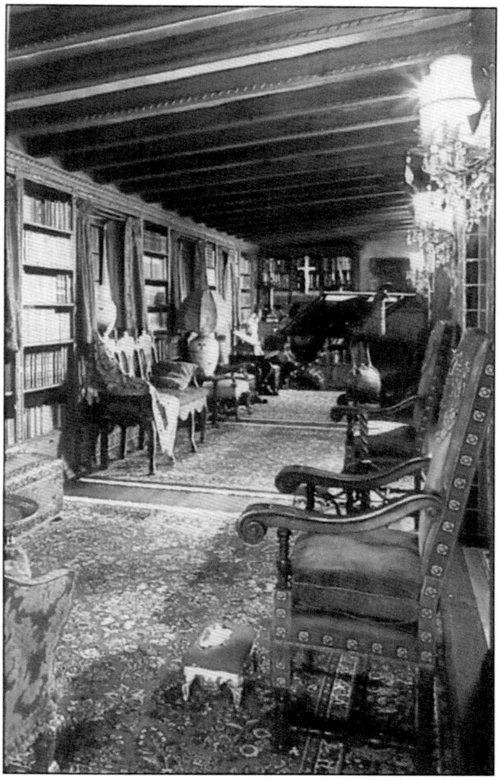

Pictured here are postcards from the Chinqua-Penn Plantation House. At right is the library. Pictured below is the reception hall. The Chinqua Penn Farm and Dairy, completed in 1926, is between Reidsville and Eden at the junction of Salem Church Road and Wentworth Street. Built with hand-hewn logs and stone quarried from the estate's 1,000 acres, this Y-shaped house, the home of Thomas Jefferson Penn and Betsy Penn, was conceived by New York architect Harry C. Ingalls. (Courtesy of the Jerri B. Griffin Collection, Madison, NC.) (Copyrighted postcards used with permission of Aerial Photography Services, Inc., 2511 S. Tryon Street, Charlotte, NC.)

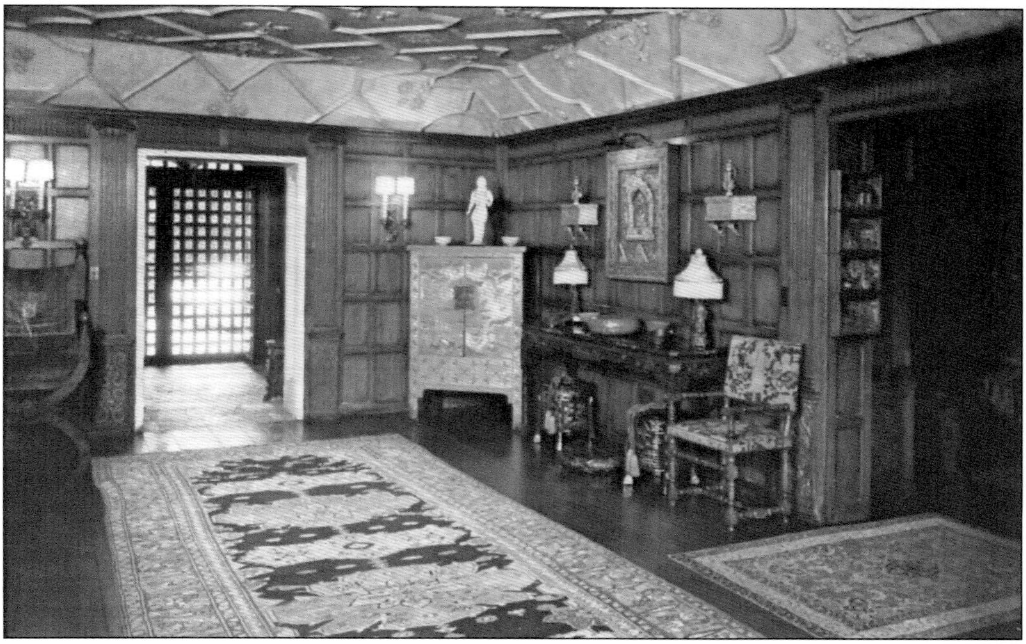

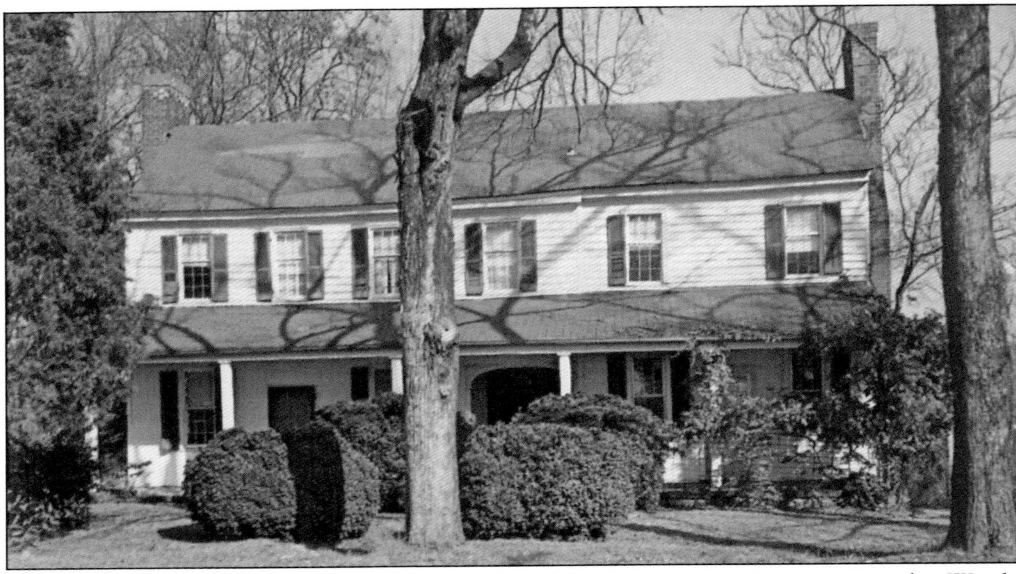

Among the many treasures of the Rockingham Historical Society's properties, the Wright Tavern-Reid House and Post Office, located on NC 65 in Wentworth, is one of the better known structures. The postcard above is postmarked 1994 in commemoration of the structure as a Bicentennial Station. The card was actually created around 1969 near the completion of the restoration spearheaded by the society. Today the tavern is a favorite stop for residents and a treat for visitors who have never enjoyed open-hearth meals. Below is Zelma Joyce Scott, the city historian of Stoneville, preparing fish for friends—Southern hospitality at its best in Rockingham County, North Carolina. (Courtesy of the Jerri B. Griffin Collection, Madison, NC.) (Copyrighted postcard courtesy of Aerial Photography Services, Inc., 2511 S. Tryon Street, Charlotte, NC.)

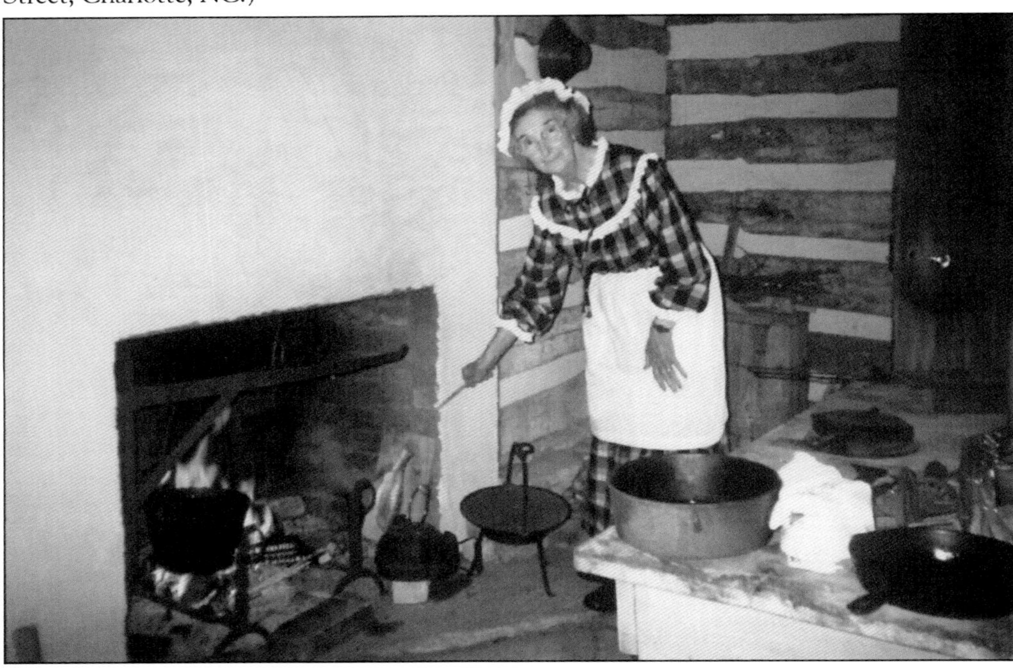